Internet Spaceships Are Serious Business

University of Minnesota Press

Minneapolis

London

# INTERNET SPACESHIPS
# ARE SERIOUS BUSINESS

## An *EVE Online* Reader

MARCUS CARTER, KELLY BERGSTROM, AND DARRYL WOODFORD, EDITORS

Published by the University of Minnesota Press
111 Third Avenue South, Suite 290
Minneapolis, MN 55401-2520
http://www.upress.umn.edu

Printed in the United States of America on acid-free paper

The University of Minnesota is an equal-opportunity educator and employer.

22   21   20   19   18   17   16        10   9   8   7   6   5   4   3   2   1

Library of Congress Cataloging-in-Publication Data
Names: Carter, Marcus, editor of compilation. | Bergstrom, Kelly, editor of compilation. | Woodford, Darryl, editor of compilation.
Title: Internet spaceships are serious business : an EVE online reader / Marcus Carter, Kelly Bergstrom, and Darryl Woodford, editors.
Description: Minneapolis : Univ Of Minnesota Press, 2016. | Includes bibliographical references and index.
Identifiers: LCCN 2015036848 | ISBN 978-0-8166-9907-0 (hc) | ISBN 978-0-8166-9908-7 (pb)
Subjects: LCSH: EVE (Computer game) | BISAC: SOCIAL SCIENCE / Media Studies. | GAMES / Video & Electronic. | BUSINESS & ECONOMICS / E-Commerce / General (see also COMPUTERS / Electronic Commerce).
Classification: LCC GV1469.27 .I67 2016 | DDC 794.8—dc23
LC record available at http://lccn.loc.gov/2015036848

To the past, present, and future players of *EVE Online*, who make their world worth studying

# Contents

# Glossary of *EVE Online* Jargon

Whereas other massively multiplayer online games (MMOGs) have some degree of crossover of terms and slang, *EVE Online* has been relatively isolated; consequently, its players use specialized language—contributing to its difficulty. This glossary covers many of the common expressions found in this collection and should be used as a quick-reference guide for unfamiliar terms.

alliance
: Organizations of corporations formally recognized by *EVE Online*. Alliances can claim sovereignty over in-game territory and enable access to shared resources and communication venues. The leader of an alliance is known as an executor.

botting
: The use of automatic programs to play the game, typically to generate resources. Botting is against the rules of *EVE Online*.

coalitions
: Informal associations of alliances not recognized by *EVE Online*. These are typically military associations, similar to organizations like NATO.

CONCORD
: *EVE Online*'s nonplayer, in-game police force, which intervenes in unprovoked conflict in high-sec space. *See also* high-sec.

corporation
: A group of players formally recognized by *EVE Online,* similar to guilds or clans in other MMOGs. Corporations can enable member access to shared resources and communication venues. The leader of a corporation is known as the CEO.

CSM
: Council of Stellar Management, the democratic council of *EVE Online* players who advocate player needs and wishes to *EVE Online*'s developer. The CSM has annual elections.

high-sec
: Common *EVE Online* colloquialism for solar systems where *EVE*'s

in-game police (CONCORD) will respond to unprovoked attacks and destroy the attacker. *See also* null-sec.

ISK      *EVE Online*'s virtual currency, standing for "interstellar kredit."

null-sec      Common *EVE Online* colloquialism for "0.0 security" solar systems, that is, systems where *EVE*'s in-game police (CONCORD) are entirely absent and players can be attacked at any time with no protection from the game. Player alliances can claim sovereignty over null-sec solar systems and build upgrades, such as space stations at which players can dock and trade. *See also* high-sec.

PLEX      Pilots License Extension, an in-game item that can be redeemed for one month of game time or purchased with real money and sold on the in-game market.

PVE      Player versus environment combat.

PVP      Player versus player combat.

scam      Refers to when a player steals in-game items or money from another *EVE Online* player. This is legal within the game world and requires misplaced trust.

Serenity      Chinese *EVE Online* server run by Tiancity. Owing to Chinese online gaming legislation, Chinese players are the only nationality not present on *EVE Online*'s main server, Tranquility. *See also* Singularity, Tranquility.

Singularity      The *EVE Online* test server that all players can access. Developers use this server to trial changes to the game, and eSport teams use Singularity to practice. It is regularly reset to match the status of the Tranquility server, allowing players the unique opportunity to play without consequence. *See also* Serenity, Tranquility.

Tranquility      The main *EVE Online* server. *See also* Serenity, Singularity.

# Introduction

*Marcus Carter, Kelly Bergstrom, and Darryl Woodford*

**The strangest thing** about *EVE Online* is that people play it at all. The game's design, user interface, and community all scream "don't play me" at a new user. *EVE* players pay US$15 a month for the privilege of playing in a world that heavily disadvantages new players, where real-time skill training means it takes *years* to fly the most powerful ships. To fly these ships, players will have to form relationships and trust other players in a game where the number one rule is not to trust anyone, because other players *will* ruthlessly lie, cheat, deceive, and steal at any opportunity. They will devote countless hours to earning in-game credits to fly ships worth as much as a small car, only for them to be permanently removed from the game if destroyed. They'll join communities that are like small nation-states, with thousands of players around the world with whom they might never even interact, let alone meet. They'll set alarms at 3:00 A.M. to defend the territory of these virtual nations from other strange *EVE Online* players and live multiple online lives to bring down their enemies from the inside with sabotage and subterfuge.

If a video game should always be fun, then *EVE Online* isn't a very good video game. It is ruthless and unforgiving, and what counts as "play" is often terrifying, brutal, and demoralizing for the uninitiated player. It actively promotes and fosters a cold harshness that would be unthinkable in other virtual worlds. For many, if not most, of the potential gamers who start a trial account, it's an unplayable, even terrifying game. But many of those who survive the learning curve can't imagine playing anything else. First released by CCP Games in 2003, the space-themed sandbox remains one of the few massively multiplayer online games (MMOGs) to successfully grow its player base in the years after its release, breaking five hundred thousand active subscriptions shortly after its tenth anniversary. This accomplishment—achieved despite an overall decline in subscriptions in the MMOG market—can be attributed to the unique assemblage of design and culture that make *EVE Online* so unusual, and so terrifying. *EVE*

*Online* is a true sandbox, but the real charm lies deep in the back of the sandbox, where players are melting the sand into glass shards and stabbing each other in the eyes.

*EVE Online* deserves attention precisely because it is so radically different from the rest of mainstream online gaming. In a gaming culture dominated by *World of Warcraft, Candy Crush,* and *Call of Duty, EVE Online* stands out as an antigame, purposefully flouting the conventions that are otherwise understood to be necessary for making a MMOG successful. *World of Warcraft,* with its peak of 12 million subscribers, demands to be treated as a behemoth gaming phenomenon (Corneliussen and Rettberg 2008) but isn't particularly different to those games that preceded it, or those that have followed. Without understating its influence, *World of Warcraft* is part of a clear evolution of online virtual world games that trace a messy history from 1980's Multi-User Dungeons (MUDs) to the 3-D, humanoid-avatar games of today. *EVE Online,* conversely, comes out of nowhere—technically, socially, and conceptually.

Perhaps because it is so difficult to play, *EVE* has been the perpetual exception in game studies. In *The Ethics of Computer Games,* Miguel Sicart (2009, 188) notes *EVE* as an example of a game "closest to the goal of ethical soundness" but only mentions it twice. When *EVE* is referenced in passing, it is often only to note what differentiates it from other MMOGs: its single-server configuration (Achterbosch, Pierce, and Simmons 2008), its player-elected council (van Lent 2008), the occurrence of economic theft (Consalvo 2009; Evans 2010), the wide use of third-party communication sites during play (Lehdonvirta 2010), and the impressive breadth of social experiences present (Korhonen, Montola, and Arrasvuori 2009). Various virtual world legal analyses also mention *EVE Online* in passing to support their arguments for why virtual worlds should (White 2008), or should not (Cifrino 2014), be subject to real-world property law. Our concern is that by only mentioning these characteristics as odd exceptions, opportunities for better understanding games as cultural, sociological phenomena, or as virtual worlds with blurred boundaries, and their communities as meaningful and "real" third places, or as played and experienced artifacts, are lost to this exceptionalism. In other words, *EVE Online*'s strangeness offers an opportunity to better understand game mechanics, play experience, game communities, and online culture, and the essays in this book capture both the weird and the wonderful, written by scholars and players who have genuinely understood, and grown to love, this virtual world.

This book is for both the uninitiated reader interested in gaming cultures and the dedicated capsuleer. Our contributors unpack and help make sense of a world filled with bizarre and concealed practices and communities that challenge many underlying conceptions about online games and play. For those who can recall exactly where they were and what they were doing when they first heard about the Battle of B-R5RB (a battle in *EVE Online* that resulted in damage translatable to US$300,000 in real-world dollars), these essays draw from and contribute to ongoing conversations about *EVE*'s technical and social dimensions and larger philosophical questions. Finally, no other game has yet successfully replicated a fraction of what makes *EVE* so attractive to its players, so we also invite game designers to use this collection as an opportunity to better understand how *EVE*'s underlying design affords its unique emergent play.

*EVE Online* challenges the very notion of what a game can be, and the essays in this collection take up the additional challenge of describing what *EVE* is and what it's like to play it. To define *EVE* in comparison to games like *World of Warcraft* is a poor way to capture what makes this game so unique. By providing a comprehensive look at the very real universe of New Eden, we offer readers a chance to understand what makes it so special, to capture the *feeling* of being an *EVE Online* player and why it has been so successful.

Our early chapters set the scene for the collection, describing what it is like to interact with *EVE Online*. Each chapter stands alone, but together they provide a foundation that highlights how intricately tied together *EVE*'s design and its emergent activities and game play are. Alongside the chapters authored by researchers, we include pieces by other *EVE Online* experts—players and developers—to best provide an account of the spirit and emergent play practices of *EVE* that are otherwise hidden from outsiders. These chapters allow the reader to vicariously become an *EVE Online* player and in turn better appreciate the later chapters, which discuss how it's possible for a game to have history and why it is important that this history be preserved.

We have divided the collection into three themes. The structure of a game's universe, its cosmology, obviously structures how the game play unfolds. Consequently, our first theme explores the technical configuration and design of *EVE Online*'s New Eden. Included is an *EVE Online* glossary intended to provide the necessary background and key vocabulary for nonplayers (or for those who rage-uninstalled the client after the first hour). Our second theme examines what has emerged from *EVE*'s design—its complex player culture, persistent communities, and unique styles of play—whereas our third theme explores questions of history, curation, and preservation. Our collection captures the complexities of *EVE Online* and what it means to the half-million players who engage with the complex virtual world each day. Not only do these chapters highlight what differentiates *EVE Online* but together they explain why the unusual, difficult, and harsh MMOG is poised to persist for another decade and remain one of the most important games of this generation.

## Designing New Eden

*EVE Online* isn't a game that you can dabble in. If this book were about *World of Warcraft*, it would be possible for you to pick up a copy of the game and play for a few hours to get a general sense of what *World of Warcraft* is: how it's played, how you create a character, the feel of the virtual world, and the rhythm of combat. Although it wouldn't be possible to fully understand the game world or its culture, the foundation of what it is to play and enjoy *World of Warcraft* is accessible to a new player. *EVE,* in comparison, is difficult, complex, and closed off. In our second chapter, Christopher Paul explores the rhetorical harshness of *EVE*'s design and richly describes how various elements of it effectively push players away from the game. Readers who attempt, but abandon, playing *EVE Online* should take heart in the fact that even many now-dedicated *EVE* players gave up following their first intrusion into the unforgiving virtual world.

In response to this, the volume begins, in chapter 1, with an introduction to the play of *EVE Online* by Kelly Bergstrom and Marcus Carter. We begin with the notion of sandbox, a concept most frequently invoked by *EVE* players to describe the game to nonplayers, outlining the technical and economic realities of access, the variety of play styles and social culture that have emerged from the collisions of its unusual design decisions. This is by no means comprehensive, because we recognize that numerous pockets of the *EVE* universe are left uncovered by our accounts, but it provides the necessary foundation for understanding the interrelations of our chapters, such as how *EVE*'s largest and most violent player communities rely on the pacifist, solo miners with whom they share their virtual universe and whom they so frequently deride. From this foundation, it becomes clearer how the rhetorical force of the dissuasive elements Paul discusses in chapter 2 hones the community of *EVE* players like any other form of hazing, forcing players (who survive) to reach out to other players and find a community with which to play, socializing *EVE* players into the fact that *EVE* is not a solo game. *EVE*'s harshness doesn't just impact who is left playing it but the very type of play that emerges.

The virtual universe of New Eden is set twenty thousand years into our future, depicting a particular space-future for humanity characterized by greed and war. William Sims Bainbridge, whose doctoral dissertation analyzed the history of the space-flight social movement, including observations of the last human launch to the moon in 1972, explores in chapter 3 these prophetic dimensions of *EVE Online* as a simulation of possible interstellar colonization. In his contribution, Bainbridge employs the methodology of *impersonation*, exploring *EVE* through an avatar based on Hermann Oberth, with his choices and direction within the sandbox informed by what we know about Oberth and his personal attitudes as an antiauthoritarian, eccentric intellectual. In contradiction to *EVE*'s key norms, but in alignment with Oberth's real character, Bainbridge's interrogation of *EVE* focuses on the solo mining and manufacturing play of *EVE*, providing excellent and detailed introductions to the actualities of this side of *EVE Online* play, which is often overlooked in the gaming press.

To finance the initial development of *EVE Online*, CCP Games founders Reynir Harðarson, Thorolfur Beck, and Ívar Kristjánsson designed and released *Hæuttuspil* (Danger Game), a board game that taught children the dangers of drinking and drug use, which prepared the company for its later rounds of financing. The origins of *EVE Online*, however, are even earlier in the Icelandic dot-com company OZ.com, founded in 1995 with the ambitious goal of creating OZ Virtual, a 3-D Web browser with voice chat, personalized avatars, and the ability to see everyone simultaneously visiting the same URL. With the enviable job title of "universe architect," former CCP Games employee Kjartan Pierre Emilsson's essay (chapter 4) is a history of *EVE Online*'s development from this virtual browser to explain one of the most distinguishing design features of *EVE*: its single, persistent server shared by all players (except those on the sequestered Chinese server). It is this developmental history that Bainbridge identifies in his contribution, noting how *EVE* does not replicate the cosmos (at least in any way that we understand it) but rather a system of information, with interstellar travel resembling hyperlinks connecting distributed worlds, reflecting a particular (possibly real) prophecy for human's real space-future.

EVE's persistent, shared-world host means that New Eden is a truly global virtual world. As we explain in chapter 1's introduction to *EVE*, one of the most well publicized facets of *EVE* play is its player-formed alliances and corporations, some with ten thousand or more members, who wage vicious wars with each other over control of in-game territory, resorting to the espionage and complex organizations further explored in chapters 9 and 10. These wars are both cold and hot, with the cloak and dagger of diplomacy, espionage, and subterfuge always simmering in the background, exploding into flashpoint battles involving hundreds, occasionally thousands, of combatants. The consequence of making *EVE* a globally shared virtual universe is that these battles occur around the clock. As a result, *EVE*'s communities that operate within the lawless regions of space, called "null-sec," are similarly global and transnational, and Oskar Milik's contribution (chapter 5) examines how two of these groups—TEST Alliance Please Ignore and Goonswarm Federation—establish a shared appreciation of global time that has been weaponized in *EVE*'s ruthless combat. Milik notes how *EVE* alliances attempt to deny their opponents fun to grind them into the virtual ground, with persistent, mundane, and un-fun experiences. Detachments like these between concepts like "play" and "fun" demonstrated throughout this volume are of wide relevance in the continuing study of modern games and reflect the opportunities *EVE* presents for game studies.

Alongside these negotiations of a global time are the negotiations of a globalized community and the subsequent interactions that occur between players of different cultural backgrounds, divided by time, space, and language. One of the most prominent non-English-speaking groups is the Russian bloc, who are widely characterized by Western players as intrusively ruthless and powerful. Contrary to existing game studies research that has typically characterized international conflicts within online games as the result of Western players pushing back against nonnormative, non-Western players, Catherine Goodfellow's contribution to the collection (chapter 6) demonstrates how both Russian and Western players appropriate "Russianness" in strategic ways, reflecting the unique values of *EVE Online* players. Drawing on both English- and Russian-language player discourse, Goodfellow also highlights parallels between "real-world" characterizations and conflicts that reflect the complex ways that the different players of *EVE* contribute to and alter its constitution. Both Goodfellow's and Milik's research paves the way for understanding contemporary gaming and gaming culture as it becomes increasingly globalized and diverse, a transition that *EVE* is at the forefront of, exemplifying the importance of studying *EVE Online*.

## *EVE Online*'s Emergent Play: Player Battles, Piracy, and Espionage

In early 2012, The Mittani, the infamous leader of the powerful Goonswarm Federation (a community in *EVE* with more than ten thousand members), led an assault on the center of the in-game economy, a solar system called Jita. In this "high-sec" system, nonplayer police will intervene if someone attacks another player unprovoked. This allows miners and manufacturers to safely move their goods around, or so they thought. Goonswarm players and their allies built and flew enormous fleets of cheap ships that were able to collectively deal out a colossal amount of damage in a single volley, destroying these undefended industrialists before the nonplayer police could arrive to destroy the aggressors. Despite Goonswarm announcing the event thirty days prior, thousands of players lost goods worth billions of in-game credits in the assault, commonly known as Burn Jita. In most online worlds, an explicit effort to shut down the game's economy would see intervention on behalf of the developer. But in this case, *EVE Online* senior producer described this spectacular example of space piracy as "fucking brilliant" (Yin-Poole 2012). In contrast to other MMOGs, often referred to as theme parks for their on-rails, linear design where play is typically the result of interaction with the game client, *EVE Online*'s play is "emergent"; that is, the play *emerges* from interactions between players. Though the game has a story, with optional quests to complete, player-organized events such as piracy and battles are what provide the major dramatic moments in the game's history. Many attribute CCP Game's philosophy of enabling emergence as what allows *EVE* to continue to grow a decade after its release. Consequently, our second theme explores the topic of emergence in *EVE* through documenting and exploring key, and often evocative, examples.

A concept Bergstrom and Carter note in chapter 1 the pervasive rule hammered into each new player (typically in all capital letters), "DON'T TRUST ANYONE," as scamming, theft, and espionage (all of which can have very real implications for their victims) are pervasive within *EVE* (see Carter 2015). The exception to this rule is the player Chribba, who occupies a unique role in the virtual universe as the *only* trustworthy player in New Eden. As CCP offers no protection from scams that exploit misplaced trust, Chribba acts as a broker in large trades that cannot be completed through the in-game marketplace, having brokered the virtual equivalent of US$6 million. Chribba's contribution to the collection (chapter 7), an account of the nature and history of his role, and commentary on his status as a celebrity in a virtual universe, provides insight into the confluence of various emergent play behaviors that characterize *EVE*'s violent sandbox.

*EVE* players who pick up this collection will be unsurprised by the mammoth presence of the Goonswarm Federation throughout the volume. Drawing its members, and culture, from the Something Awful forums, this player group has changed the very way that *EVE* is played and is feared, admired, loathed, and loved by the broader *EVE* community. Goonswarm aggressively utilizes time as a weapon—as documented in Milik's chapter—and was the first Western alliance to build a relationship with the previously ostracized, but powerful, Russian Bloc. Chapters 9 and 10 feature contributions from senior Goonswarm Federation members who provide intimate, personal accounts of the types of play unthinkable to someone unfamiliar with *EVE Online*. Building on Alex Golub's phenomenological approach to raiding in *World of Warcraft*, we preface these two player contributions with a study of Goonswarm by Richard Page (chapter 8), who argues that the project—of "playing Something Awful" rather than "playing *EVE*"—makes play meaningful for Goonswarm members. Through this perspective, Page demonstrates how the emergent play described throughout the volume is not just a practice that emerges from an interaction between player and code but a pervasive practice that originates in communities and cultures outside of the game world. This understanding will assist researchers in better approaching how social worlds intersect with virtual worlds, while also further challenging formalist approaches to understanding contemporary games.

In her exploration of the characterizations of Russian players in *EVE*, Catherine Goodfellow provides some examples of Cold War–era propaganda, reworked and recontextualized to apply to *EVE Online*'s wars (see also Carter 2014). Though these images often invoke the camaraderie and individual sacrifice necessary for group success within *EVE*—with humor throughout—the references to the Cold War appeal to and legitimize the pervasive use of espionage in *EVE* play. For example, key contributors to the "digital grind" Milik describes in his chapter were acts of sabotage, such as where the spreadsheet used by TEST logistics directors to coordinate the work required to support the war effort was routinely and regularly sabotaged—subtly enough to avoid detection—by an enemy agent player. In chapter 9, Keith Harrison, aka "Endie," the leader of the Goonswarm Intelligence Agency, overviews the work and play involved in this espionage, which often exceeds the contribution of military battles to war efforts. Overviewing the distinctions between "human intelligence" and "signals intelligence," Harrison demonstrates the dramatic impact of commodifying trust in *EVE Online* and the challenge of negotiating the boundaries of emerging play in virtual worlds. This dimension of *EVE*, well established and accepted by the player community, tests existing academic approaches to trust, consent, and labor in multiplayer games.

This play and strategy that surround and facilitate *EVE*'s viciously fought wars are often referred to by its players as the metagame. Harrison defines the metagame as "those aspects of the game that occur outside of the game-play mechanics of the *EVE* client and server software," emphasizing that it is *part of the game* rather than a peripheral activity that surrounds it. *EVE*'s metagame has such substance that, as chapter

10 demonstrates, it's possible to play only the metagame, rarely (if ever) logging into the game at all. To these players, such as The Mittani, orchestrator of the Burn Jita event, former chairman of the CSM (*EVE*'s player-elected council), and feared leader of the Goonswarm Federation, *EVE Online* "is a chat program, a kanban board, and a network of connections, institutions, organizations and cultures which myself and my compatriots have worked to create, defend, and strengthen," and not a spaceship virtual world. The Mittani, in chapter 10, contributes to this volume rare insight into what it means to play *EVE*'s metagame and into the emergent nature of *EVE* player organizations that support and demand the styles of play that occur. In coordination with Harrison's and Page's contributions, and Milik's detailed account of *EVE* warfare, chapter 10 provides a rich and comprehensive portrayal of how much of *EVE* is played outside of the game client and how much this metagame impacts the *EVE* world, exemplifying the importance of examining these interrelations in MMOG studies.

The majority of portrayals of *EVE*, particularly in popular culture, focus on the harshness of the game and its community: massive thefts, key betrayals, and high-cost battles. Milik notes in chapter 5 the impact of these "undeniably cool" dimensions of *EVE Online* on player subscriptions, and the majority of academic work (and, indeed, this volume) focuses on these dimensions of *EVE* that characterize its "don't play me" rhetoric. However, within this ruthless and combative virtual world are deeply personal and meaningful communities and relationships. In chapter 11, Martin R. Gibbs, Marcus Carter, and Joji Mori explore these through documenting and examining the in-game memorializations that occurred following the murder of Sean Smith in the 2012 attack on the U.S. Embassy in Benghazi, Libya. A U.S. Foreign Service employee, Sean Smith was also Vile Rat, the chief diplomat of Goonswarm Federation and former member of the CSM. Smith had an enormous impact on the diplomacy-play that emerged alongside Harrison's espionage in *EVE*'s large communities, and the memorializations that followed his passing reflect his impact on the game world. These memorializations, many which appropriated in-game weapons and items with recontextualized meanings, reflected the bricolage characteristic of physical-world public community mournings. Their extent through the *EVE* community reflects the significance of *EVE*'s community to its players and the camaraderie that is often overlooked in sensationalized media accounts.

Unlike the vast majority of other MMOGs, which maintain 30 to 40 percent female players, *EVE Online* has an aberrantly low 4 percent female player base. In chapter 12, Kelly Bergstrom notes that discussions around gender in games, in both academic and popular discourse, typically focus on women's play (or lack thereof). Furthermore, these discourses also assume that those women who *do* play are either outliers or need to be specifically courted with female-friendly games. Reapplying such an approach to *EVE* would fail to reveal the underlying rhetorical and social practices that gender *EVE* play, and Bergstrom unpacks how certain styles of emergent play are privileged over others through the framework of hegemonic masculinities

(Connell and Messerschmidt 2005). Bergstrom focuses on the emergent player event of Hulkageddon, an annual coordinated event similar to Burn Jita where pirate players attack undefended mining ships in high-sec space, exploiting the same mechanic. Through identifying the intersections between gender and play hierarchies in such an explicitly gendered game, Bergstrom emphasizes the fact that—applicable to all game studies—examinations of gender in games must focus not just on female players (or lack thereof) but on the *entire* community.

Reflecting the pervasiveness and *intensity* of *EVE*'s emergent play, events like Hulkageddon and Burn Jita are organized and coordinated for profit by metagame players like The Mittani and Endie. Key contributors to the war described in Milik's chapter were changes to where players could find technetium, an ore that can be mined in the game and sold or used to build spaceships. These changes, introduced into the game by CCP, brought down the Organization for Technetium Exporting Corporations (a riff on OPEC), a coalition that had secretly been manipulating the price of technetium for increased profit (for more on this, see Carter 2014). These powerful corporations had been (and likely still are, in some fashion) manipulating the game market through these events; the ships destroyed in Jita demand high quantities of the technetium that *EVE*'s large communities mine and sell from the moons orbiting the planets in the solar systems they control. Destroying mining ships throughout the game world thus drove up demand for the resource they controlled. The scale of these intertwined events that involve hundreds of groups and thousands of players impacting every *EVE* player through the in-game market, driven by the players as an emergent play style, is incomparable to the game play of any other contemporary online game.

This collection overwhelmingly focuses on the Tranquility *EVE Online* server, the shard that hosts nearly all *EVE* players and the world we have described so far. The exception to this is the Chinese *EVE* community, who have access only to the Serenity server, a separate replicate server operated by Chinese firm Tiancity. In consequence, a separate *EVE* world has developed with a meaningfully different community that has begun exploring *EVE*'s ruthless, consequential, and treacherous world on its own, in isolation. We are delighted to be able to include in the collection a chapter contributed by Mantou (translated by Richard Page), the most famous player on *EVE Online*'s Chinese server (chapter 13). As the leader of one of Serenity's most powerful alliances, Mantou reflects on the autocratic nature of all *EVE Online* communities—that power is always consolidated into the hands of a single player and leader—something that The Mittani similarly identifies as a strength in *EVE* warfare. Mantou's commentary on how it is not possible to bring democracy in *EVE*, as players do not possess the underlying circumstances to enact it, is a fascinating contribution on behalf of the Chinese *EVE* community. Mantou further discusses the changes that would need to be brought about in *EVE Online* to make a democratic social system in the game.

## Curating and Archiving a Universe

The themes of design and emergence are deeply intertwined in *EVE,* each contextualizing and reinforcing the other, developing organically over the game's decade-long history. The *EVE* archived within this volume is distinct from the *EVE* of 2003 and will undoubtedly continue to evolve. This is remarkably unusual for digital games; though some of the earliest virtual worlds remain online, their subscriptions are at a fraction of their peak, and ongoing development has all but halted. Consequently, our third theme explores these questions of history and preservation, attempting to understand what it means to be a game that looks like it will continue to grow for another decade or longer.

*EVE*'s history is heavily characterized by the unusual relationship between CCP Games and *EVE* players, which has already been hinted at in the Burn Jita event. As Jedrzej Czarnota notes in his contribution (chapter 14), CCP Games approaches its relationship to *EVE Online* as a janitor, not as a god, which encourages the sandbox game's emergent play. Drawing on interviews with *EVE Online* developers, Czarnota provides detailed insight into the mechanisms and strategies in place to facilitate the communications and cooperation between *EVE Online* players and the developers. As a form of co-creation, this practice has been instrumental in shaping the *EVE Online* of today. Explicit strategies include Fanfest, the annual convention held in Reykjavik each year, attended by more than twenty-five hundred *EVE Online* players; the Council for Stellar Management, *EVE*'s player-elected council; and CCP's engagement with players on forums and social media. Though none of these events is unique to *EVE,* Czarnota establishes how their centrality to the ongoing development of *EVE Online* will be crucial for the game's continued longevity.

One emblematic effort to involve players in the ongoing development, preservation, and publication of *EVE Online* was the 2013 True Stories project, explored in depth in Nick Webber's contribution to the collection (chapter 15). Carrying the tagline "History is made by those who write it," the project offered players the opportunity to recount and celebrate the "important stories of actual events" from *EVE*'s first decade of game play. This part storytelling contest, part PR exercise, and part repository of game histories saw 750 stories submitted, with the winning story—penned, unsurprisingly, by The Mittani—captured in a fully illustrated comic book.

As in Webber's analysis of the discourse that surrounded this competition, there are pressing tensions between the competing player histories, "real" histories, and fictive histories (see also Carter et al. 2015). *EVE Online*'s fictive, imagined history is linked into a possible future of our current day: a dystopic galaxy filled with ruthless corporations in perpetual war over limited resources. In this dystopic future, a natural wormhole—called "EVE"—was found that allowed travel to a new, virgin galaxy named "New Eden." After a century of colonization, the wormhole collapsed, and those few colonies that survived persisted, grew, and eventually rediscovered space travel and other colonies, leading to more destructive warfare. The first four of these make up the current nonplayer factions in *EVE Online,* locked in a temporary armistice between equally powerful factions and maintaining the nonplayer police in approximately one-third of the playable solar systems. This fictive is crucially important for the emergence of *EVE*'s ruthless play styles, but although a small community of *EVE* role-players exists, this fictive history has little bearing on in-game events and has hardly progressed in the past ten years.

*EVE*'s player history, conversely, is incomparably rich, evolving, and unpreserved, and contributions to the True Stories project enabled players the opportunity to articulate and record their own game play history. As this collection demonstrates, the acts of a lone player can have enormous impact on the entire world and how it has unfolded. This means that these player stories can be as important to the universe of *EVE* as its fictive lore, but, as Webber demonstrates, tensions around the legitimacies of these different histories remain present. The maxim that "history is written by the victors" is true both in the history of global conflict and in the universe of New Eden. By examining this explicitly historical competition, Webber contributes to our understanding of video game history as well as providing insight into the values of *EVE Online* culture and how players make and take meaning from online games—and the role that game histories can play in this process.

While this project reveals the values of many *EVE Online* players, it also highlights emerging conflicts in the ongoing efforts to preserve digital games and virtual worlds. In late 2012, New York's Museum of Modern Art (MoMA) acquired fourteen digital games, *EVE Online* among them, for its permanent collection. *EVE* was acquired as part of this effort in recognition of its function, design, and visual architecture that allow players to participate freely and is the first MMOG to be acquired by a museum. In their closing contribution to the collection, Kristin MacDonough, Rebecca Fraimow, Dan Erdman, Kathryn Gronsbell, and Erica Titkemeyer discuss the preservation strategy MoMA deployed and how many of the properties that make it attractive for acquisition, such as its lack of a linear timeline or player-driven world, make it incredibly problematic for preservation and conservation. They conclude that many of the key elements of player–player interaction—which this volume considers the essence of *EVE Online*—are unpreservable.

This volume acts to preserve it, or at least a part of it. *EVE Online* is constantly evolving in response to player actions and the developer's gentle hand. Drawing on a plurality of voices, we capture the complexities of *EVE Online* and what it means to its players. Its unique, single-server universe has created a rich culture in which individual players and their actions *matter.* This culture has demanded new and sophisticated global communities and afforded new styles of emergent play that challenge firmly held notions of what "play" can be.

## BIBLIOGRAPHY

Achterbosch, Leigh, Robyn Pierce, and Gregory Simmons. 2008. "Massively Multiplayer Online Role-Playing Games: The Past, Present, and Future." *Computers in Entertainment* 5, no. 4: Article 9.

Carter, Marcus. 2014. "Emitexts and Paratexts: Propaganda in EVE Online." *Games and Culture* 10, no. 4: 311–42.

———. 2015. "Massively Multiplayer Dark Play: Treacherous Play in EVE Online." In *The Dark Side of Game Play: Controversial Issues in Playful Environments,* edited by Torill Elvira Mortensen, Jonas Linderoth, and Ashley M. L. Brown, 191–209. London: Routledge.

Carter, Marcus, Kelly Bergstrom, Nick Webber, and Oskar Milik. 2015. "EVE Is Real." Paper presented at the Digital Games Research Association Conference: Diversity of Play, Luneberg, Germany, May. http://www.digra.org/digital-library/publications/eve-is-real/.

CCP Games. 2009. "EVE Online: Old Storyline Intro" (trailer). http://www.youtube.com/watch?v=T84nrp08MWo.

Cifrino, Christopher. 2014. "Virtual Property, Virtual Rights: Why Contract Law, Not Property Law, Must Be the Governing Paradigm in the Law of Virtual Worlds." *Boston College Law Review* 55, no. 1: 235–64.

Connell, Raewyn, and James W. Messerschmidt. 2005. "Hegemonic Masculinity: Rethinking the Concept." *Gender and Society* 19, no. 6: 829–59.

Consalvo, Mia. 2009. *Cheating: Gaining Advantage at Video Games.* Cambridge, Mass.: MIT Press.

Corneliussen, Hilde, and Jill Walker Rettberg. 2008. *Digital Culture, Play, and Identity: A "World of Warcraft" Reader.* Cambridge, Mass.: MIT Press.

Evans, Monica. 2010. "Murder, Ransom, Theft, and Grief: Understanding Digital Ethics in Games." In *Videogame Cultures and the Future of Interactive Entertainment,* edited by Daniel Riha, 81–89. Oxford: Inter-Disciplinary Press.

Korhonen, Hannu, Markus Montola, and Juha Arrasvuori. 2009. "Understanding Playful User Experience through Digital Games." In *Proceedings of the International Conference on Designing Pleasurable Products and Interfaces,* 274–85. New York: ACM Press.

Lehdonvirta, Villi. 2010. "Virtual Worlds Don't Exist: Questioning the Dichotomous Approach in MMO Studies." *Game Studies* 10, no. 1. http://gamestudies.org/1001/articles/lehdonvirta.

Sicart, Miguel. 2009. *The Ethics of Computer Games.* Cambridge, Mass.: MIT Press.

van Lent, Michael. 2008. "The Future Is Virtually Here." *IEEE Computer* 41, no. 8: 87–89.

White, Ethan. 2008. "Massively Multiplayer Online Fraud: Why the Introduction of Real World Law in a Virtual Context Is Good for Everyone." *Northwestern Journal of Technology and Intellectual Property* 6, no. 2: 228–42.

Yin-Poole, Wesley. 2012. "CCP: Players' Attempt to Destroy Eve Online Economy Is 'F***ing Brilliant.'" http://www.eurogamer.net/articles/2012-04-27-ccp-players-attempt-to-destroy-eve-online-economy-is-f-ing-brilliant.

## *EVE Online* for the Uninitiated

*Kelly Bergstrom and Marcus Carter*

How do you describe *EVE Online* to someone who has never played it before? The most stripped-down explanation is probably that

> *EVE* is a space-themed massively multiplayer online game (MMOG).

But not only does this description require you know what an MMOG is, it doesn't provide any information about the important parts of *EVE* that make it different, such as how the developer (CCP Games) has a laissez-faire approach to the community or how scamming and theft are permitted and, consequently, pervasive. These facts about *EVE* are what make it relatively unique in the broader MMOG landscape and therefore are important to explaining what *EVE* is like. So, then, this short description would have to be expanded to something along the lines of the following:

> *EVE* is a space-themed MMOG with little developer intervention. Aside from hacking/modifying the software code, players are free to do whatever they like, including scamming, cheating, and assassinating other players.

But this does not account for other affordances of the game's design that also make it unique in the MMOG marketplace, for example, *EVE*'s permanent death or its single-server configuration, and the consequences of these design decisions for the types of play that occur. So perhaps the description could be revised as follows:

> *EVE* is a space-themed MMOG that is played on a single-shard server. There are many in-game affordances that result in high-stakes play (e.g., permadeath). Furthermore, the game's developer rarely intervenes. Aside from hacking/modifying the software code, players are free to do whatever they like, including scamming, cheating, and assassinating other players.

And yet, this third revision to the description does not account for how only a small portion of *EVE* is actually played within the game client. The majority of the communication, strategy and planning occurs on forums and in chat rooms outside of *EVE*, meaning many *EVE* "players" rarely log into the game client at all (see chapter 10). The preceding description also does not account for the unusual representations of the player within the game client, the disposable nature of ships, or the player-driven nature of the economy. In fact, it would take an entire book chapter even to begin to provide a "brief description" that does any justice to the task of explaining to someone who has never played *EVE* just *what EVE Online* is.

This is our attempt at that chapter; we do our best to provide a brief (or as brief as possible) explanation of what *EVE* is for someone who has yet to play it. Our goal is to provide the helpful context and background for the following fifteen chapters. Whereas with other games it would be helpful to spend a few hours playing the tutorials (*EVE* provides a limited free trial), this doesn't apply to *EVE*. Other games can be reasonably well understood after a few hours of play, or even after watching a video of play, but many elements of *EVE* are inaccessible to outsiders encountering the game for the first time, unless there is a more experienced player there to help guide their way. This is not to say that learning to play *EVE* is a Sisyphean task, but as chapter 2 illustrates, *EVE*'s tutorial system has a steep learning curve and leaves out important information. New players enter *EVE* with little understanding about how the game works and, in consequence, must reach out to other players for help, to build a social group with which to play, and to learn what it is to be an *EVE* player (Bergstrom et al. 2013). So, then, our goal for this chapter is to supplement the introduction provided by the trial account and/or in-game tutorial, taking the place of a friendly current player helping to guide you through your first steps into *EVE*.

In other words, the purpose of this chapter is to introduce the reader to what *EVE* is. This chapter provides the background and key vocabulary necessary for understanding the following chapters for the reader who has never played *EVE*; consequently, those familiar with the game should feel free to skip it. This description of course comes with the necessary caveat that *EVE* is constantly evolving, and this information represents a snapshot at a particular point in time (early 2015). Studying an MMOG means studying a moving target: with each expansion or patch, things will inevitably change. However, we have written this chapter to be focused on the bigger-picture elements of *EVE*, and we hope that our snapshot will not become hopelessly dated by the time this book reaches print. Finally, we note that this chapter is organized around a series of headings to allow the reader to skip over the information she doesn't necessary need and to zero in on the parts of *EVE* that are unfamiliar and/or need further contextualization.

## The Sandbox of *EVE Online*

In addition to being a sci-fi and/or space-themed MMOG, one of the most frequent labels applied to *EVE* is that it is a sandbox-style game. When applied to games, *sandbox* is usually taken to mean an open world in which players have free rein to choose their own in-game activities based on what they find most interesting (CCP Games n.d.). CCP Games often refers to (and advertises) *EVE Online* as "the Sandbox." For example, in 2009, CCP Games released a trailer (CCP Games 2009a) that has since attracted more than 1.5 million views. This trailer, titled *The Butterfly Effect*, begins with a voice-over stating,

> In chaos theory, there's a concept known as sensitive dependence on initial conditions. Most people call it the butterfly effect. In *EVE*, we call it the Sandbox.

This trailer depicts the consequences of a simple decision: one player deciding to lend a hand to another player in trouble. This momentary act of kindness ultimately leads to an "epic battle between thousands of players." The voice-over concludes,

> Hundreds of thousands of people could hear about this battle. Why so many? Because it all happened in one universe, not in separate realms, just one big Sandbox, where the actions of one person can resonate throughout the game world. In *EVE*, the choices you make shape the outcome of events. . . . What matters most is that the experience was emergent. Unscripted. Because in the Sandbox, all player actions, no matter how subtle or bold, always have an impact.

*The Butterfly Effect* trailer provides insight into what CCP, and *EVE* players, means when it refers to *EVE* as a sandbox, emphasizing how play is player driven rather than scripted or linear. This promotional text also highlights the importance of the single-shard server configuration, which allows a single *EVE* player to affect the entire virtual world of New Eden far more dramatically than typically afforded in other MMOGs (see, e.g., chapters 7 and 10).

## Inside the *EVE Online* Client

### ACCESSING *EVE ONLINE*

To begin at its most basic, *EVE Online* is a piece of software. It was initially available to buy in 2003, and briefly again in 2008, as a physical, boxed game that required installation from a CD-ROM. However, for most of its history, the *EVE* software has been digitally distributed through a downloadable executable file from CCP directly or through platforms like Steam. The current (January 2015) version is a little larger than six gigabytes. *EVE* requires an active Internet connection to play, and upon running the program, the user has to sign into a personal account using a username and password. Once signed in, the user is able select from a maximum of three characters and enter the virtual universe of New Eden as one of these characters. In these regards, *EVE* is entirely unremarkable and quite similar to many of the other MMOGs available for purchase and play.

Also unremarkable is that once a new account's trial period has ended, the account requires a subscription to remain active, with a monthly fee of €14.95, £10.00 for British customers, or US$15.00 for the rest of the world. Though *EVE*'s contemporaries in 2003 often charged a subscription, such a business model has grown increasingly rare during the rise of free-to-play games. *EVE Online* remains one of the few MMOGs to charge a subscription, which is interesting to note in the context of big-budget MMOGs like *Rift, Star Wars: The Old Republic,* and *The Secret World,* which have had to move toward various freemium business models. Although *EVE*'s subscription price is similar to that of market dominator *World of Warcraft,* we note that Blizzard Entertainment (*World of Warcraft*'s developer) charges for major additions to game content (referred to as "expansions"), whereas CCP does not; rather, *EVE*'s expansions are made available to all current *EVE* players twice a year (usually, one spring and one fall release) without charge.

The currency used within the game world is known as interstellar kredits (ISK), not to be confused with the Icelandic krona (also abbreviated ISK). This in-game currency functions similarly to what is seen in other MMOGs, with a notable exception that as of 2008, ISK can be converted into a Pilots License Extension (PLEX). This item can be purchased with in-game money or with real money for approximately US$19.95 (or less, if bought in bulk). One unit of PLEX can be redeemed to a user's account for one month's subscription; in other words, in-game currency can be used to pay for the game's subscription fees. This has the effect of allowing virtually wealthy players the opportunity to pay for their subscriptions with ISK and virtually poor players the opportunity to subsidize their play with real-world currency. Commended at its introduction for integrating virtual and real economies without disadvantaging players unwilling or unable to pay, PLEX provides a tenable exchange rate for the value of virtual goods in real life (US$19.95 is worth approximately 800 million ISK). It is currently against the rules of *EVE Online* to sell ISK for real money, though such practices are widespread on black market sites.

## *EVE ONLINE*'S IMAGINARY

*EVE* is set far into the future, in a dystopic sci-fi imaginary. As humankind expanded across the galaxy, "ruthless corporations rose to power, seizing every world within their grasp" (CCP Games 2009b). When the galaxy was filled, these corporations turned against each other, catalyzing centuries of war. In this future, a natural wormhole—called "EVE"—was discovered that allowed ships to travel to a new, virgin galaxy named "New Eden." After a century of colonization, the wormhole collapsed, "severing young colonies from the home worlds that sustained them" (CCP Games 2009b). Millions died, and those few colonies that survived persisted, grew, and eventually rediscovered space travel and other colonies that had survived, leading to more destructive warfare. The first four of these make up the current nonplayer factions in *EVE Online,* locked in a temporary armistice. The fiction of *EVE* is thus a harsh and ruthless future, in which war and destruction are commonplace (for more on *EVE*'s histories, see chapter 15). The four nonplayer factions are as follows:

> **Amarr Empire**: the largest nation in this fictional world; a society based on slave labor, ruled by a theocratic monarchy with an omnipresent religion
>
> **Caldari State**: a corporate dictatorship prizing strength, efficiency, and dignity
>
> **Gallente Federation**: the only "true" democracy of New Eden; a society focused on both liberal ideology (brotherhood and equal rights to all) and scientific advancement
>
> **Minmatar Republic**: emancipated slaves from the Amarr Empire; the postslavery society is characterized by tribal leadership and individualism

Players take on the role of "capsuleers," functionally immortal space pilots as a result of advanced cloning technologies. Upon logging in to the game for the first time, new players are asked to choose one of these four empires as their character's race and then to select a subrace. As mentioned earlier, each *EVE* account holds a maximum of three characters, and each of these characters has a unique pseudonym affording a persistent identity. When starting a character, the player can take tutorials that introduce him to the basics of manufacturing and combat (see chapter 2 on these tutorials and their failures in more detail), or the player can disregard the tutorials completely and venture out into the corners of the virtual universe. As Richard Page notes (see chapter 8), the play that emerges from player interactions with the client is not inevitable but swayed by the intersecting social worlds that meet in New Eden. It is also worth noting that no matter what race a player selects for her avatar, she is able to interact with and freely communicate with any other player in the game.

### AVATARS IN *EVE ONLINE*

As well as breaking from a few key conventions of the MMOG genre, which is primarily populated with fantasy-themed games (orcs, elves, and magic), for most of *EVE Online*'s history, players could not move through the game world via a humanoid or anthropomorphized avatar, a feature commonly found in other MMOGs. Instead, players saw passport-sized "photographs" of their own characters and were consequently mostly known to each other by usernames rather than virtual appearance (on this, see Carter, Gibbs, and Arnold 2012). When looking at another player's character in the virtual environment, the player sees a spaceship and the avatar's name. Even this spaceship is not a permanent representation of a player within the game world, with spaceships being regularly changed, depending on the pilot's goal at any particular time. Little customization is available, players frequently change ships depending on their purpose, and ships can be permanently destroyed.

In a recent expansion ("Incarna," released June 2011), CCP introduced fully rendered avatars and a sophisticated character creator that allows players to modify their avatars' bodies in great detail, providing control right down to the level of modifying muscle group development. That new avatar is only visible to an individual player as the avatar walks around inside his personal Captain's Quarters, which are not accessible to any other players. As of the most recent *EVE* expansion ("Rhea," released December 2014), players continue to interact with each other via their spaceships, and Captain's Quarters remain inaccessible to other players.

### THE *EVE* GAME WORLD

*EVE* is divided into two types of environments, but in both the player can communicate with any other player through EveMail (an in-game e-mail service), public and private chat rooms (such as the help channels described in chapter 2), and in local chat, a chat room shared by all players in a solar system and that identifies friends or foes nearby.

The first type of game world environment is when a player is docked in a space station, where the player's character cannot be attacked. Here the player can trade on the in-game market, manufacture goods, and load the cargo hold of her ship. The other environment is when a player is undocked, piloting her ship through *EVE*'s vast virtual universe comprising thousands of solar systems. An *EVE* solar system has hundreds, if not thousands, of celestial objects that can be flown to in a few seconds, and each solar system is connected to others through a network of jump bridges that teleport the user vast virtual distances in moments. Each solar system has a security status. In high-security systems, or high-sec, the in-game police (CONCORD) will swiftly respond to unprovoked aggression, but if an attacker is quick enough, players can still be destroyed, a mechanic exploited in player events like Hulkageddon (see chapter 12) and Burn Jita (see chapter 8). High-sec is where the nonplayer empires hold sovereignty, granting all players with good standing access to space stations for trade and manufacturing (on this type of play, see chapters 3, 7, and 12). In contrast, null-sec is where *EVE*'s huge player alliances (of tens of thousands of players) can claim sovereignty and build space stations and infrastructure only for their allies, and this is also where *EVE*'s notable wars are waged (on this, see chapters 5 and 8–10). Other solar systems include low-sec, where nonplayer groups provide space stations but no protection from CONCORD, and wormholes, systems without local chat (and thus without knowledge of who occupies the space around you) or space stations but with the most rewarding player versus environment (PVE) play.

### "LEVELING UP" IN *EVE*

In nearly all other MMOGs, a new player starts out much less powerful than older players, and through play, the player develops experience (XP), which levels up his character, making the character more powerful and unlocking new abilities, eventually allowing the character to become as powerful as a player who has been playing for significantly longer. Often this is critiqued as forcing players to "grind"—engage in repetitive actions—to level up their characters. Although, similar to other MMOGs, new *EVE* players are at a distinct disadvantage, this gap is much more difficult to close. This is because new abilities are unlocked through skill training, something that takes real time and is not accelerated by interactions within the game world.

Skills unlock the ability to do specific things (such as fly logistics ships or use a heavy missile launcher) and increase efficiency at doing them (such as flying faster or increasing manufacturing efficiency). Skills can be trained up to level 5, with the first level taking only a few minutes and the fifth level sometimes taking weeks of real time to train. The player does not have to be logged in to the game to train skills but—until the "Pheobe" release (2014)—could only queue skills up to twenty-four hours in advance, leading to the pejorative nickname for *EVE*: "skill queues online." As these skills take real time, it is consequently not possible for a new player to be as powerful as one who has been playing for several years.

With only one character able to be learning a new skill at any given time on a single subscription, it is very rare for an *EVE* player to start over with a new character for the sake of revising her in-game identity (common in other MMOGs). Instead, it is far more likely for a player to have multiple accounts, as described by some of the *EVE* players interviewed as part of Taylor et al.'s (2015) study, which is discussed further in the final section of this chapter.

### DEATH IN *EVE ONLINE*

Another major departure *EVE* takes from the player–player interaction seen in other games is that death carries harsher consequences in *EVE*'s game world. If a player-controlled ship sustains enough damage from attacks by other players or NPCs, it will explode. Any items (including PLEX) being carried by the ship will either be destroyed or will remain floating in the wreckage and available for any nearby players to pick up and keep as their own. Often these ships and their cargo are worth the equivalent of hundreds, occasionally thousands, of real-world dollars and represent an enormous investment of time and energy. A player whose ship has been destroyed can attempt to flee the wreckage in an escape pod that is vulnerable to attack. If the pod is destroyed and a player wishes to continue, a clone that is being held in stasis must be activated from one of the space stations scattered around the universe. Until the "Rhea" expansion (2014), if this clone hadn't been recently updated, the player lost a percentage of his trained skill points, further increasing the harsh consequences of death in *EVE*. Killing another player's pod offers no advantage or reward but is to be expected in this ruthless MMOG.

### A SINGLE-SERVER UNIVERSE

*EVE* is relatively unique in that the game is played on a single-shard server. All players interact in a single persistent universe, capable of handling more than fifty thousand simultaneous connections. Unlike most MMOGs, where players are divided into multiple smaller servers that house parallel versions of the game world, all *EVE*

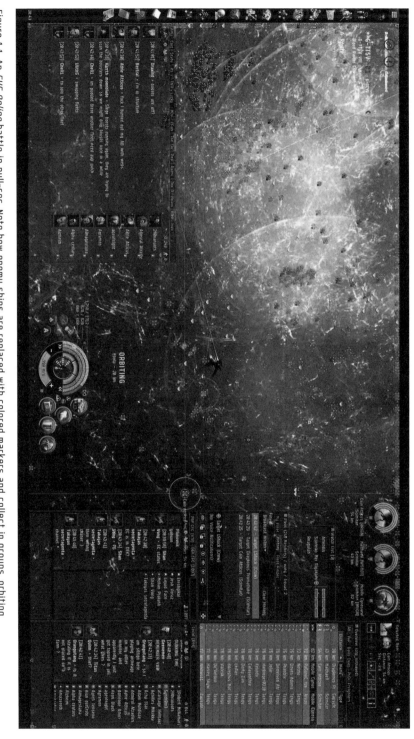

Figure 1.1. An *EVE Online* battle in null-sec. Note how enemy ships are replaced with colored markers and collect in groups, orbiting around "anchor" ships. The lower left is the chat window, and the panels on the right are depicting information such as the other ships nearby, friendly fleet information, and the enemy ships targeted. The status of the player's ship is displayed on the console in the middle of the screen. This particular battle (via Pronger 2014) involved more than seven hundred players simultaneously.

players are on the same server and can interact with and impact any other player. Multiple servers allow players to create "a clean slate" by transferring their characters to new servers, but this clean slate is unavailable to *EVE* players unwilling to start their long training queues over again. All of these qualities point toward a game world in which players become heavily invested in a single, persistent player identity.

## COMBAT IN *EVE ONLINE*

In chapter 3, William Bainbridge provides a detailed description of how *EVE*'s mining and industrial play functions, so we only describe *EVE*'s combat in this chapter. Players' control of their spaceships is not mapped to a direct input (e.g., using the W, A, S, and D keys to move); rather, players can command their ships to go in a particular direction, such as aligning with a celestial object (such as a sun or planet), or clicking in a direction of space, or orbiting another object at a defined distance. They select enemy ships by clicking on them in the game world or selecting them from a list of nearby ships (which can be arranged by distance, type, and so forth). There are a variety of different weapon types in *EVE*, but (for the sake of some simplicity) the main three types are lasers, projectile turrets, and missile launchers, and these can be fitted to do four types of damage: electromagnetic, thermal, kinetic, and explosive. The different ship types (coming from the four fictional empires in high-sec) are geared toward different weapon types; for example, Amarr ships have a high energy reserve to power several laser weapons. Ships are also typically geared toward different types of defense, for example, Caldari ships have powerful shields but low armor and are thus less resistant to electromagnetic damage. Combat therefore becomes a version of rock-paper-scissors, with players attempting to bring the right offense and defense to best deal with their opponents' ship types.

The type of offense and defense defines the way combat occurs. Missile launchers fire powerful explosives that travel three to four kilometers per second, exploding on or near their targets. A missile can only last five to ten seconds before detonating, limiting the aggressor's distance. A player who has trained the appropriate skills can often extend these factors by up to 25 percent. Missile-based ship combat thus typically involves orbiting the enemy at a distance of thirty-five to forty kilometers, firing once every ten to fifteen seconds. In groups, players orbit their fleet commander (FC) at a close distance, and the FC then orbits the enemy ships. Projectile turret-based weapons are more complex; they require better accuracy, something affected by a ship's signature radius (the smaller the "sig," the harder it is to track, and the harder it is to lock the target). The damage that a projectile weapon does is affected by the enemy ship's radial, transversal, and angular velocities. Fast but weak ships will orbit an enemy in a fast, tight circle to increase their angular velocity, making themselves harder to hit. Consequently, players use other types of offensive modules to increase an opponent's signature radius (making them easier to target and track), slow down enemy ships (making them easier to hit), and stop them from activating their warp drives to escape.

In large fleet battles, thirty to forty players firing at once on a coordinated target can kill their opponent immediately. However, solo or small-group combat typically involves exchanges of volleys that can last for several minutes. Furthermore, logistics ships can repair damaged ships while being fired upon, negating enemy attacks. This reduces the possible impact of lag, meaning players in Australia, thousands of kilometers from *EVE*'s servers in London, are not disadvantaged, permitting the single-shard virtual world so important to *EVE Online*'s unique experience. In summary, the actualities of *EVE* combat are incredibly complex, demanding intimate game knowledge and the assistance of third-party programs and Excel spreadsheets to correctly calculate damage in different circumstances. Although understanding them is useful for contextualizing the topics of discussion in the following chapters, it is not required.

## *EVE Online* Outside the Client

Though the elements of the *EVE Online* client described earlier are important for understanding the *EVE* experience, it is often what occurs outside the client that is most foreign to nonplayers and crucial for understanding *EVE*. An enormous amount of the practices involved in playing *EVE* occur outside of the *EVE* client, perhaps more so than for any other MMOG. These are not chores associated with understanding or coordinating play within the game but spaces in which play is legitimately occurring. As Darryl Woodford (2012) has noted, the widespread practices that occur outside of *EVE* present both conceptual and methodological challenges to game studies research (see also Lehdonvirta 2010; Carter, Gibbs, and Harrop 2014). An enormous portion of what constitutes *EVE* play happens in these spaces. To play *EVE* without engaging in these spaces is to not really play *EVE* at all, and thus acknowledging the practices outside of *EVE* is crucial for understanding it and researching it.

### *EVE ONLINE*'S API

The key piece of technology that makes this sprawling of play possible is *EVE Online*'s application programming interface (API). This is a piece of software that allows third-party applications to request information from a player's account without having to know the player's username and password. Players can create custom APIs that only give out specific information and then give these API keys to third-party applications. This means players are able to securely share information about their accounts with programs and others and verify their identity on platforms not managed by CCP Games.

One result of this has been a wide range of third-party applications that help curb *EVE*'s harsh learning curve and difficult mechanics. EVE Fitting Tool (EFT), a program Chris Paul notes in chapter 2, is "compulsory for anyone making informed decisions about key components of the game" and allows players to mock-fit ships with different modules and view what their speed, damage, and defense would be as well as what skills would need to be trained to fly it. EVEMon is a similar program that allows players to plan their skill training years in advance toward different goals and calculate how long it will take to pilot new ships; it is capable of running in the background to notify players when they are not training skills or when a piece of manufacturing has finished.

## SOCIAL GROUPS IN *EVE ONLINE*

When traveling through the universe of New Eden with allies, players can join together into temporary groups or *fleets.* This is a way of preventing friendly fire and allows players to communicate with each other easily. More permanent groupings in *EVE* are *corporations.* Corporations, like guilds *(World of Warcraft, EverQuest),* cabals *(The Secret World),* or linkshells *(Final Fantasy XIV),* are a way for players to join together under the banner of a common group name, pool resources, and communicate with other members easily in a private corporation-only chat channel. Corporations can also align themselves with other corporations as part of an *alliance.* Alliances can hold sovereignty over an area of the universe, and this territory can be assaulted by other alliances as part of a hostile takeover and attempts to increase empire. Alliances can declare war on each other, and these wars can last months or even years. Long-standing grievances and wars become part of the game's history and are chronicled on wikis or websites such as the EVElopedia (see chapter 15). The largest alliances have more than forty thousand members (see chapter 10 on the organizational demands of running a group this size). A robust and customized technical infrastructure is necessary to support these organizations, the majority of which require *EVE*'s API to function.

First, corporations and alliances use forums hosted on third-party websites to facilitate the development of a community and coordinate players. These are typical gaming forums, with subforums dedicated to different *EVE*-specific topics (military strategy, industrial, market, services for sale, etc.) and to general interests (music, other games, etc.). Corporation and alliance leadership typically use their forums to discuss leadership strategy and planning and to announce these plans to the members of the group. The API tool means that players can sign up to these forums and verify their in-game identity, meaning that players can trust that "John Smith" posting on the forums is the same "John Smith" that can be found in-game, the persistent identity to which, as we emphasized in the previous section, players have a significant attachment. In addition to forums, alliances typically also have IRC chat and voice servers that players are able to use to communicate even when not playing the game; typically, players have these running whenever their computers are running. For example, this allows groups to send announcements and notifications to all members who may be able to log in to the game and defend territory. During battles, voice servers are integral to coordinating the hundreds of players in fleets and consequently are often the focus of DDoS attacks and infiltration (see chapter 9).

Leaders in TEST Alliance—the group at the center of Carter's ethnography (Carter 2015c)—often suggested that their IT infrastructure was one of the group's most valuable assets. In addition to the communication infrastructure, this was also because of the third-party programs *EVE* players had developed that use the API function to help manage tens of thousands of players. For example, typical of an *EVE* alliance, TEST has HR teams that review applications to join the alliance. They also have re-imbursement teams that review ships destroyed in combat for the alliance and sub-sequently remunerate players who died, and they have other groups for players with specific skills (such as a group only for players who can pilot a certain kind of ship). Such is the logistical complexity of coordinating thousands of players; applications like these are crucial to an alliance's in-game success.

## *EVE Online* Play Styles

In this section, we overview some of the common play styles that have emerged in *EVE*. What follows should not be taken as an exhaustive list of the types of play styles present in the game. Instead, these should be viewed more as *EVE* archetypes that help elucidate the sorts of play that can happen within this sandbox to better contextualize the discussions present throughout the remainder of this book. However, we stress that play preferences are fluid, and they are not mutually exclusive. Simply put, a player who enjoys mining may also enjoy participating in player versus player (PVP) combat. Expressing a preference for one does not (and will not) prevent participation in any of the other ways of playing *EVE*. However, we note that because of *EVE*'s real-time skill training system, players often focus a character's training on a specific career to maximize efficiency, in turn attaching their player identities to specific styles of play.

### MINERS AND INDUSTRIALISTS

The vast majority of in-game ships and items are manufactured by *EVE Online* players, using minerals mined by other players. Miners orbit asteroids until their cargo holds are full, firing mining lasers at them, before taking the minerals to a space station. Often miners will leave the minerals in space in secure cargo containers and re-turn with ships with large cargo holds or will coordinate with other players to increase the efficiency of their play (a notion measured by "ISK per hour"). It is also not rare for dedicated miners to run multiple accounts simultaneously and do all this teamwork themselves. As players train their characters to be more efficient, they can fly larger ships that mine more quickly and make more money from play. Mining is commonly denigrated as one of the most "carebear" styles of play for its solo nature and low skill requirement (see chapters 7 and 12 on this colloquialism), but many players enjoy this relatively passive style of play because it does not demand their entire attention and can mesh with other simultaneous practices (see Carter, Nansen, and Gibbs 2014).

These minerals can then be used to manufacture ships, modules, weapons, and ammunition using blueprints (see chapter 3 for a detailed description of the manu-facturing process), a process similarly made more efficient by specific skill training.

Manufacturers are players who focus on turning minerals (either mined themselves or more often bought on the game market) into modules that can then be sold at a profit. Manufacturing takes real time, broken up into "runs," but can make significant profit from minimal, regular effort. Third-party programs using *EVE*'s API system often facilitate calculating the potential profit from manufacturing runs and may offer suggestions for how to improve this profit.

### PLAYING THE MARKET

Often in distinction from this industrialist play style, market players are those who do not necessarily manufacture goods themselves but rather focus on buying low and selling high. This is possible because purchased items in *EVE* are not magically teleported to the buyer's location; rather, they are purchased in a specific space station, and the player has to attend that space station to use it. The virtual universe of *EVE Online* is enormous, comprising thousands of solar systems each often having multiple space stations, thus market players profit off the laziness of other players. While goods are mined and manufactured across the universe (predominantly in high-sec), market players work on buying goods at the best price possible before either relisting them at a higher price or moving them to a different location to sell for profit (sometimes this job is contracted out to "freighter" players). Several trading hubs, the largest being the Jita solar system, typically sell at the lowest price, whereas goods typically cost the most in null-sec.

Market players often use Excel spreadsheets and third-party programs to maximize profit, but the richest can make enough to subsidize the subscriptions of multiple accounts just by logging on for twenty minutes each day to update buy and sell orders. Like the rest of *EVE*, its market is unforgiving and ruthless, with the game's most powerful players manipulating the market through political maneuvers and monopolizing resources, earning vast amounts of income to fund wars and political agendas.

### PLAYER VERSUS ENVIRONMENT

*EVE*'s market is driven by the permanent destruction of destroyed ships in the various iterations of *EVE*'s combat and the expense of ammunition. Rarely losing their ships, PVE players are those who fight nonplayer enemies, receiving bounties from the nonplayer empires and sellable salvage for doing so. There are a variety of player identities within this play style, with PVE players who fly incredibly expensive ships in the security of high-sec, eking out efficiencies where possible, and null-sec PVE players who look for valuable enemy spawns but are constantly on the lookout for enemy pirates. Some PVE resembles "raids" in *World of Warcraft* (see Chen 2012), where groups of players must carefully coordinate small fleets to beat dangerous enemies in "incursions." The most difficult form of PVE is found in wormholes where local chat does not function, making it difficult to determine if any enemies are nearby. These systems also do not have space stations, meaning players must carry with them everything they could possibly need until they can find their way back into charted space through a maze of wormholes that are constantly collapsing.

PVP combat similarly has a variety of forms, from engaging in solo PVP to commanding fleets of hundreds of pilots.

### PLAYER VERSUS PLAYER

PVP within *EVE* comes in many different forms, ranging from highly skilled solo PVP to tight-knit teams in "gang warfare" and the deindividualized large fleet battles, often having more than five hundred pilots on each side. Most important to note for someone unfamiliar with this game world is that PVP can at times be nonconsensual. If a *World of Warcraft* player decides that he wants to engage in combat against fellow players, he has a few options: he can create a character on a specifically designated PVP server, he can queue for a battleground and be matched against other players wishing to PVP, he can turn on his personal PVP flag and then venture out into contested space and hope to come across opposing players "in the wild," he can challenge players of his own faction to a duel, and so on. The common theme is that players are able to make the choice to be open to PVP, whether by selecting a PVP server or purposefully queuing for a battleground. For those who do not enjoy PVP, there is another designation of PVE servers available, where players are free to go about their business without fear of ambush. Similar safe zones just do not exist within New Eden, as evidenced by player-organized events such as Hulkageddon, which is discussed in chapter 12.

### SCAMMERS

Particularly unusual, *EVE Online* features pervasive treacherous play: the exploitation of misplaced trust for in-game advantage (Carter 2015a). Unlike all other MMOGs that design out the possibility for dark play involving theft, treachery, malfeasance, and betrayal, CCP Games has designed for such activities at a massive and unparalleled scale. Except for disallowing technical exploits, players are not restricted from deceiving, tricking, lying, and generally being dishonest toward other players in the pursuit of game goals, including in *EVE*'s eSport (see Carter and Gibbs 2013; Carter 2015b, 2015c). This has manifested in the pervasive and common occurrences of scamming, stealing, and espionage and in what Nick Combs (2007) refers to as a "culture of mistrust." This ruthlessness of *EVE* has permeated every fiber of its play, and the number one rule hammered into each new player is "DON'T TRUST ANYONE," but at numerous levels, *EVE* players are forced to trust one another to access certain styles of *EVE* play. In chapter 9, Keith Harrison, a player who runs the largest and most feared intelligence agency in *EVE,* unpacks the practices around espionage in *EVE* in more detail.

OTHER PLAY STYLES

This list of player identities unpacks some of the most common play styles found in *EVE Online* but is by no means comprehensive. A small community of role-players exists within *EVE Online,* situating their efforts and play within *EVE*'s rich fictional history. Similarly, many players follow, document, and discuss *EVE Online*'s lore and the occasional additions to it that often foreshadow future expansions and changes to the game world or simply document explorations of the *EVE* universe (e.g., see Mark726 2015). With a presence on Twitter (around the hashtag #tweetfleet), blogs, and *EVE* and other gaming forums, small communities of interest like this emerge and contribute to *EVE*'s nature as a pastime (see Carter, Gibbs, and Harrop 2014) in that a wide range of leisure practices are associated with playing *EVE* that are not confined to the *EVE* client. Finally, we note that there are definite hierarchies between these play styles in *EVE*'s heterogeneous community, which are unpacked in further detail by Taylor et al. (2015) and by Kelly Bergstrom in chapter 12.

## Conclusion

*EVE* is unusually difficult to understand for the nonplayer; as detailed as we have been in this chapter, we have still greatly simplified many of our descriptions and overlooked many styles of play or elements of *EVE*'s design that a player may consider important. Furthermore, *EVE* is a game that is constantly evolving, featuring many styles of play now that have only emerged as the community has grown (the emphasis on propaganda, for instance, is a relatively new development) over the past ten years. This description, and indeed this book, is only able to capture a small slice of *EVE,* a slice defined by the time the work was written and the topics of the chapters.

BIBLIOGRAPHY

Bergstrom, Kelly, Marcus Carter, Darryl Woodford, and Christopher A. Paul. 2013. "Constructing the Ideal EVE Online Player." Paper presented at DeFragging Games Studies, Atlanta, Ga. http://www.digra.org/digital-library/publications/constructing-the-ideal-eve-online-player/.

Carter, Marcus. 2014. "Emitexts and Paratexts: Propaganda in EVE Online." *Games and Culture* 10, no. 4: 311–42.

———. 2015a. "Massively Multiplayer Dark Play: Treacherous Play in EVE Online." In *The Dark Side of Game Play: Controversial Issues in Playful Advances,* edited by Torill Mortensen, Jonas Linderoth, and Ashley Brown, 191–209. Routledge: London.

———. 2015b. "The Demarcation Problem in Multiplayer Games: Boundary-Work in EVE Online's eSport." *Game Studies* 15, no. 1. http://gamestudies.org/1501/articles/carter.

———. 2015c. "Treacherous Play in EVE Online." PhD diss., University of Melbourne.

Carter, Marcus, and Martin Gibbs. 2013. "eSports in EVE Online: Skullduggery, Fair Play and

Acceptability in an Unbounded Competition." In *Proceedings of the Eighth International Conference on the Foundations of Digital Games*, 47–54. Chania, Greece: SASDG.

Carter, Marcus, Martin Gibbs, and Michael Arnold. 2012. "Avatars, Characters, Players and Users: Multiple Identities at/in Play." In *Proceedings of the Twenty-Fourth Australian Computer–Human Interaction Conference*, ed. Vivienne Farrell, Graham Farrell, Caslon Chua, Weidong Huang, Raj Vasa, and Clinton Woodward, 68–71. Melbourne: ACM Press.

Carter, Marcus, Martin Gibbs, and Mitchell Harrop. 2014. "Drafting an Army: The Playful Pastime of Warhammer 40,000." *Games and Culture* 9, no. 2: 122–47.

Carter, Marcus, Bjorn Nansen, and Martin Gibbs. 2014. "Screen Ecologies, Multi-gaming and Designing for Different Registers of Engagement." In *Proceedings of the First ACM SIG-CHI Annual Symposium on Computer–Human Interaction in Play*, ed. Lennart E. Nacke, 37–46. Toronto: ACM Press.

CCP Games. 2009a. "The Butterfly Effect." https://www.youtube.com/watch?v=08hmqyejCYU.

———. 2009b. "EVE Online: Old Storyline Intro." https://www.youtube.com/watch?v=T84n rp08MWo.

———. n.d. "Find Your Path in the Sandbox." http://www.eveonline.com/sandbox/.

Chen, Mark. 2012. *Leet Noobs: The Life and Death of an Expert Player Group in World of Warcraft*. New York: Peter Lang.

Combs, Nick. 2007. "A Culture of Mistrust in EVE-Online." *TerraNova*. http://terranova.blogs.com/ terra_nova/2007/11/culture-of-mist.html.

Lehdonvirta, Vili. 2010. "Virtual Worlds Don't Exist: Questioning the Dichotomous Approach in MMO Studies." *Game Studies* 10, no. 1. http://gamestudies.org/1001/articles/lehdo nvirta.

Mark726. 2015. *EVE Travel* (blog). https://evetravel.wordpress.com/.

Pronger, C. 2014. "EVE Online Battle of G-TT5V." https://www.youtube.com/watch?v=vG -2Yw7O59U.

Taylor, Nicholas, Kelly Bergstrom, Jennifer Jenson, and Suzanne de Castell. 2015. "Alienated Playbour: Relations of Production in EVE Online." *Games and Culture* 10, no. 4: 365–88.

Woodford, D. 2012. "Hanging Out Is Hard to Do: Methodology in Non-avatar Environments." *Journal of Gaming and Virtual Worlds* 4, no. 3: 275–88.

## *EVE Online* Is Hard and It Matters

*Christopher Paul*

*EVE Online* is an oddity. It shares several things in common with onetime massively multiplayer online game (MMOG) giant *World of Warcraft (WoW)*. Both games charged a subscription fee while competitors went free-to-play. Both games grew for sustained periods of time after their respective launches, unlike other games that had a burst of interest and then quickly shrank. However, these two industry-leading games also have marked differences. *WoW* featured far more subscribers than *EVE*, as it attracted and retained more than 12 million players for years (Blizzard Entertainment 2011), and *WoW* is considered to be a much easier game for players to learn, even though the game lost approximately 70 percent of its trial players before they reached level 10 (Burnes 2011). Having debuted in 2003, *EVE* is older than *WoW*, but even with its age, *EVE* is still growing and planning for its second decade, which is an opposite path to *WoW*'s steady decline in subscriptions. Primarily distributed via Steam and featuring regular, free expansions to the game, *EVE* is further distinctive because of its space theme, its sandbox design, and its level of interaction with players, which includes a Council of Stellar Management that is staffed by players elected to serve as representatives in communication with the game's Icelandic developer CCP Games as well as an annual Fanfest in Iceland.

It is within the world of *EVE* that a peculiar thing happens. Elements of *EVE*'s design push players away from the game, as the early moments of the game effectively tell new people that they do not belong, that this is not a game they should be playing. In doing so, *EVE* presents a complex rhetorical message, one predicated on honing its community of players and ensuring that those who do make it through those frustrating early moments are far more committed than players of other games. The impact of this approach is somewhat counterintuitive as, by developing a well-deserved reputation for a maddening tutorial process, *EVE* gathers a committed, unified player base on which to sustain the game and build a cohesive community. Players of any game are constructed by the game itself in a process of co-creation, and *EVE* is a particularly interesting example of how typical players of a game and their processes of play can be shaped by a game and the structures around them (Bergstrom et al. 2013). Although players are frequently vocal about developer decisions pertaining to the game, the outspokenness is driven by passion, which keeps the game going and the subscriptions flowing. From a rhetorical standpoint, telling new players not to play is exactly what helps *EVE* grow, offering a counterintuitive pathway for the success of digital games and a warning to be heeded before any major changes are made to the new player experience.

Understanding the ramifications of *EVE*'s design requires a brief exploration of rhetorical analysis, with a discussion of both the traditional role of rhetoric and how rhetoric has been applied to games. With that theoretical background established, it is appropriate to move to a discussion of *EVE* in general and then to the new player experience in *EVE* and how CCP has sought to make it somewhat more accessible. Finally, the combination of a rhetorical perspective and knowledge of *EVE* articulates how the game persuades people not to play and what *EVE*'s design indicates about digital games more broadly.

## Rhetoric, Briefly

Rhetorical analysis has been defined in many ways, but a contemporary baseline definition argues that "rhetoric is the study of what is persuasive" (Campbell and Huxman 2009, 5). Influenced by the works of Kenneth Burke, rhetoric is about how elements of the ways in which we communicate influence people to act in particular ways. Burke was fascinated by language and symbol systems, as he thought "the whole overall 'picture' [of reality] is but a construct of our symbol system" (Burke 1966, 5) and that language works as "*a symbolic means for inducing cooperation in beings that by nature respond to symbols*" (Burke 1969, 43).

In the wake of Burke's work, the role of rhetoric expanded, as scholars connected rhetoric to ways of knowing, contending that "rhetoric may be viewed not as a matter of giving effectiveness to truth but of creating truth" (Scott 1967, 13). The end result of this articulation of rhetoric finds the discipline offering "another perspective, one that accounts for the production, circulation, reception and interpretation of messages" (Zarefsky 2008, 635).

In the midst of an analysis about *EVE*, one particular element of Burke's work is notable: identification. Burke held that people were inherently divided from each other, but we sought to come together, which required us to identify with something that we shared with other people. Burke held that in aspiring to something greater than ourselves, we needed to act with other people to facilitate "a way of life [that] is an *acting-together*; and in acting together, men have common sensations, concepts, images, ideas, attitudes that make them *consubstantial*" (Burke 1969, 21). In seeking to come together, we need to find something outside of ourselves to which we can latch on, something that brings us into connection with others. Burke generally sought to find that link in language, but more recent scholars have held that "identification, in short, becomes as much a process and structure as a discrete perlocutionary act" (Jordan 2005, 269), which certainly opens the door to explore how people come together with and through digital games.

This link to finding something greater than ourselves can be found riddled throughout MMOGs, as they are predicated on interaction with others within the context of something greater. As T. L. Taylor (2006, 9) noted about play in *EverQuest,* "shared action becomes a basis for social interaction, which in turn shapes the play." The interactions within the games, the play, are the pieces that encourage identification with either other players or the game itself; those are the elements that establish a consubstantial connection. In *EVE,* the question is about how those elements of identification and consubstantiality are specifically deployed to attract some precisely because they weeded out others and what that indicates about games as a whole.

The final element of rhetoric to consider is how contemporary scholars in game studies have applied the ideological approach to the study of games. One approach is to consider how, in video games, "the main representational mode is procedural, rather than verbal" (Bogost 2006, 168), which requires analyzing the procedural rhetoric of video games, with a focus on the "practice of using processes persuasively" (Bogost 2007, 29). This approach is grounded in the belief that video games "make arguments with *processes*" (Bogost 2008, 125). The key recognition of procedural rhetoric is that communication in video games functions differently than communication in other media forms, thus procedural elements in digital games are particularly worthy of study.

Game studies scholars have also examined rhetorical functions of games beyond the procedural elements contained in the code and programmatic design of games, like the ways in which rewards in games interact with player discourse surrounding games (Paul 2010b), how changes in game design impact a game's rhetorical environment (Paul 2010a), and how player discourse functions to define the terms on which games are played (Moeller, Esplin, and Conway 2009). The tools of rhetoric enable a critical examination of how the words, design, and play of games create meaning and shape how games are constructed as cultural objects (Paul 2012). Rhetoric places focus on specific elements of interaction between players, games, and designers, as "the form of the player-game interaction has to be taken seriously if critics are to come to terms with the rhetorical force" of certain games (Voorhees 2009, 256).

Rhetorical analysis is particularly well suited to examining how specific elements of communication seek to establish a message and impact behavior. In the case of games, words, design, and play can perform many different functions, from changing a person's view of the world to encouraging her to play in a specific way. *EVE* is interesting in that the first few moments of a player's experience in the game are designed in such a way that a new player quickly receives the message that he does not belong, that he should not be playing this game. This consistent message forms the base of the new player experience in New Eden.

## *EVE Online*: An Overview

*EVE Online* is certainly willing to let as many people as they want try the game—developer CCP regularly offers free trials ranging from fourteen to twenty-one days to give people a chance to do just that—but the design of the game pushes most people away, honing the audience of the game and shaping the context of its player base through specific game design choices.

In addition to previously discussed difference such as the single-shard world, space theme, and unusual circumstances of play that exist both within and outside of the game client, some specific elements of *EVE*'s design warrant attention. Character embodiment is also fundamentally different, as players are primarily interacting with the ships they are flying, and any character can pursue any and all skills for which she possesses the prerequisites. Players in the game are often represented through what is commonly known as a passport photo, which looks very much like the offline equivalent. Frequently reduced to a single 2-D image of a character, personalization of one's avatar is different than in other MMOGs. A player also must learn that his ship is a tool, a frequently disposable asset and one that may often need to be sacrificed in service of a greater good.

Further differentiating *EVE* is the means by which players skill up in the game. Instead of picking a class that dictates their abilities, any player in *EVE* can decide what she wants to do, and if she subsequently changes her mind, the player can change her training to add her newly desired skills. *EVE* does not have an analogue to the frequently found experience points that determine levels, instead using a training system where characters level up around the clock, whether online or off. This mode of training is particularly friendly to spending less time in-game, as the amount of time spent playing does not dictate one's ability in the game, but it firmly and permanently tilts the balance of power toward those who have played longer and acquired more skills. New players can learn many introductory skills quickly enough to be competitive in key aspects of the game within about a month, but they will have less versatility than those who have been playing for years, and they cannot ever catch up to those who keep playing. This mode of training also impacts the way that alternate characters work, as players have little incentive to level up another class to fulfill different roles in a group. However, only one character on each account can train skills at any given time, which means that those in *EVE* interested in having a character dedicated to a particular task, such as trade, mining, industry, or player versus player (PVP) combat, will likely choose to get a second, third, or fourth account to train multiple skills at once, specializing each of the characters in a particular role.

Although these differences, and more, separate *EVE* from its competitors, the most notable difference is the brutal, harsh, cold, and unfriendly learning curve that distinguishes the game. *EVE*'s learning curve is routinely summarized in similar ways, with notes that it is "mind-numbingly harsh for those who want a pick-up game, or a game that cares if you make it beyond your first 30 days—or even 30 hours" (Smith 2010), and that it has "the deserved reputation for being the hardest MMO to get a grasp of" (Egan 2009). *EVE* has a virtually vertical learning curve, with a deep and complex world that has so many differences from other games that there is a veritable ton of information to learn. Even the game developers, CCP, note the difficulty of learning the game when beginning to play, stating that "you don't have to learn everything at once and that some things you won't ever need to learn" and that "despite all our efforts to help players learn, most still gain the majority of their knowledge from other players which is the natural way of things in an MMORPG" (CCP 2010b).

This last note is perhaps the most interesting, as it presents part of the reason why the developers do not necessarily have a problem with the game's reputation as the most difficult MMOG to learn. The difficulty encourages player interaction, as new players must interact with older players to ascertain how to play the game. Player interaction in the game is designed to create identification among players, developing a more tightly knit community where those experienced in *EVE* are placed in a position to welcome those new to the game. This has led to the development of groups like EVE University[1] and Brave Newbies Inc.,[2] player-run corporations dedicated to educating players new to the game. Players have to reach out to others, and groups like these are some of the few entities that are broadly protected by most in the game. Brave Newbies was formed with a goal "to inspire all those that have tried *EVE Online* or are thinking about trying it but are put off by the slow start. It doesn't have to be this way and Brave Newbies Inc. seems to be determined in proving that to everyone who joins" (CCP Phantom 2014). Warring factions can generally agree on the utility and importance of groups like EVE University, as they train new pilots and help keep the game growing. The difficulty is notable and important, precisely because it has a tremendous impact on the rhetorical force of *EVE*: as it shapes the terms on which the initial patterns of identification are formed for new players. Tutorials and advice are typical to most games, but in *EVE*, they happen in a special way, because the most useful lessons are largely left to the players and their interactions inside and outside of the game client.

Two other key design components distinguish play in *EVE*. First is the near-constant refrain, reinforced in both word and deed, that you should trust no one (Schaefer 2010). The developer's FAQ about the game concludes with the warning that "this is general advice" and that CCP "cannot guarantee any standard of behavior towards you" (CCP 2010b). Although vague, the intent behind this warning is reinforced by the numerous in-game actions that have thrown the *EVE* world, individual corporations (the *EVE* versions of guilds or clans), or player accounts into chaos. In *EVE*, it is legal to steal from others or engage in a creative use of game mechanics to garner an advantage, which could range from a suicide attack to destroy another player's ship and obtain the loot rights to the cargo and materials, to stealing the equivalent of US$45,000 in game currency in a massive investment scam, to defrauding your corporation of billions in game currency or engaging in corporate espionage to dissolve a competitor (Chalk 2010).

Account hacking results in a ban, and a very few activities are frowned on by the developers, but in the course of *EVE*, there is no protection from scams or other activities that would be deemed illicit by game managers of many other MMOGs. A new player is likely to be outside his starting space station with lootable items with names like "Welcome Gift" or the somewhat less savvy "Free Shit," only to learn upon looting that looting items makes a player fair game for players who get their jollies from blowing up the ships of those foolish enough to fall prey to a scam. Much like e-mail spam, local channels in *EVE* abound with "investment" opportunities that are too good to be true, and the unlucky saps who invest will quickly find their in-game currency drained with no recourse, because if they were foolish enough to fall victim to a nefarious scam, they certainly deserved it in the world of *EVE*, and it is hoped that they will have learned a lesson for next time. The sandbox-style design means that *EVE Online* has a massive amount of emergent, unexpected game play, as players are given free rein to do just about whatever they like in the game world to gain the play experiences they seek. This can compound the disorientation of new players, as they are learning game mechanics, social norms, and details of the rich history of a society. New players do not just need to learn how to play a game, they also have to learn to play the players of *EVE*.

The companion game concept to this is that you will die in *EVE Online*; it is simply a matter of when and how often. The first commandment of *EVE* is that "the only place where you're safe in *EVE* is either docked or offline, otherwise you're mostly fair game" (CrazyKinux 2010). For many, the idea of death or risk in a game may not seem like a particularly big deal, as players die in games all the time. However, the penalty for dying in *EVE* hearkens back to the penalties invoked in older games, such as *EverQuest*. A player who is not properly prepared for the risk of death may lose almost all of her net worth and months' worth of training in one fell swoop. In a world where a single ship can cost about as much as a small used car would in the real world (Stigg 2010), the central role of PVP and death is quite meaningful. In *EVE*, "you do not have any safety, like you do in a PvE Warcraft realm. You do not flag on PvP. It's always on" (Hammer 2007d). Any *EVE* player can attack any other *EVE* player in any zone in the game. Nonplayer character (NPC) police will attack those with malevolent intentions in certain areas of the game world, but the CONCORD police are there merely to react to what has happened rather than to prevent the attack in the first place. As a result, other players can destroy your ship, knowing they will be destroyed by CONCORD, for their friends to loot the materials your ship contained. Any ship carrying too much cargo or particularly valuable items is likely to be destroyed at any point in any system in the game. There is no safe haven while flying in the space of New Eden.

When your ship is destroyed, and "you will lose a lot of ships while you learn the ropes" (Hammer 2007b), you are jettisoned into space in your pod. NPCs will not attack the pod, but players can, resulting in you getting "podded." Although being podded is "nothing personal" (CrazyKinux 2010) for *EVE* players, it can result in a loss of "*a month's full-time* training or more" (Hammer 2007b). The month of training can never fully be recovered. Certainly you can train those skills all over again, but being podded can result in catastrophic consequences, compounding the damage from a loss of a ship. *EVE* does have game mechanisms to mitigate losses from death, including ship insurance and clones that can store your skill points in case of podding, but the existence of both programs speaks to the regularity of death in *EVE* and its potentially dire consequences. An up-to-date clone can offset much of the damage from being podded, but insurance does not cover all components of the ship, making death in *EVE* a significant, harsh experience that can be especially cruel to the unprepared.

These two elements are fundamental parts of how *EVE* functions rhetorically, as they create the terms of a dystopian world where players are required to watch their backs. Romanticizing elements of a free-for-all-style Wild West world, *EVE* is a haven for those who enjoy griefing, which encourages those with more altruistic intentions to identify with something greater than themselves, while also providing a clear space for griefers to come together as the pirates who are just as crucial to game play in *EVE* as anyone else. Interactions in *EVE* are necessarily social, as players' activities, from a PVP victory to market arbitrage to mining, potentially impact every other player in the game and shape the terms of identification in a dynamic, unstable world. This world is not for everyone, though, as the harsh terms of engagement are designed so that players are either in or out, because the fundamental underpinnings of the sandbox world do not change; it is merely a question of how a player will either exploit them or shut the game down and move on to something else.

## Beginning *EVE*

Logging in to *EVE* means being greeted with a message about the number of other players sharing the server with you, a number that frequently totals in the mid-five figures. An introductory cinematic introduces players to the world of New Eden, which was discovered when explorers left Earth and used the EVE gate to pass through a wormhole in space. The gate later collapsed, leaving "thousands of small colonies" in a state of "complete isolation to fend for themselves, cut off from the old world" and "clinging to the brink of extinction" (CCP 2010a). Players are encouraged to forge their own fates in an emergent world where the bold are rewarded and the meek are punished. The narrative background for *EVE* is harsh and dark, depicting a galaxy where exceptional individuals shape the world they navigate. This setting perfectly suits the game, as the early moments in *EVE* are likely to make many players feel as if they are completely isolated and on the brink of extinction, just like those early settlers of New Eden. The tutorial has been changed many, many times over the years, as new features have been added to the game and when key trouble spots have been identified. The changes have tended to make the game more accessible in an attempt to smooth the learning curve, with the general intent of making "the sci-fi sandbox less like ancient Sanskrit and more like an intuitive MMO" (Reahard 2012).

Part of the most recent major redesign of the *EVE* tutorial as of this writing was to prepare for the "increased awareness of and interest in" *EVE* given the launch of *Dust 514* (CCP Greyscale 2013). Anticipating an influx of new players, CCP gave one of its teams one month to redesign the tutorial in an effort to address the roughest edges. Changes were made, from altering the order of certain tasks to introducing new "dead-sexy in-space pointers" (Figure 2.1) that can make key objects in space far more visible (CCP Greyscale 2013). These changes were generally praised by the *EVE* commentariat, although there are often reservations that range from the fact that new players can quite literally get lost in space to the fact that all of the instructions must be meticulously read on-screen (Drain 2012). The tutorial and the way it introduces players to *EVE* are at the center of how the game functions rhetorically to push players away.

After the initial cinematics that welcome new accounts, players are given a series of choices about their race, bloodline, and other key elements of their characters. Originally these decisions had a substantial impact on play, but those consequences have been watered down over time to prevent new players from hamstringing their efforts before they know what they are doing. Creation of the actual character is an awe-inspiring process, as the graphic details of *EVE* have been substantially upgraded over time, and choices for what players want their characters to look like seem both endless, from tattoos to hair to wrinkles, and limited, in the case of skin tones and biological sex, at the same time. A player then moves into the world of *EVE*, where his character is seen walking in a space station before boarding his spaceship, which has the likely effect of helping the player understand that "they are a character in the escape pod and that their ships are just replaceable tools" (Drain 2012). Once he boards

Figure 2.1. An example of the "dead-sexy in-space pointers" introduced to improve *EVE*'s usability.

his ship, the player is treated to a crash course tutorial about the basic mechanisms of *EVE*, including early lessons in piloting his ship, and then ends up in a space station where he can pursue a variety of different tutorial missions that are vaguely matched to potential careers within the game.

Despite efforts to make learning the game less frustrating and to smooth elements of the learning curve, the current state of development can still be mind-numbing. The user interface likely resembles little the player has ever seen in a game. Players are flying spaceships, so there is no flat ground from which to orient oneself. The choices to make and the menus to wade through are both deep and complex, throwing players into information overload almost before they get started. Complicating matters even further are the frequently incomplete instructions that infuse the early game experience with a level of frustration that borders on keyboard throwing. Players are told to do things, such as to add something to their overview, but they are not told *how* to do those things or why they might want to do them when faced with life outside of the tutorial. One mission warns players that it may lead them through dangerous space unless they adjust their autopilot settings, but there is no guidance on how to make those adjustments. These events typify the early game experience in *EVE*, and they are key to how the game socializes players, which is a huge part of what makes *EVE* what it is. Players are presented with windows that pop up over the top of other windows (Figure 2.2), muddling their view and creating what one MMO gamer

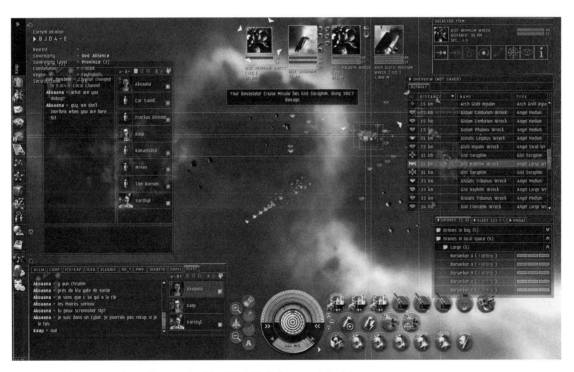

Figure 2.2. Information overload in *EVE Online*'s in-game tutorials.

refers to as "one of the most poorly laid out tutorials that I have ever seen" (Spinks 2011).

Moving into the game itself, players are faced with an array of options and are bombarded with choices that seemingly have no answer within the game itself. Without turning to other players or resources outside of the game, they are likely to be so lost that they will never be found. An array of NPC agents offer missions to complete but only scant guidance on which ones to choose, how to go about completing them, or why to complete them. Although there are different kinds of agents for different career paths, they are not labeled with the career path, just with their name and affiliation, which can lead to a situation where a new pilot engages in the advanced military tutorials before completing the basic military missions, a decision that is not likely to end well. The rewards for completing these missions are nice, but there is little guidance on how to sell or loot items and even less about what to train to excel in New Eden. The lack of training instruction is particularly mystifying, as part of the interface includes a system of certificates pilots can claim that present potential training paths, but nothing is done to direct new pilots to this information.

Part of the result of the incomplete information within the game is a cottage industry of websites and tools outside of the game that supplement the material within *EVE*. The difference between these sites and companion sites for other MMOGs, such as Wowhead or Allakhazam, is that tools like EVEMon and the EVE Fitting Tool (EFT) are compulsory for anyone seeking to make informed decisions about key components of the game. Although external sites for many games aid in making better decisions and streamlining play within the game, a tool like EFT, which is designed to help players choose what components to install on their spaceships, is necessary to weed through the thousands of choices that may or may not fit the ship a player seeks to fly. Playing without EFT or a guide found on a website would be akin to choosing talents in *WoW* without the tooltips describing what the abilities do. Information considered crucial to the game is left out, which requires players to fail or to know to seek guidance outside of the game client to make optimal choices. EVEMon aids pilots in deciding on a training path, letting players select their end result and then backfilling the pieces they will need to get to fly a particular ship or possess a specific ability. Although all the information necessary to make those decisions is technically contained within the game, one would have to be fluent in dozens upon dozens of skills and all of their prerequisites to make even a basic training decision. EVEMon is so vital to pilots that "it really should be bundled with the game" (Hammer 2007c).

## The Rhetorical Force of *EVE*

The effective function of all of these elements, from the vertical learning curve that so many will fall off to the harsh penalties to the ever-present risk of death, is to hone the community of *EVE* players, much like a secretive club seeks to stay hip and trendy by staying under the radar of most people. To get through certain sections of *EVE* is a test, one that most do not pass, but just like any other form of hazing, those who do pass the unannounced exams share something in common that can prompt them to adhere to the greater group, even if a player cannot trust them enough to loan them a beloved ship or in-game currency. Hazing discourages short-term membership in a group by chasing off those prospective group members who are not fully committed to overcoming obstacles (Cimino 2011). Hazing is ostensibly tied to building community in a group, even though it may lead to substantial mistrust that damages the group in the medium to long term (Johnson 2011). *EVE* tells new people not to play it, and if those people keep coming back for abuse, they are likely to be a good fit for the community of pilots already ensconced in the universe of New Eden, even though they may be somewhat scarred by navigating the process of establishing themselves there.

The tutorials, which lack key pieces of information, work as a lateral thinking exam, where players must turn to each other or find information on their own to complete the tasks they are given. *EVE* has built-in support personnel, from game masters (GMs) who frequently greet new players with a welcome message to an Interstellar Services Department (ISD), a group of volunteer players who spend part of their playtime answering questions for those new to the game. Accounts within their first thirty days of existence are enrolled in a rookie chat channel where senior players, GMs, and members of ISD are available to answer common questions and point players in the direction of useful resources. These elements are built in to socialize players into the fact that, at least initially, *EVE* is a game where one is necessarily playing with other people, one that is not practical to solo, and one that is not confined to the bounds of its computer program. These socializing devices smooth the hazing in an attempt to give players a slight boost and offer at least a chat channel as an outlet for frustration and conversation with other players.

Although players should not fully trust anyone, *EVE* "has quite a mature community, and a very friendly group of people who loiter in the New Citizens forum watching for a new post to answer," and the *EVE* "community is helpful and positive" (Hammer 2007a), even if they might blow your ship up later. A wealth of informational guides are available to new players, often specifically designed to supplement the information the in-game tutorial omits (CrazyKinux 2008); a player only has to know that she needs to look for them.

The game is harsh, and many players will set out to shoot you down in a heartbeat, but if a player is actually interested in *EVE* and does his own due diligence, a substantial portion of the *EVE* community will bend over backward to provide new players with the information they need to survive their early days in *EVE*. The rhetorical force of placing the role of primary positive socializing force on the players in the game is that CCP quickly weeds out those who do not care to reach out to others, as one has to ask questions and find answers to survive in *EVE*. The real focus of the rhetorical dimensions of the early game in *EVE* is not necessarily about learning how to play the game but rather about learning how to reach out to the greater community of players to establish consubstantiality and ensconce new players in what it means to play *EVE*, shaping the rhetorical environment of play for those who remain. *EVE* is a game more likely to be played in social interactions among players than through the algorithms that govern the game. Turning away those who do not get it enables CCP to build a community of players who do get it and who can continue to find spaces in which to build the emergent style of game play that typifies *EVE*.

By producing a series of tutorials that cannot be completed without filling in the gaps, *EVE* persuades players into either quitting the game in frustration or reaching out to others. In doing so, CCP has created a game that features the emergent behaviors of players as the crux of the game and enhances the identification among those interested in a game where the players make it what it is. *EVE*'s design redefines the early game experience, as by implicitly pushing players away from the game, CCP hones the community of players and increases commitment to the game. As a result, CCP has facilitated the development of an active, committed group of players on which to keep *EVE* going. Although the game is unlikely ever to break *WoW*'s record number of subscribers, it is in a position to thrive alongside other large AAA MMOG titles and last far longer than them, largely because it is designed to be inaccessible. The social focus of *EVE* also facilitates emergent game play, which may be a key part of why it is beginning its second decade and CCP is planning for many more. In the case of *EVE*, rhetorical analysis indicates the substantial value of doing something different than other games, as it pushes the masses away to attract a committed sliver of the gaming populace.

## NOTES

1  http://www.eveuniversity.org/.
2  http://www.reddit.com/r/Bravenewbies/.

## BIBLIOGRAPHY

Bergstrom, Kelly, Marcus Carter, Darryl Woodford, and Christopher A. Paul. 2013. "Constructing the Ideal EVE Online Player." Paper presented at the conference of the Digital Games Research Association, Atlanta, Georgia.

Blizzard Entertainment. 2011. "World of Warcraft Subscriber Base Reaches 12 Million Worldwide." October 7. http://us.blizzard.com/en-us/company/press/pressreleases.html?101007.

Bogost, Ian. 2006. "Videogames and Ideological Frames." *Popular Communication* 4, no. 3: 165–83.

———. 2007. *Persuasive Games: The Expressive Power of Videogames.* Cambridge, Mass.: MIT Press.

———. 2008. "The Rhetoric of Video Games." In *The Ecology of Games: Connecting Youth, Games and Learning,* edited by K. Salen, 117–40. Cambridge, Mass.: MIT Press.

Burke, Kenneth. 1966. *Language as Symbolic Action: Essays on Life, Literature, and Method.* Berkeley: University of California Press.

———. 1969. *A Rhetoric of Motives.* Berkeley: University of California Press.

Burnes, Andrew. 2011. "World of Warcraft: 70% of Trial Players Give Up before Level Ten." *Voodoo Extreme* (blog), February 11. http://ve3d.ign.com/articles/news/52996/World-Of-Warcraft-70-Of-Trial-Players-Give-Up-Before-Level-Ten.

Campbell, Karlyn Kohrs, and Susan Schultz Huxman. 2009. *The Rhetorical Act: Thinking, Speaking, and Writing Critically.* Belmont, Calif.: Wadsworth Cengage Learning.

CCP. 2010a. "EVE Online: Backstory." http://community.eveonline.com/backstory/.

———. 2010b. "EVE Online: FAQ." http://www.eveonline.com/faq/faq_01.asp.

CCP Greyscale. 2013. "Upcoming Tutorial Revisions." July 25. http://community.eveonline.com/news/dev-blogs/73075.

CCP Phantom. 2014. "Community Spotlight—Brave Newbies Inc." December 2. http://community.eveonline.com/news/dev-blogs/74260.

Chalk, Andy. 2010. "More *EVE Online* Shenanigans: GoonSwarm Ganks Band of Brothers." *The Escapist,* February 5. http://www.escapistmagazine.com/news/view/89219-More-EVE-Online-Shenanigans-GoonSwarm-Ganks-Band-Of-Brothers.

Cimino, Aldo. 2011. "The Evolution of Hazing: Motivational Mechanisms and the Abuse of Newcomers." *Journal of Cognition and Culture* 11: 241–67.

CrazyKinux. 2008. "10 Posts for the Eve Newbie." *CrazyKinux's Musing* (blog), August 20. http://www.crazykinux.ca/2008/08/10-posts-for-eve-online-newbie.html.

———. 2010. "EVE Blog Banter #16: The Three Pillars of Wisdom." *CrazyKinux's Musing* (blog), March 15. http://www.crazykinux.ca/2010/03/eve-blog-banter-16-three-pillars-of.html.

Drain, Brendan. 2010a. "EVE Gambling Website SOMER.Blink Is the Target of 125 Billion ISK Theft." *Massively* (blog), November 16. http://massively.joystiq.com/2010/11/16/eve-gambling-website-somer-blink-is-the-target-of-125-billion-is/.

———. 2010b. "EVE Online Player Steals $45,000 Worth of ISK in Massive Investment Scam." *Massively* (blog), September 11. http://massively.joystiq.com/2010/09/11/eve-online-player-steals-45–000-worth-of-isk-in-massive-investm/.

———. 2010c. "Questionable EVE Attack Deals 30 Billion ISK in Damage." *Massively* (blog), October 10. http://massively.joystiq.com/2010/10/10/questionable-eve-attack-deals-30-billion-isk-in-damage/.

———. 2012. "EVE Evolved: EVE Online's New Tutorial." *Massively* (blog), August 19. http://massively.joystiq.com/2012/08/19/eve-evolved-eve-onlines-new-tutorial/.

Egan, James. 2009. "The Lowdown on EVE Online's New Player Experience." *Massively* (blog), February 18. http://massively.joystiq.com/2009/02/18/the-lowdown-on-eve-onlines-new-player-experience/.

Hammer. 2007a. "About Hammer's Guide." *Hammer's Eve* (blog), May. http://hammer-eve.blogspot.com/2007/05/about-my-guide.html.

———. 2007b. "Death and Clones." *Hammer's Eve* (blog), May. http://hammer-eve.blogspot.com/2007/05/death-and-clones.html.

———. 2007c. "Eve: For Experienced Gamers." *Hammer's Eve* (blog), May. http://hammer-eve.blogspot.com/2007/05/eve-for-wow-gamers.html /.

———. 2007d. "Eve Is Harsh: You Get Ganked." *Hammer's Eve* (blog), June. http://hammer-eve.blogspot.com/2007/06/eve-is-harsh-you-get-ganked.html.

Johnson, Jay. 2011. "Through the Liminal: A Comparative Analysis of Communitas and Rites of Passage in Sport Hazing and Initiations." *Canadian Journal of Sociology* 36, no. 3: 199–227.

Jordan, Jay. 2005. "Dell Hymes, Kenneth Burke's 'Identification,' and the Birth of Sociolinguistics." *Rhetoric Review* 24, no. 3: 264–79.

Moeller, Ryan M., Bruce Esplin, and Steven Conway. 2009. "Cheesers, Pullers, and Glitchers: The Rhetoric of Sportsmanship and the Discourse of Online Sports Gamers." *Game Studies* 9, no. 2.

Paul, Christopher A. 2010a. "Process, Paratexts, and Texts: Rhetorical Analysis and Virtual Worlds." *Journal of Virtual Worlds Research* 3, no. 1.

———. 2010b. "Welfare Epics? The Rhetoric of Rewards in World of Warcraft." *Games and Culture* 5, no. 2: 158–76.

———. 2012. *Wordplay and the Discourse of Video Games: Analyzing Words, Design, and Play.* New York: Routledge.

Reahard, Jef. 2012. "EVE's Inferno Build Patched to 1.2, Newb-Friendly Tweaks Abound." *Massively* (blog), August 8. http://massively.joystiq.com/2012/08/08/eves-inferno-build-patched -to-1-2-newb-friendly-tweaks-abound/.

Schaefer, Beowolf. 2010. "*Trust No One!* Zen and the Art of Internet Spaceship Management." March 19. http://eve-zen.info/blog/?p=699.

Scott, Robert L. 1967. "On Viewing Rhetoric as Epistemic." *Central States Speech Journal* 18: 9–17.

Smith, Chris. 2010. "If EVE and Battletech Got It On." *Levelcapped* (blog), November 10. http:// levelcapped.com/2010/11/if-eve-and-battletech-got-it-on/.

Spinks. 2011. "Brief Look at the EVE Character Creator." *Welcome to Spinksville!* (blog), January 24. http://spinksville.wordpress.com/2011/01/24/brief-look-at-the-eve-character-creator/.

Stigg. 2010. "Eve: Ship Costs, USD, Time Spent." *The Black Temple* (blog), February 10. http:// www.knightly-slumber.com/worldofwarcraft/node/2860.

Taylor, T. L. 2006. *Play between Worlds: Exploring Online Game Culture.* Cambridge, Mass.: MIT Press.

Voorhees, Gerald A. 2009. "I Play Therefore I Am: Sid Meier's Civilization, Turn-Based Strategy Games, and the Cogito." *Games and Culture* 4, no. 3: 254–75.

Zarefsky, David. 2008. "Knowledge Claims in Rhetorical Criticism." *Journal of Communication* 58: 629–40.

# 3

## Virtual Interstellar Travel

*William Sims Bainbridge*

*EVE Online* is called a game, but it could be considered a simulation of possible human interstellar colonization. As a space-themed game, it is unusual in setting the action between planets rather than on the surface of an alien planet, but this may be an especially realistic feature for a simulation, given how inhospitable most of the thousands of known planets undoubtedly are (Horowitz 1986; Launius 2010). *EVE* relates to real-world space exploration in two distinct ways: as a simulation of what might actually be accomplished using rocket technologies invented during the twentieth century and as a projection of a very different kind of progress that could be accomplished in astronautics by means of new information technologies to be developed during the twenty-first century. This chapter documents both prophetic dimensions of *EVE Online* through an avatar based on Hermann Oberth, who was historically the most significant pioneer in the development of space rocketry and an uninhibited technological visionary of the first order. Science fiction virtual worlds only very approximately simulate the technical realities of space travel, yet they can capture human hopes and the metaphors people use to conceptualize the universe.

### Impersonating a Spaceflight Pioneer

Among the most appropriate social science research methodologies for studying online role-playing games is *impersonation* of a real human individual whose knowledge and perspective provide excellent preparation to discover truths and stimulate hypotheses. The first extensive use of role-playing as a tool for gaining insight was probably the *psychodrama* method, developed by Jacob Moreno for use in group psychotherapy, especially for clients who already understood their own minds but were still having difficulty handling other people (Moreno and Toeman 1942; Moreno 1946). A more recent application is the ancestor veneration avatar (AVA), an impersonation of a deceased family member meant not only to serve as a modern version of ancient rituals of respect or as mourning therapy but also to teach about life from the perspective of a loved one who is no longer present to serve as a living role model (Bainbridge 2013a; 2013d). Extensive experimentation with AVAs in science fiction environments have been carried out in *Star Trek Online* and in the Star Trek community in the nongame virtual world *Second Life* (Bainbridge, forthcoming). In addition, *transavatars* refers to the use of virtual world role-playing as a tool for self-transcendence or even for the translation of self into artificial intelligence avatars (Bainbridge 2013e). One need not have such radical goals to benefit intellectually from imaginatively inhabiting the mentality of another person, in the guise of a character in *EVE Online*.

Therefore, when I returned to *EVE Online* after an absence of many months, I did not reenter my existing characters but created a new one based on the most significant single individual in the early history of rocket science, Hermann Oberth. My main existing character, Theo Logian, had been crafted as an archetype rather than an impersonation, representing sociologists of religion as a collective group (Bainbridge 1997) rather than any individual pioneer of that field, to better to understand Amarr religion. When I began to create the new character late in 2013, I discovered there already was one named Hermann Oberth, testimony to the fame of the real man, which had apparently been created way back in 2005 and may not have been active since the following year. So I named mine Herman Noberth, which is convenient, because here I can use "Oberth" to refer to the real space pioneer and "Noberth" to refer to the New-Oberth *EVE* character.

All histories of spaceflight heap praise on three great pioneers who separately developed the fundamental principles on which space programs were eventually based: Konstantin Tsiolkovsky (1857–1935) in Russia, Robert H. Goddard (1882–1945) in the United States, and Hermann Oberth (1894–1989) in Romania or German-speaking Europe more generally defined (Bainbridge 1976). Of the three, Goddard was the only one actually to make rockets, test-firing the world's first liquid-fuel rocket in 1926, but he struggled throughout his life to build his own personal space program and avoided significant cooperation with anyone else. Indeed, all three of these pioneers were eccentric intellectuals who kept their distance from other people. Oberth himself could be described as a brilliant crank who developed his own theosophical occult system simultaneously with his rocket theories, conjecturing, for example, that each cell in his body had its own immortal soul and believing that he could be reincarnated after death in a future spacefaring civilization (Oberth 1959). Thus Oberth himself was quite ready to be reincarnated as Noberth.

Immediately upon entering the New Eden galaxy, Noberth faced two problems. First, the beginning tutorials all involved accepting assignments from nonplayer characters (NPCs) who held higher bureaucratic status than Noberth himself did. But Oberth rejected the authority of other people, so Noberth quit the tutorials after a couple of hours. In a study of how CCP Games designed *EVE* to commit players to each other, thus leaving many gaps in the tutorials, which would require newcomers to seek advice from veterans, Christopher Paul (2011, 264) commented, "The rhetorical force of placing the role of primary positive socializing force on the players in the game, rather than building the elements into the procedures of the game itself, is that CCP quickly weeds out those that do not care or do not know to reach out to others, as one has to ask questions and find answers to survive and enjoy play in EVE." However, it is not in the nature of a radical genius like Oberth to seek guidance from other people; rather, it is his nature to explore solo beyond the conventional boundaries.

Second, even in the tutorials, *EVE* emphasizes combat, initially against NPCs, as training for the player versus player combat that dominates action after the tutorials and across most of the galaxy. The V-2 rocket program of the German army in World War II was based on Oberth's ideas, and its leader, Wernher von Braun, was a personal disciple of Oberth. But Oberth never really worked inside the V-2 program and remained rather aloof from the war for three possible reasons, all of which may be true: (1) Oberth was a genius for whom war was the ultimate act of stupidity; (2) the German authorities did not trust Oberth, because although his native language was German, his nationality was Romanian; and (3) the army, and perhaps von Braun as well, recognized that Oberth was an untrustworthy crank who had developed innovative technical ideas precisely because he was mentally deviant.

Thus Noberth was starting his new life in *EVE* in contradiction to some of its key norms. He would not undertake missions for anybody. He would not fight anybody. He would not even cooperate closely with anybody. Oberth was the archetypal solo player in life, troubled by the fact that he could not accomplish his personal goals without help and finding cooperation very alien to his nature. The only course left open to Noberth was gathering mineral resources from asteroids and using them to create new spaceships and related technologies. This suited my research purposes very well, because Noberth's goal was to understand *EVE* space technology as well as he could, to better compare it with the rocket technology Oberth had developed and to understand the possibilities for real human activity beyond Earth and the solar system.

My guide was Oberth's (1923) first book, *Die Rakete zu den Planetenräumen (The Rocket into the Planetary Spaces),* in which he provided very, very detailed plans and mathematical analyses for multistage liquid-fuel rockets. Clearly, following the obsessive character of the great space pioneers, Noberth would love the tiny details of crafting in *EVE*. My copy of *Die Rakete* is actually a photocopy provided to me forty years ago by the Houghton Library of rare books at Harvard University, and it has served for four decades as my intellectual anchor to spaceflight. Its main issue, once one gets past all the obsessive details, is that it will be just barely possible to launch rockets into space, using high-energy liquid chemical propellants and the multistage principle. But nothing in the book, or even in today's rocket technology, suggests how it will be feasible to conduct major human activities in outer space, such as those depicted in *EVE Online*.

In 1909, American astronomer Garrett P. Serviss (1911) may have been the first person seriously to propose nuclear propulsion for spacecraft, in the initial magazine-serialized episode of a science fiction novel. By the middle of the twentieth century, knowledgeable people imagined that a nuclear rocket could use the heat of a fission reactor to accelerate a reaction mass, such as hydrogen gas, perhaps achieving twice the specific impulse of the best practical chemical rocket that burns hydrogen with oxygen, as Oberth had detailed in 1923. But the American program to develop nuclear launch rocket technology ended in 1972, coincidentally the year of the last flight to the moon, and today's concerns with the dangers of nuclear technologies render this approach not merely technically difficult but environmentally unthinkable. The Space Shuttle was a fundamentally unsuccessful attempt to reduce the cost of chemical rockets through reusable vehicles that originally intended to avoid discarding stages of a multistage rocket during launch (Launius 2006). As of 2014, we are left without a serious alternative to Oberth's 1923 methods, yet they have exhausted their potential (Coopersmith 2011). These grim facts provide additional motivation for Noberth to discover how interstellar spaceflight is possible in *EVE*.

## Building an Armada

Essentially all massively multiplayer online games begin with a process in which the user selects the name, gender, ethnicity, starting place, and action capabilities often called "class," which, however, *EVE* does not limit. Once I had selected "male" and the name "Herman Noberth," I imagined that he made all subsequent decisions. At his entry into *EVE*, Noberth needed to select a society and tribe. His natural choice was the rebellious Minmatar Republic, joining the Sebiestor tribe within it, who were noted as innovative engineers and compulsive tinkerers. His entry point was the Malukker solar system, and from completing part of one tutorial at the very beginning, he received a very useful Venture frigate, built by an NPC mining syndicate called Outer Ring Excavations (ORE). He also gained a somewhat strange frigate that also was not a Minmatar spacecraft. Its official description reads, "This Magnate-class frigate is one of the most decoratively designed ship classes in the Amarr Empire, considered to be a pet project for a small, elite group of royal ship engineers for over a decade." Noberth surmised that this Amarr frigate had been intended for my earlier main character, Theo Logian, but wound up in Noberth's spaceship hangar instead. The Venture and Magnate frigates suggested to Noberth that he should himself manufacture a full collection of all the other constructible frigates, as many other ships belonging to the technically adept Minmatar as he could afford, and a variety of ship accessories, to understand the range of designs feasible in the *EVE* galaxy.

As a loyal subscriber to *EVE Online*, I received a birthday gift when the game became ten years old in the form of a splendid Gnosis battlecruiser. However, Noberth was not planning to engage in any battles, so he left the Gnosis in storage for a long time, took it on a few test flights, and then sold it, to have money to invest in his construction project. Shrewd enough to notice that the price of a ship varied from place to place, he flew it from Malukker to the Rens solar system, earning considerably more than if he had sold it where he originally kept it. Rens was also the place where he bought many specialized components for his research, but he did not do any experimentation there, because the local factory was overwhelmed by other clients, and he really did not enjoy their company. Figure 3.1 shows the Gnosis leaving Malukker for the last time under Noberth's ownership.

In the early stages of his work, Noberth jumped around from one experiment to another, settling into a well-designed research plan only after a few weeks. Therefore, for sake of clarity, we describe his progress here in a more logical sequence than he actually achieved it. The Venture frigate came already equipped with a low-efficiency mining laser, so Noberth could fly it to one of the nearby asteroid belts, park it a couple thousand meters from an asteroid, and fire the laser to collect some ore. Presumably, the laser vaporizes the surface of the asteroid and some electromagnetic system draws the dust or vapor into the ore hold of the Venture, which can contain five thousand cubic meters. The composition of the ore, and thus how much of which mineral resources can be refined from it, depends on the particular kind of asteroid among many types. When the ore hold filled up, Noberth would fly to the nearest space station, where he could either sell the ore directly on the computerized market for *EVE*'s currency, which is denominated in interstellar kredits (ISK), or refine the ore into pure materials from which he could construct things.

In his brief tutorial experience, Noberth had received an improved Miner I laser, but he needed the ability to make more of them to install on multiple mining ships. Manufacturing an item has five main requirements: (1) a blueprint to guide the manufacturing, (2) sufficient ratings on the required skills, (3) raw materials of the right kinds and quantities, (4) access to a manufacturing facility, and (5) a small price for the manufacturing if the facility does not belong to the user. The blueprint for a Miner I laser cost 92,700 ISK on the local market, which was quite cheap. The required skill,

Figure 3.1. The Gnosis battlecruiser leaving a space station.

Industry I, was low. Skill books need to be bought and placed in a training queue, each of five skill levels simply taking time from minutes to weeks to complete. The minimum materials required to build a Miner I laser are 1,311 units of tritanium (n.b. not titanium), 476 units of pyerite (n.b. not pyrite), and 118 units of mexallon. The actual quantities required were somewhat greater, because Noberth's technical skills and manufacturing facilities were not perfect. Noberth always did his manufacturing in a space station that had the right equipment, at low cost.

His Venture could handle two Miner I lasers, so he built a pair. It could also handle mining drones, tiny, unmanned machines that would fly near the asteroid, use their own lasers to mine, then periodically bring the ore to the ship. Three skills are required to operate a mining drone: Mining level II, Mining Drone Operation level I, and Drones level I. However, his Venture could operate two drones, in addition to its two onboard mining lasers, and one additional level of Drones skill is required for each additional drone operated simultaneously. Improved mining lasers, using two rather than one, and adding mining drones do not increase the quality or quantity that can be mined in one expedition to an asteroid belt but merely reduce the time to complete the task. At one point, Noberth manufactured a mobile depot where he could temporarily place ore mined from asteroids, but the jaunt to a nearby space station was almost as quick, so he never used it.

Scanning the market, Noberth saw that his next, improved ship for mining should be an ORE Procurer. Making one would be quite impractical, given that its blueprint would cost 1.7 billion ISK, more money than he was likely ever to accumulate, so he bought one for 16.5 million ISK, less than 1 percent the original amount. It needed a strip mining laser, three times the power of ordinary mining lasers, the blueprint for which was affordable but high at 16,130,050 ISK, so Noberth simply bought a premade one for 2,449,978 ISK, figuring he already knew the principles from having made regular lasers and drones. He used his Procurer for all subsequent mining, and thus it became his flagship. Figure 3.2 shows it in the process of mining an asteroid, firing a bright beam from its laser, as five mining drones fire their smaller lasers at the same target, which they are orbiting.

The process of mining with the Procurer went like this. After entering an asteroid belt, Noberth would click on several of these huge rocks to get information about what mineral they were and to move his ship within range of one of them. Properly prepared, a tabular display also allowed him to find and select asteroids composed of the desired material. As he neared twenty kilometers from one, he could lock his ship's sights on it. Nearer than fifteen kilometers, he could start his mining laser, and within ten, he would launch all five of the mining drones and set them to "mine repeatedly." He would then lock his sights on the next promising nearby asteroid and wait for the mining of the first to finish. After a few minutes, the first asteroid would have vanished into his ore hold. He would again tell the drones to "mine repeatedly," and they would get to work on the second asteroid, which he had already locked on, as would his ship's strip miner when he restarted it. He would lock the ship's sights on a third asteroid in

Figure 3.2. A Procurer spaceship mining an asteroid, with a laser and five mining drones.

preparation for mining it if the second asteroid were exhausted. The ore hold capacity of the Procurer was twelve thousand cubic meters, and when it was full, the first step was to tell the five mining drones to return to their separate holds. Then Noberth would direct the Procurer to return to the space station to empty the ore hold to get ready for another mining expedition.

Having resolved to avoid combat, Noberth needed to stay in high-sec solar systems, where he would never be attacked. This limited the range of minerals he could mine to three: (1) veldspar, which produces titanium; (2) scordite, which produces both titanium and pyerite; and (3) plagioclase, which produces titanium, pyerite, and mexallon. The other minerals he needed to build ships could be obtained by purchase on the market.

As Noberth progressed, he established himself in five solar systems, visiting many others but using these to store all his ships and other resources. As his starting point, Malukker was the location for storing miscellaneous junk and making spaceship accessories at the Minmatar Republic University station. One interstellar jump away was the Ameinaka system, where he set up his collection of Minmatar ships in the Six Kin Development Warehouse. One interstellar jump from Ameinaka was the Arlulf system, which linked to the Brundakur and Alf systems, which linked to each other. Using the arrangement of systems as a category scheme, Noberth placed his Caldari ships in Arlulf, his Gallente ships in Brundakur, and his Amarr ships in Alf. Each of these three systems had a chemical tech factory, so Noberth used those sites. Figure 3.3 shows information about the Minmatar ships that made Ameinaka their home, beginning with the Reaper rookie ship he received for free, followed by the six frigates.

The cost of blueprints for the six Minmatar frigates totaled 15.2 million ISK, for an average of 2,5333,333 ISK each. Because Noberth was himself Minmatar, building his own society's ships was cheaper than building ships for the other societies. The average blueprint cost for the six Caldari frigates was 4,449,914 ISK, for the six Gallente frigates 5,287,166 ISK, and for the five remaining Amarr frigates, given that he already had a Magnate, 6,395,000 ISK. Altogether, the twenty-three blueprints cost him 105,597,479 ISK. He earned about 1.7 million ISK for each mining expedition on his Procurer, so counting the additional costs of materials, he invested more than one hundred mining expeditions into completing his spaceship collection.

The Cyclone mentioned in the Thrasher description was one of three models of Minmatar battlecruiser, and the cheapest price Noberth found for a blueprint was 517 million ISK, so he never built one. He was, however, able to check the list of materials required and found that they were all the ordinary minerals he was used to dealing with, expensive given the quantities required but not likely to provide scientific discoveries. Far more interesting would have been constructing a Ragnarok, the Minmatar Titan warship, but its blueprint cost fully 67.5 billion ISK. Building one did not require any minerals but the assembly of a vast number of manufactured components, such as a minimum of 440 power generators, 550 propulsion engines, and 550 jump drives. Just one propulsion engine would have cost him 8 million ISK. Visiting

| Ship | Blueprint ISK Cost | Description from the Ship's Owner User Interface |
|---|---|---|
| Reaper | - | Not constructible but "very cheap and is used en masse in daring hit-and-run operations by Minmatars either side of the law" |
| Breacher | 2,800,000 | "The Breacher's structure is little more than a fragile scrapheap, but the ship's missile launcher hardpoints and superior sensors have placed it among the most valued Minmatar frigates when it comes to long range combat." |
| Burst | 2,500,000 | "had been a small and fast cargo vessel. This all changed after the redesign, when the Burst found its small-time mining capabilities curtailed in lieu of logistics systems that moved its focus to shield support for friendly vessels." |
| Probe | 2,700,000 | "large compared to most Minmatar frigates and is considered a good scout and cargo-runner. Uncharacteristically for a Minmatar ship, its hard outer coating makes it difficult to destroy, while the limited weapon hardpoints force it to rely on drone assistance if engaged in combat." |
| Rifter | 2,800,000 | "a very powerful combat frigate and can easily tackle the best frigates out there." |
| Slasher | 2,100,000 | "cheap, but versatile... extremely fast, with decent armaments, and is popular amongst budding pirates and smugglers." |
| Vigil | 2,300,000 | "an unusual Minmatar ship, serving both as a long range scout as well as an electronic warfare platform. It is fast and agile, allowing it to keep the distance needed to avoid enemy fire while making use of jammers or other electronic gadgets." |
| Shuttle | 50,000 | cheap to make for one-way travel |
| Hoarder | 4,525,000 | "possesses an extra cargo bay... a static-free, blast-proof chamber, and as such is meant to be dedicated solely to ferrying consumable charges of all kinds, including ammunition, missiles, capacitor charges, nanite paste and bombs." |
| Mammoth | 9,375,000 | "the largest industrial ship of the Minmatar Republic" |
| Wreathe | 3,225,000 | "an old ship of the Minmatar Republic and one of the oldest ships still in usage... incapable of handling anything but the most mundane tasks" |
| Talwar | 7,837,500 | "built to rush around at speed without getting caught, and to hit very hard and very, very fast" |
| Thrasher | 7,500,000 | "Engineered as a supplement to its big brother the Cyclone, the Thrasher's tremendous turret capabilities and advanced tracking computers allow it to protect its larger counterpart from smaller, faster menaces." |

Figure 3.3. Noberth's collection of Minmatar spaceships.

the kill-board on the website of EVE University[1] revealed daunting statistics about how many hundreds of millions of ISK space warriors could earn by murdering each other, vast sums far beyond the reach of a solo pacifist like himself.

## The Means for Spaceflight

Herman Noberth was very pleased to discover that spaceships in *EVE* were propelled by rockets, and to show his dedication to that technology, he invested a month of his training time completing the top level of Rocket Science, level V. However, Hermann Oberth late in life had reportedly believed that flying saucers were spaceships from other worlds, which implies that the preeminent rocket pioneer could imagine other forms of propulsion. Yet the rockets in *EVE* do not follow the principles of the ones developed on twentieth-century Earth.

The first anomaly Noberth noticed was that his spaceships did not require any kind of fuel and seemed to have infinite range. That clearly was a mystery, because when he fired the rockets, they expelled exhaust, in a manner that seemed similar to chemical rockets. Even if the engines were nuclear, they would have required some kind of reaction mass to exploit the equal and opposite reaction that accelerated a rocket in one direction, as the reaction mass was accelerated in the opposite direction.

Central to each ship in the display was a capacitor, but it seemed only to power accessories, not the ship itself. The official *EVE Online* wiki[2] explains, "A ship's reactor provides power to essential ship systems, but many modules in order to be activated require a burst of power which the reactor is unable to provide. Capacitors therefore are installed to meet this need. The reactor fills the capacitor with power, the capacitor stores this power until modules are activated. As modules are activated, power is drained from the capacitor, which then causes the reactor to add more power." But if those essential ship systems include the propulsion engines, how can they function without expendable fuel or reaction mass? Constructing his vast collection of spaceships had given Noberth no insights about such questions, because the process did not require him to build components, such as engines and fuel tanks, then assemble them to make a complete ship. The only components he could build were accessories. One was an afterburner, which increased ship speed, but only jet fighters on Earth use afterburners, not rockets, so Noberth could never figure out how they worked in *EVE*.

The best opportunity to test the ordinary rocket engines was when Noberth was in an asteroid field, because he could fly a ship toward any of the asteroids then turn in the direction of another. Starting up the rocket took several seconds, as did switching it off, but what happened in between did not match conventional physics. In one series of runs with his Procurer, Noberth found it would accelerate at about one-third the acceleration of gravity on the surface of Earth to a velocity of about eighty meters per second, then acceleration would diminish until velocity reached a maximum value just under ninety-two meters per second. Then the ship continued moving at that constant velocity despite the fact that the rocket engine was still operating. To decelerate, Noberth merely needed to switch the engine off, a process that took a while to complete. Ordinary terrestrial rocket theory would have required firing the ship's engines in the direction of travel, using fuel to decelerate.

By accident, Noberth discovered the complex physics of orbiting in the *EVE* universe. When mining, he typically parked his ship near an asteroid, and it would naturally hold its position rather than being drawn toward the asteroid by its tiny gravity or moving in relation to asteroids in other orbits, because each asteroid belt tended to be a stable circle or arc of boulders, with nothing at the center of curvature. But once, while mining with his Venture and two drones, he chose to go into orbit around the asteroid. This required operating his engine constantly, something that would not be true for orbiting in Earth's own solar system. At this point, I irresponsibly left him alone and went away from my computer to do a household chore. When I returned, I discovered to my dismay that the asteroid had been mined to extinction, which had released the Venture from its orbit, and it had rocketed several hundred kilometers away. Noberth began to return to the asteroid belt, then realized that the two mining drones had also been released from their orbits. He was able to figure out where they were but was too far away to recall them to the Venture's drone hold, and despite several attempts, there was no way to move the ship close enough to them, so they were lost and needed to be replaced.

Maneuvering followed a mixture of conventional and unconventional principles. Once the USSR and United States had orbited real spaceships, conventional wisdom established complex relationships between the engines that accelerated the vehicle versus the engines rotating it. At launch, many liquid-fuel rockets swiveled the main engine to steer, but orbital vehicles used their main engines only very briefly to accelerate and employed small steering jets to turn in the desired direction. When Noberth instructed his ship to go in a direction other than the one it was already pointing, it would behave rather like an aircraft, firing the main engine and then banking into a turn, rolling more than 45 degrees in the direction of the turn for reasons that Noberth could never figure out. This was all quite unconventional but at least not an obvious violation of physical principles.

The conventional part of spaceship control in *EVE* was actually slightly controversial with players. A pilot instructed the ship to head toward a specific destination, and its autopilot would do the rest. It was not possible to control the ship freely with a joystick, as one would with an aircraft, which would have allowed Noberth to retrieve his two lost drones. Real-world spacecraft controls vary somewhat, but the fundamental principle is computer control rather than manual. One reason is that all movement must be done very precisely to avoid wasting any fuel. But *EVE* ships apparently do not need fuel. There may be several reasons why *EVE* uses the control system it does, including the complex system of virtual world instancing it uses, which constantly moves a player from one part of the database to another, but in a way that seamless flight would violate.

Many computer games depicting spaceflight, notably the rather excellent system in *Star Trek Online* or the more realistic method in the now-defunct *Jumpgate,* do give the player freedom to control the direction of movement. Others, such as several of the Star Wars games, employ the metaphor of flying fighter aircraft via joystick, which many players seem to find very exciting. Writing on the *Massively* blog in 2013, Brendan Drain reported, "Ever since its release in 2003, *EVE Online* has been bombarded with requests for direct flight controls and dogfighter-style game play. Most ships in *EVE* are huge lumbering hulks compared to real-world aircraft, more akin to large seafaring ships than nimble jetfighters. Even tiny agile Interceptors can't be controlled directly, instead having the player issue commands to fly in a particular direction or move toward or orbit an object. As a result, combat in *EVE* has become much more heavily about the strategy of directing fleets of dozens or hundreds of ships than any kind of piloting skill or twitch control."

One feature shared by fighter aircraft and seagoing ships is bilateral symmetry: left and right, or port and starboard, to use nautical terminology, are mirror images of each other. That is not strictly necessary for spacecraft, most obviously in cases like the Voyager, Galileo, and Cassini probes to outer planets, which have components mounted in various directions, some on extension beams. Bilateral symmetry means that up and down are very distinct directions, and the top and bottom of the craft could be exceedingly different from each other, whereas in outer space, there exists no up and down. The Gnosis and Procurer shown in Figures 3.1 and 3.2 could hardly look more different from each other, yet both have bilateral symmetry. There are a few exceptions in *EVE,* however, and Figure 3.4 shows Noberth's rookie ship, his Reaper, which is exceedingly asymmetrical, despite having a definite top and bottom.

Because *EVE* ships do not seem to use fuel, they do not require the multistage principle that Oberth analyzed in detail in *Die Rakete.* For launch from Earth, liquid-fuel chemical rockets must accelerate the payload to a velocity of at least five miles per

Figure 3.4. An asymmetrical Reaper novice spaceship warping.

second—seven if the payload must leave Earth's gravity altogether—but this means accelerating much of the fuel to high velocities as well, not to mention the fuel tanks and the large engines required for liftoff. Oberth recognized that it is essentially impossible to loft the entire vehicle into orbit, so the biggest tanks and engines must be jettisoned. Apollo used a complex multistage system not only to get to the moon, but also to land there and return. Although staging would not be required to get from Earth orbit to the asteroid belt between Mars and Jupiter, it would be if the goal were to collect ore there and return, as is the case frequently in *EVE*.

Noberth found only one situation in which rocket staging was required for *EVE* missions, and it is illustrated in Figure 3.1. He could fly his Gnosis back and forth between the Malukker and Rens solar systems hundreds of times without refueling, but how could he return from Rens to Malukker after selling his Gnosis there? The answer is that the Gnosis in Figure 3.1 is carrying a small shuttle, packaged to make it storable, inside its cargo hold. So the shuttle was the second stage of a two-stage system, with the Gnosis as the first stage. Ships with much smaller cargo holds than the Gnosis has cannot carry a shuttle, even packaged up, but all ships can carry a shuttle blueprint, and only a small quantity of tritanium is required to manufacture one of these tiny ships, which, like all larger ships, are, however, capable of flying great distances. Arranging all his ships and equipment across five solar systems required Noberth to construct many shuttles from all four societies, using them for return journeys after delivering a different ship to its destination. Thus, even if the physics of spaceflight differs greatly between the New Eden galaxy and our own, the same kind of logistics and logical thinking are required in both.

## Warps and Jumps

The Reaper shown in Figure 3.4 is in the process of starting a warp run inside a solar system, which begins with the rocket engines flaring, then the vehicle rushing forward until empty space begins streaming past as if made of clouds or water. The planet in the background, Ameinaka IV, shows some distortion on the left edge, which is always seen early and late in warping, apparently because the space around the ships has been warped unevenly, causing a lensing effect. Warping allows travel from one planet to another, or from a space station to an asteroid field, in less than a minute, compared with the months or years required for real spacecraft.

My favorite example is the unmanned probe Voyager 2, because I was doing sociological research at its home base, the Jet Propulsion Laboratory, during its encounters with Saturn and Uranus. Launched August 20, 1977, Voyager 2 reached Jupiter on July 9, 1979, Saturn on August 25, 1981, Uranus on January 24, 1986, and Neptune on August 25, 1989. That is twelve years from Earth to Neptune, and at its current velocity, Voyager 2 will not reach the distance of the nearest other solar system for about fifty thousand years. A classic analysis of the potential of nuclear fusion rockets implied at best that they might reach 20 percent of the speed of light, or 10 percent if the goal were to decelerate at the destination, which could reduce the time of an interstellar flight to perhaps one human lifetime, but not to a minute or two, as in *EVE* (Horner 1963).

Science fiction has developed several literary conventions to contract the duration of space voyages so they can fit within the limited time and space of a humanly meaningful narrative (Bainbridge 1986). Chief among these are warps, jumps, and wormholes. *EVE* uses all of these, but none of them has a good scientific basis. Yes, the duration of a voyage would be shorter if space were warped to reduce the effective distance that needs to be traveled. But the only force that can warp space is gravitation, requiring an immense mass like that of the sun to produce enough warp to notice, let alone to use effectively. *Star Trek* popularized the warp metaphor, but if it were a real technical possibility, the means to achieve it would have become apparent by now (Bainbridge 2014).

Interstellar travel in *EVE Online* is accomplished through huge jumpgates fixed often at multiple edges of a solar system, some of which appear to be electromagnetic catapults and may be using the warp principle on a higher level to throw a spacecraft farther and faster than its own engines could accomplish. In an earlier publication, I wrote (Bainbridge 2011b, 123–24),

> Whenever a ship jumps, a ball of light appears inside the gate, expands into something like an arrow of light, and shoots away. The physics involved is unknown. Users do get much experience in the control system, however, and a ship's autopilot can handle several jumps in a row, to any given destination. Indeed, the navigation system in *EVE* is complex, functional, and realistic, allowing the user to look at the galaxy, rotate it, focus on particular systems, and search for the best routes.

Returning to *EVE* years afterward, I discovered that it had become possible for users to manufacture much weaker jump devices, and one of them, the Mobile Micro Jump Unit (MMJ), was within Noberth's construction capabilities. To build the MMJ unit, Noberth had first to develop the right skills, specifically reaching level II in both Graviton Physics and Molecular Engineering, each of which cost him 10 million ISK for its skill book and required him already to have reached the top level V in both Science and Engineering. The reference to *graviton* suggested that the physics concerned the fundamental nature of gravity, something that terrestrial science has not yet achieved, and the skill description includes the phrase "spatial distortion devices." This sounds like warping space, not jumping across it. The blueprint for the MMJ was somewhat expensive, costing fully 30 million ISK.

The raw materials required were not excessive: just 13,500 units of titanium and 675 each of pyrite and zydrine. But four kinds of crucial components were also needed, all of which Noberth bought from the market: two nuclear reactors, two high-tech transmitters, three smartfab units, and four guidance systems. As an illustration of how the manufacturing was done, Noberth had it built at the Republic University in orbit around Malukker I but did not do the work himself. Rather, he collected the raw materials and submitted the package to the Science and Industry Factory, paying it a mere 1,730.57 ISK and waiting two hours and fourteen minutes for delivery of the finished product. That meant he learned nothing about the scientific principles on which the device operated by managing the construction. He had hoped to learn how the reactors worked by training in Nuclear Physics up to level V and building a Nuclear Reactor Unit, which he did. But in the process, he gained no intellectual insights, and ironically, it turned out that the Nuclear Reactor Unit was not suitable for use as a nuclear reactor in the MMJ unit.

Figure 3.5 is two images of the start of a jump, just seconds apart, in which Noberth is flying his Breacher frigate. In the top screenshot, the star of the solar system is in the background, just above the mobile microjump unit, which is floating motionless. The strange asymmetric assortment of pipes, fins, and compartments that fills the right two-thirds of the picture is the Breacher, with its rocket still firing to bring it to the jump unit. At that instant, Noberth activated the MMJ, and the Breacher turned and zoomed away in the direction from which it had come. In the lower screenshot, the Breacher is moving fast to the right, and a space-time distortion bubble has formed around the ship, greatly distorting the image. Exactly why the ship's rockets need to fire is not clear, unless it is merely to add more drama, because the MMJ logically is

Figure 3.5. Two steps in a jump by a Breacher frigate.

doing all the work. For another couple of seconds, the Breacher zooms away as if in an ordinary warp, but with the bubble seething with activity, then there is a flash of light, and suddenly the ship is one hundred kilometers distant from the jump unit.

In experimenting with the MMJ unit, as soon as Noberth had placed it, he immediately locked his ship's guidance system onto it, so he could tell the ship to return to that exact location after each test jump. His first tests were done with the Amarr Magnate frigate, but the information lock transferred to his Breacher when he returned to his collection of Minmatar ships. If an MMJ unit is not activated for two days, it will disintegrate. Noberth did not find a practical use for the MMJ, although he imagined it was one way to escape an attacker during a battle, a situation he never intended to face, and he learned very little from building and operating the unit.

To be sure, Noberth could do what was called *research* during his manufacturing, but this resulted in a reduction of the raw materials required to manufacture something rather than telling him how the device worked. He maximized training in Minmatar Starship Engineering, but unless he were to decide to go into business mass-producing the ships for which he owned blueprints, this would be of no value. He longed to buy the skill book for Astronautic Engineering but never found one for sale. Its description claimed, "Skill and knowledge of Astronautics and its use in the development of advanced technology." But rumor had it that this was the only skill book that added absolutely nothing to the student's abilities. Not being able to buy something that was absolutely useless had a certain logic to it.

## Hyperspace versus Hypertext

The technical discrepancies between *EVE Online* and real space technology as pioneered by Hermann Oberth are not flaws in *EVE* but in the universe we inhabit. Arguably among the most ridiculous web pages currently in existence is the Wikipedia article for "wormhole," which goes to great rhetorical lengths to justify the concept used to provide verisimilitude to the *EVE* idea that a galaxy different from our own could be reached by a short jump, albeit one that vanishes after the first waves of colonists have passed through. In its more sober passages, the Wikipedia article admits that there is neither evidence nor a good conceptual model of how a wormhole might function as a transit gateway, not to mention the issue of how any solid structure, such as a human body or spaceship, could tolerate the gravitational distortions upon entry. The same applies to the warp drives and interstellar jumps used regularly by Noberth and his virtual colleagues. Yet if technologies like those simulated in *EVE* are impossible, so, too, is interstellar travel.

There does, however, exist a real-world technology that allows one to jump from one world to another in an instant, namely, hypertext links on web pages. Perhaps human exploration of the cosmos will be conducted by avatars in the form of space probes and robot landers. Our bodies can remain on Earth, just as we do not need to voyage to London or Reykjavik but rather can log in to *EVE* from our homes.

Conceptualizing the cosmos as a system of information, not a scattering of planets, may be most conducive for an interesting human future.

Subjectively, an *EVE* player does not perceive the virtual universe from inside a ship but looks at the ship from outside. Indeed, to see the surroundings without obstruction, the user may almost instantly zoom backward, until the ship is a mere speck on the computer screen. In terms of game industry concepts, that means it is not a first-person shooter but a hybrid third-person role-playing game and strategy game. The highly convenient navigation tools for flying from one planet, asteroid belt, or solar system to another are rather like graphical network-based Internet browsing tools. Changing ships is easy when one is in a hangar that contains more than one ship, and although defeat in battle can be traumatic, the loser escapes in a capsule that represents a virtual world vantage point more than a complex machine. Thus *EVE* has many virtues as a simulation of how human beings might experience future virtual exploration of the real universe. This is especially so once fleets of space probes have collected detailed information over a period of decades and a virtual representation of a solar system is ready for much more rapid analysis by scientists or learning by students.

During the decade in which *EVE Online* has earned worldwide admiration, human spaceflight has entered a period of stagnation or even decline. The last Space Shuttle landed in July 2011, and NASA has wandered from one antique-style launch system to another, without any clear goal. China proved its space mettle with a lunar lander but did not surpass much earlier Russian and American accomplishments. Although there is ample room to debate what the goals of the world's space program should be, at present, they are aimless. Perhaps we should abandon human spaceflight, at least until fundamentally better launch technologies have been developed, and learn a lesson from *EVE* about how interstellar travel could be accomplished. Information systems designed for personality capture could produce artificial intelligences based on real human individuals and transport them to the stars, not the original biological organisms (Bainbridge 2011a, 2013c). That is to say, with artificial intelligence, Noberth could become not an avatar but an NPC.

The space programs of planet Earth may have lost much of their former ability to inspire people (Delgado 2011). Yet millions of "players" find online role-playing "games" to be inspirational (Bainbridge 2013b). *EVE Online* can inspire players to contribute to the advance of science and technology, and the complexity of *EVE*'s manufacturing and travel systems is good training for logical thinking more generally. Thus *EVE* is a school for spaceflight without needing to represent exactly the technologies Hermann Oberth envisioned. Indeed, *EVE* teaches how technology can mediate cooperation and conflict, two challenges that Oberth himself never mastered.

NOTES

1  http://killfeed.eveuniversity.org/.

2  http://wiki.eveonline.com/en/wiki/Capacitor/.

## BIBLIOGRAPHY

Bainbridge, William Sims. 1976. *The Spaceflight Revolution*. New York: Wiley-Interscience.

———. 1986. *Dimensions of Science Fiction*. Cambridge, Mass.: Harvard University Press.

———. 1997. *The Sociology of Religious Movements*. New York: Routledge.

———. 2011a. "Direct Contact with Extraterrestrials via Computer Emulation." In *Civilizations beyond Earth: Extraterrestrial Life and Society*, edited by Douglas A. Vakoch and Albert A. Harrison, 191–202. New York: Berghahn Press.

———. 2011b. *The Virtual Future*. London: Springer.

———. 2013a. "Ancestor Veneration Avatars." In *Handbook of Research on Technoself: Identity in a Technological Society*, edited by Rocci Luppicini, 308–21. Hershey, Pa.: Information Science Reference.

———. 2013b. *eGods: Faith versus Fantasy in Computer Gaming*. New York: Oxford University Press.

———. 2013c. *Personality Capture and Emulation*. London: Springer.

———. 2013d. "Perspectives on Virtual Veneration." *The Information Society* 29, no. 3: 196–202.

———. 2013e. "Transavatars." In *The Transhumanist Reader*, edited by Max More and Natasha Vita-More, 91–108. Chichester, U.K.: Wiley-Blackwell.

———. 2014. *The Meaning and Value of Spaceflight*. Berlin: Springer.

———. Forthcoming. *Star Worlds: Freedom versus Control in Online Gameworlds*. Ann Arbor: University of Michigan Press.

Coopersmith, Jonathan. 2011. "The Cost of Reaching Orbit: Ground-Based Launch Systems." *Space Policy* 27: 77–80.

Delgado, Laura M. 2011. "When Inspiration Fails to Inspire." *Space Policy* 27: 94–98.

Drain, Brendan. 2013. "EVE Evolved: Merging Valkyrie with EVE Online." *Massively* (blog), October 27. http://massively.joystiq.com/2013/10/27/eve-evolved-merging-valkyrie-with-eve-online/.

Horner, Sebastian von. 1963. "The General Limits of Space Travel." In *Interstellar Communication*, edited by A. G. W. Cameron, 144–56. New York: Benjamin.

Horowitz, Norman H. 1986. "Mars: Myth and Reality." *Engineering and Science*, March 4–9, 35–37.

Launius, Roger D. 2006. "Assessing the Legacy of the Space Shuttle." *Space Policy* 22: 226–34.

———. 2010. "Can We Colonize the Solar System? Human Biology and Survival in the Extreme Space Environment." *Endeavour* 34, no. 3: 122–29.

Moreno, Jacob L. 1946. "Psychodrama and Group Psychotherapy." *Sociometry* 9: 249–53.

Moreno, Jacob L., and Zerka Toeman. 1942. "The Group Approach in Psychodrama." *Sociometry* 5: 191–95.

Oberth, Hermann. 1923. *Die Rakete zu den Planetenräumen*. Munich, Germany: Oldenbourg.

———. 1959. *Stoff und Leben*. Remagen, Germany: Reichl.

Paul, Christopher A. 2011. "Don't Play Me: *EVE Online*, New Players, and Rhetoric." In *Proceedings of the Sixth International Conference on Foundations of Digital Games*, 262–64. New York: ACM.

Serviss, Garrett P. 1911. *A Columbus of Space*. New York: D. Appleton.

# 4

## Universes, Metaverses, and Multiverses

*Kjartan Pierre Emilsson*

**What is the nature of reality?** What does it mean to be somewhere? What are things? Why should we care?

These metaphysical questions sound like assignments you might get in a philosophical class in university and not something you would ever need to think about in the context of making a game. But strangely enough, all of these questions came up at some point during the initial design of *EVE Online,* and though the idea was never actually to answer them, the process of thinking about them influenced many design choices. In this chapter, I focus specifically on the design choice of keeping *EVE* as a *single shard,* meaning that all participants of the game interact in a single common game universe, instead of being segregated into multiple instances of the same game universe. This design choice was and still is fairly uncommon in the industry, and it has various particular consequences, both good and bad. Nevertheless, even today, after operating the *EVE* universe for more than ten years, we are still absolutely convinced that this was the best design choice for *EVE* and that it has been key to both its longevity and its uniqueness.

To understand what led us to this design choice, we must look back beyond *EVE* at the confluence of various historical factors that ultimately made this decision both obvious and unavoidable, but first it is important to understand the mind-set that we as creators had during the early stages of the design and the cultural background we were in.

CCP Games was founded in 1997, in the midst of the dot-com boom, with the idea of creating a massively multiplayer online game (MMOG). Many of the people working at CCP at that time and during the early phase of the game's design over the next five years had worked together previously in a truly early dot-com company, called OZ.com, that had started off in 1995.

OZ.com, founded by Gudjon Mar Gudjonsson, had started as a small, 3-D visual effects shop for advertising agencies, but by 1995, it had attracted a handful of like-minded people who were both passionate about 3-D graphics and early adopters of the Internet, which was just emerging as a commercial opportunity. Some of the people involved at this early time were Reynir Hardarson, a graphic designer who became the founder of CCP; Matthias Gudmundsson, a programmer who became lead tech director of CCP; Fridrik Haraldsson, a graphic designer who later became the main user interface designer/programmer of *EVE Online*; Hilmar Veigar Pétursson, a programmer who later became CEO of CCP; Sigurdur Ólafsson, an artist who became CMO of early CCP; and me, a physicist working as the CTO of OZ.com, later to become the lead game designer of *EVE Online* at CCP.

None of us were game developers, and even though we were all gamers, gaming wasn't what defined us. The grand idea that united all of us then was the promise of building a true virtual reality, the Metaverse, as popularized in influential novels by writers such as William Gibson and Neal Stephenson.

As the foolhardy and naively optimistic young people we were, we felt that the Web, with its 2-D representation of information, was just a minor stepping-stone to a much more grandiose vision of a truly global, networked information space that a user could navigate as an avatar and through which she could interact outside the limitations of physical constraints. The instrument of discovery was the browser, the tool that projected a user into this virtual space and allowed her to interact with the space and other participants.

In 1995, Netscape had just shaken the financial world by being the first large Internet initial public offering, riding on its ubiquitous HTML browser. This set the tone for all the other Internet companies. And just as the old 2-D Web was constructed by HTML and TCP networks, the brave new world would need some kind of fundamental primitives to be built upon, and this is where we started on the quixotic journey to work on designing this operating system for virtual reality.

OZ's vision was to create a 3-D browser, called OZ Virtual, using the then-emerging VRML markup language, with which a person could navigate this new virtual reality Web. But we didn't settle for just browsing this new world; we also wanted to let users have physical representations in these worlds that they could share with others such that they could interact, both visually but also through other forms. The idea was to use space and spaceflight as metaphors for how people browsed this virtual reality, going from place to place. Early versions of this product were presented at the Internet World Expo in San Jose, California, in 1996.[1]

It was during this phase that we started thinking about the meaning of a "place" or "location." Could someone be in multiple places at once? Could the actions that a person performs in one place influence things in a different place? How could we compartmentalize places but yet have them networked into a gigantic, coherent union? How would we model agency into such a global system?

An important thing to note here is that in all of these thoughts, there was always an implied understanding that the Metaverse was a unique phenomenon. Just as we

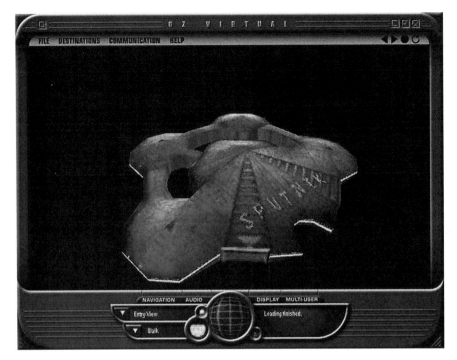

Figure 4.1. Approaching the Sputnik space station in the OZ Virtual browser, 1996.

talk today of the World Wide Web as a single thing, the augmented Metaverse was also unique: a true alternative reality in which a person could participate and to which he could contribute but which was an independent whole. The notion of instancing the Metaverse, creating multiple identical copies of it where different groups of people would reside without being able to communicate, was so alien to us that I don't think it ever crossed our minds. I think therein lies one of the influential factors that led us to the single-shard design for *EVE*: we were so immersed in this holistic concept of a singular virtual reality that we simply couldn't conceive of anything else.

When CCP was founded, it inherited part of this vision from OZ but was much more game focused. It was always understood that games would be part of the Metaverse, but at the same time, it was dawning on us that this huge vision wouldn't become reality anytime soon and that focusing on a game was a way to bring some of these grandiose ideas into a more concrete and manageable project. Nonetheless, the idea of having a single world, a true coherent alternate reality that encapsulated a degree of verisimilitude of interactions and agency, was an essential part of our vision of virtual reality.

Now putting aside this cultural background, let us consider another factor that was also very influential, namely, the technical side.

Regardless of the choice of a single shard, it was always a clear requirement that we wanted to create a large world that could sustain a large population. At the time, the only references we had were pioneers of the MMOG genre, such as *Ultima*

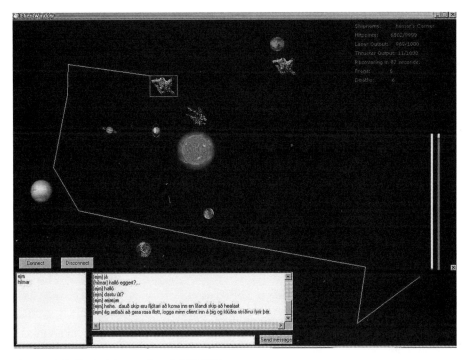

Figure 4.2. Earliest alpha version of *EVE*, 2000.

*Online* and *Everquest,* which had shard populations in the low thousands running on single CPUs. We felt we could do much more than that by adopting a clustered server architecture. This architectural approach was relatively novel at the time, especially for traditional game companies, and mostly came from the newly emerging Internet companies that had to create solutions that scaled to millions of online users. Again, the fact that our background was much more on the Internet side of things, rather than in gaming, meant that we were fortunate to have bright individuals already familiar with such architecture and who were unafraid to go down that path. The important characteristic of a clustered architecture is that it scales with the number of CPUs in the cluster rather than with the computational capacity of an individual CPU. As such, we were never faced with a hard technical constraint of supporting a maximum number of simultaneous players, which would have influenced our game design. Of course, such a constraint exists even for a clustered solution, but we were fortunate enough with *EVE* that the population size grew relatively slowly compared to other games, and the steady evolution of computing power encapsulated in Moore's law—the prediction that computing power doubles approximately every two years—could easily cope with our growth; we have never hit that hard ceiling, even to this day.

Now, to make use of a clustered architecture, computational tasks must be easily distributed. In our case, it came back to being able to segment the game world into simulation chunks that were mostly causally independent of each other, such that global dependencies became a manageable overhead.

Fortunately, and maybe not completely coincidentally, the cosmos offers naturally such a segmentation. Solar systems are far from each other, and causality can be easily constrained within them, without straining verisimilitude. The same goes with corporations (the guild equivalent of *EVE*), which naturally segment social networks into manageable chunks.

Furthermore, the physics model we chose for the spaceship dynamics was a perfectly deterministic one, which allowed us to hide a lot of the lag difference between users from different parts of the world. This, combined with relatively slow-paced combat, meant that there were no segregation needs arising from having to group together people from similar geographical locations.

As such, the genre we chose for our first game was a symbiotic fit with the architecture we had in mind, and this combination naturally avoided the problem of sharding. How much the genre choice and technical solution envisioned influenced the single-shard design decision, or inversely, is impossible to say. It all just fit together naturally.

Once that confluence of cultural background, genre choice, and technical vision was clear and we had confidently aimed for a single-shard design (or at least as far as we could take it), another strengthening factor emerged that solidified this to a point of becoming a design principle rather than a design choice: the fundamental belief that a single-shard approach would lead to new and unexpected patterns of player interaction that would make the game more deep and enjoyable by their own merit. In essence, the network effect applied to game design.

The concept of the network effect, which states that the "value" of an interconnected network increases exponentially with the number of nodes in the network, doesn't come from the gaming world but from the world of telecommunications, and at that time, it was also becoming a common term in various Internet services, especially those focusing on social networks. Funnily enough, that was another domain in which OZ and thus many early CCP people had become involved between 1997 and 2000, working closely with telecommunications provider Ericsson on social network applications.

In the context of a game, we always had a clear vision that it would ultimately be people who create content for other people and that the most fundamental form of content would be social. Indeed, as we had chosen a genre that is mostly devoid of actual content, space being mostly empty, the only way for us to scale up our worlds to the number of people we wanted was to make sure that they created entertainment for each other; otherwise, we would be forced to perpetually create new content for our players at great cost. A lot of the team had had a very formative experience playing early *Ultima Online* at a time when it was a completely open sandbox and had experienced very powerful emotions in doing so. We knew that the emotional attachment to virtual property you and your friends had built is much stronger and meaningful than attachments to ready-made, duplicated, linear content. One of our early design

Figure 4.3. *EVE* alliance influence map, 2014.

principles was to maximize human interaction anywhere applicable, whether through combat, trading, or just talking.

As we launched the game, our population grew slowly but steadily, and the social structure observed was mostly contained within the framework of small corporations with approximately 150 members each. But as the total population grew, we started observing larger coalitions forming as informal alliances of corporations. This emerged because there was enough space for it in the overall social network of the game. Also note that at this point, the game didn't offer any tools to support these metaorganizations, so they all existed outside of our control. This evolution has continued, leading to various large-scale social structures whose existence would simply be impossible in a smaller network. For us, this was a wonderful evolution that

Figure 4.4. Thousands of players interacting.

emphasized the "meta" aspect of our game and how it seemed to be able effortlessly to cross boundaries between game, players, and communities.

I have a background in chaos physics, so I have always felt that there is an analogy to the emergence in physical systems. When you take a physical system, for example, water, and constrain it, the shape it can take is largely dominated by the vessel it is in. The smaller the vessel is, the stronger the influence it has on the state of the system can be. In a way, the vessel *selects* the possible states the system can be in. When you increase the size of the vessel, its influence dwindles, and the physical system can suddenly assume myriad states that are innate to it rather than dictated. Contrast the difference between water enclosed in a small bottle and the rich, intricate patterns that water assumes in its flow through oceans and Earth's atmosphere.

To reiterate, the reasoning that led CCP to choose a single-shard architecture is most probably anchored in our background as early Internet developers rather than as gamers, in terms of technological choices but also in terms of the philosophical mindset of what it means to create a virtual world. What has converted that decision to a principle is the beautiful emergence to which it has led, creating a richness and depth in our world that doesn't come from us as creators but from the intertwined lives and destinies of our players.

NOTE

1   See http://www.metroactive.com/papers/metro/05.09.96/networld-9619.html.

# The Digital Grind

## Time and Labor as Resources of War in *EVE Online*

*Oskar Milik*

The digital universe of *EVE Online*, as discussed in previous chapters, is unique in its use of a single-server system. This means that players of the game logging on from every single country in the world (with the exception of Chinese players) are able to interact and participate on a scale not experienced in any other prior massively multiplayer online game (MMOG). The single-server design of *EVE Online* is important because it defines the social reality players experience in the game; it determines the scale of the economy, the political and social systems, and the size of conflicts and wars. This is an important aspect for both the developer and many players, because the scale of these interactions leads to increased visibility and additional marketing opportunities for the company as well as increased player investment in the game world.

Although the hardware and game code that allow such a system to take place are impressive, the single-server system creates additional challenges for players, some of which do not exist in any other MMOG. One such issue is that players from every time zone in the world are operating on a single server rather than being primarily placed into localized "hubs," with a server time that is based on the host region. What this means is that everything that takes place in the universe of *EVE Online* happens in UTC, which is GMT – 1 (one hour prior to Greenwich Mean Time) during daylight savings. This particular time zone was selected because CCP Games (the company that developed and runs *EVE Online*) is headquartered in Iceland, which is within UTC. Much like the monetary system is named ISK (interstellar kredits, but based off the same acronym for Iceland's currency), the time zone was selected because of its connection to the country. Both players and CCP generally refer to this time zone as "EVE time." By default, the EVE time is shown at the bottom left corner of the screen, with the player's local time not at all presented. Given the wide distribution of the player base across the world, it would not be possible to create any form of sustained organization without the players being able to establish a shared appreciation of time, within which everything from simple communications to massive battles can take place.

This chapter discusses the way that players of *EVE Online* negotiate the concept of time, and it addresses this through three central themes. First is the way that the players and leaders of *EVE*'s ten-thousand-plus-strong global alliances understand time and the impacts that this understanding has on in-game interactions and on an individual's allocation of resources. This also ties into the single-server system that *EVE Online* uses and the way that a player's virtual life affects his offline life. Second, it develops how time is used by players and in-game alliances as a weapon in war situations and the way that time changes the operational parameters of a conflict. Finally, because many different understandings of time may arise in the course of interaction and participation, this chapter discusses the different individuals who have power to determine how time is used and the process by which this understanding is shared with other members. This can be seen in *EVE Online* when certain time zones are given greater consideration in the course of conflicts and in the specific timelines and times of operation for conflicts that are established by a select few, ensuring that they have better control of the events as they occur.

## A Note on Methods

To answer these questions, I acted as a participant member of TEST Alliance (a large null-sec alliance) between September 2012 and August 2013. My role in the organization was that of a battle participant as well as being on the TEST Alliance tournament team, or ATXI. This involved participating in organized events that had between twelve (ATXI) and two thousand (Alliance war) members. General ethnographic notes were made on play performed in null-sec space, with specific focus given to chat logs and recordings that were made during large battles during this time. Null-sec refers to regions in *EVE Online* space that do not have any of the protections of other areas. This means that it's focused more on player versus player (PVP) conflict and allows territorial claims by alliances. In addition to these general notes, this research uses collected recordings of leaders of different alliances giving official speeches. These speeches are made publicly available and are used as methods of information exchange but also as propaganda pieces to push forward the interests of the alliance. Notes from secondary sources such as Jabber and forums were also gathered for this research. Owing to ethical considerations, data were only recorded or archived when access was granted by a leader in the alliance. Any time recordings were taken, other members in the channel received automated messages informing them of the recording, so no players were recorded without being aware of it. Finally, no information from the speeches that suggested they were uttered by an individual under the age of eighteen was transcribed or analyzed. Names of individual characters are changed in the interest of anonymity of participants of this study.

In an effort to best analyze these data for the specific social context of *EVE Online,* the data were analyzed through a framework that is based off of symbolic interactionist thought (Lofland et al. 2006; Goffman 1959) and Garfinkel's (1967) eth-nomethodology. The coding and data analysis were performed through a framework of grounded theory, as described by Charmaz (2006). This iterative method was used in this project to ensure that any ensuing theory would be rooted closely in the data. As Woodford (2012) discussed, this means that the tools for analysis were modified to match the different nature of interaction in *EVE Online*. The lack of a distinct avatar in space, for instance, creates an emphasis on the individual that exists behind the computer screen (Milik 2012). Because of this, an emphasis is placed on the language used by players of *EVE Online*. This chapter observes the process through which individuals explain their understanding of time and the way in which this concept is created and shared among an entire community of players, both within a specific alliance and in an overall sense throughout *EVE Online*.

## Null-Sec and Recruitment

It has already been mentioned how the single-server system of *EVE Online* is unique and extremely important to the game. The ability for players to engage in activities that affect the entire virtual world is an appealing aspect of the game. Stories players share about the game mention a singular economy that can be manipulated by skilled merchants, a need to physically transport goods that can be stolen by skilled pirates, and territorial claims of sovereignty that need to be defended by skilled groups of players. CCP Games has made an effort to encourage these stories, including those about in-game thefts (Geere 2010) and successful pirate actions (Foster 2013). A primary focus for these sorts of encouraged and shared stories tends to be on large-scale battles, as these are sometimes picked up by major news outlets outside of games journalism, such as the BBC (2013). CCP has also performed both hardware and software changes so that increasingly large groups of individuals can exist in a single small area (referred to as a system). These activities all occur on a server, called Tranquility, which is one of the most powerful supercomputers operated by a games company (Khaw 2013). The only exceptions to this are players connecting from China. Because of governmental regulations concerning Internet traffic and international corporations, players connect to an independent server (Serenity) that is mechanically identical to Tranquility but cannot share information with it.

The development of the technologies that allow events of this size and visibility was a purposeful area of focus for CCP and can be seen in the effort the company makes to cross-link news stories that discuss the largest battles in the game. When the Battle of Asakai[1] reached a total participation of more than three thousand players, CCP sent out press releases, encouraged tweets, and spread player videos regarding the event (Purchese 2013). CCP's desire to share this information suggests that there is an interest in a potential player base to experience the integrated world of *EVE Online*. This can be seen by referring to the subscription numbers for the game, which have been steadily growing, with particularly newsworthy stories leading to a rise in new player numbers. In the month following the Battle of Asakai, for instance, the number of active *EVE Online* players increased by approximately fifty thousand.[2] The overall number of hours played within the game also rises after a major event.

Following a massive battle for territory in a system called B-R5RB, the number of hours played by all players increased significantly, as seen in Figure 5.1 (Jester 2014). In the thirty days following this battle, the average number of players online in-game went up 10 percent; at a minimum, this is additional revenue of US$50,000 for CCP, although the typical player will participate over more than a single month. It is worth noting that this increase happened at the same time that other games, such as *World of Warcraft*, continued to see downward trends in active subscriptions as market competition leeched players. The fact that many games released after *EVE Online* that are far more easy to understand and play casually have a more difficult time retaining subscribers shows that the connection players have to *EVE Online* is linked to some greater aspects of the experience than usually considered by games companies. It makes sense, then, that the ability for players to discuss a shared reality within a single server is critically important to the community and to CCP.

The focus placed on these relatively rare but newsworthy events by the people running the game as well as those running alliances within it means that these relatively powerful individuals have an interest in encouraging participation in null-sec space. As such, these leaders need to ensure that they have the membership and the propagandists who can generate and share accounts. Recruitment efforts and propaganda are both tied closely to major military maneuvers and political "standings" changes that occur in large-scale player interactions. An example of this process is in the case of TEST Alliance Please Ignore engaging in the largest war for null-sec

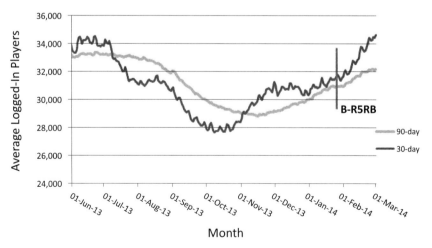

Figure 5.1. Graph showing player hours and subscriptions spiking following the major battle at B-R5RB.

space against the Goonswarm Federation, incorporating references from *Star Wars* into its website and forums, its propaganda outreach, and its recruitment efforts on other online resources. This direction for the alliance led to a change on its website, a long series of propagandistic pictures placing TEST Alliance as the rebel alliance, and many comments on posts regarding major battles on websites such as Reddit encouraging newcomers to "come fight the oppressive Goons" and "protect fun in EVE." As seen in the discussion of the Goonswarm by Richard Page (chapter 8), this emphasis on fun in the game is contrary to the strategy Goonswarm has established, which uses the removal of fun as a weapon against enemies. This use of "camping" to remove fun is addressed later in this chapter. In a speech, a Goonswarm leader states that "our foremost goal is always the denial of the enjoyment of the enemy: no fun allowed for our enemies." By focusing attention on cultural differences between TEST Alliance and its opposition, the propaganda developed during this time attempts to create a particular identity to establish TEST Alliance members as better people defending something that is worth defending. The focus on creating an image to encourage a message that will resonate with potential players shows that these alliances understand the importance of using image- and newsworthy events to best achieve their goals.

The newsworthiness of stories that occur in the universe of *EVE Online* can be seen in the example of EVE News 24, a twenty-four-hour news site that attempts to catalog occurrences throughout the universe in the game. Many other MMOGs have sites devoted to them, such as MMO-Champion or Wowhead for *World of Warcraft,* but these sites are devoted to out-of-game discussions of things such as development cycles and data collection. EVE News 24 is focused equally as heavily on in-game events as on those that occur outside it. It is the unique single-server nature of *EVE Online* that makes this focus possible. With so many players sharing a single shard, even events that occur across the universe could very well affect any player. A war declared, for instance, will change the relative value of certain ships. Similarly, a conflict over territory may alter the political landscape, leading to a player having to dedicate more hours to border maintenance.

It takes more than a handful of people to generate the resources and perform the logistics for a combat of sufficient size, and for a battle that includes thousands of users, one can imagine easily twice the number of actual combatants somehow being involved in the process. This complexity ties back to the main discussion of this chapter. Players in these alliances come from different corners of the globe, and they all need to be included in organizational and logistical considerations. Major alliances cannot survive without being willing to incorporate members from different areas and time zones around the world. As such, part of the process of incorporating a player into a group is the ability to create a shared understanding of time for both parties and to mold players into useful war-fighting members. Because these alliances are most affected by the single time system, this chapter focuses more heavily upon them, as well as on how time is treated as an object, one that proficient leaders are able to harness, much like human labor.

## TEST Alliance, Please Ignore: A Background

As mentioned earlier, a large part of this research was performed around a null-sec alliance named TEST Alliance, Please Ignore. TEST Alliance was one of the largest organizations in *EVE Online,* along with Goonswarm. The success of Goonswarm in creating an *EVE* community that was able to survive in null-sec space offered an example of how social groups may be able to grow in the game. The player numbers and popularity of *EVE Online* had been increasing steadily since its inception, and stories about large thefts, scams, and battles were growing popular on gaming-related websites, especially one called Reddit. In response, a new section of the site was created dedicated to the game of *EVE Online* (r/eve) and, within it, a movement began to start a corporation dedicated to users of the site. This movement led to the creation of Dreddit,[3] an in-game corporation that quickly grew in size and strength, until its heads formed an alliance to move to null-sec space.

With the move to null-sec, the leadership attempted to establish its base of operations as far away from Goonswarm as possible, out of fear of being targeted as another website-based group. Owing to the leader observing the map upside down, however, the final location chosen actually happened to be extremely close to the Goonswarm Federation. This story is one broadly shared with members in TEST Alliance because it reinforces a shared understanding of the culture of the alliance, and it sets up two significant points that help explain it. The first thread is how players in the organization refer to themselves and their alliance as being terrible at the game. The second concerns the fact that because TEST Alliance took up position right by Goonswarm, the relationship between the two organizations ended up being central to its growth as well as their eventual conflict in the game.

The geographical adjacency between these two alliances ties into a structural similarity as well. TEST Alliance was formed to claim sovereign space in Delve, away from an organization called IT Alliance, after a large war during which it assisted Goonswarm. As it grew, TEST Alliance maintained a reputation for being able to deploy massive numbers of players, although with weapons that were very weak and easy to access. This ability to bring members into massive conflicts was tied to the alliance's propaganda (the use of the Rifter, a very small and easy-to-fly ship, as a representation of alliance members) and recruitment (bringing in "newbros") efforts (see Bergstrom 2013 for further discussion about TEST's newbro recruitment). The rules for entry to Dreddit, the primary corporation in TEST Alliance, have not changed since its creation. The alliance HR states that Dreddit is open to any individuals who can show that they have an open and active account on the website Reddit for a sufficient amount of time. This attitude created a culture within these alliances that encourages players to identify themselves as not being excellent players or even good PVPers. This can be seen in TEST Alliance players who participate in the yearly Alliance Tournament that is run by CCP. The tournament was designed to highlight the very best players in the game, and players who participate have to practice often and be quite skilled at piloting. Being merely good is not enough to participate effectively, and yet these players still state that they are "bad at EVE." This particular approach toward membership for both Goonswarm and TEST Alliance sets them apart from the previous alliances that were strong in null-sec space. In comparison, "elite" alliances that held territory through smaller groups of dedicated and skilled players have very strict HR policies. They usually have minimums on the number of skill points a character has and on how active the player has been in PVP encounters. By using a different recruitment strategy, organizations such as TEST Alliance and Goonswarm held territory through consistent pressure only made possible by relatively large groups of newer or less elite players. In the case of TEST Alliance, a leader describes it as "massive. We have 12,496 members at the time of this posting [2013], and Dreddit itself weighs in larger than the third largest alliance in the game." By way of comparison, Pandemic Legion, which is a far more restrictive alliance, contains slightly more than two thousand active players. One can imagine that the relative scale of these groups plays into political and war-related interactions.

The strategy of mass recruitment used by TEST Alliance and Goonswarm caused both of these alliances to develop cultures that were relatively similar. As seen earlier, TEST Alliance members often portray themselves as bad at the game, and members of Goonswarm often take pride in stating that they don't have the dedication to develop skills in a computer game. These similarities can also be seen in some of the language used by players. Because the membership of these alliances are drawn from users of large, anonymous forums, certain aspects of Internet culture have become incorporated into these groups. One unfortunate aspect of this culture is the way in which offensive language is often used and encouraged. Terms such as "jew," "nazi," and "faggot" are common, and sexually suggestive references litter a majority of communication systems used. In much the same vein, the leadership refers to itself as the "short bus" (referring to a bus for students with cognitive disabilities) and widely use the term "retards" to refer to other TEST Alliance members. The use of this linguistic style helps create an us versus them mentality, where individuals who take this language seriously or with offense will be treated as outsiders of the group. These aspects of similarity between the Goonswarm and TEST Alliance caused the two alliances to work together very closely for many years, fighting other, more "serious" alliances.

Such a mentality and acceptance of language use are tied to the importance leaders place on developing a collective identity for their organizations in *EVE Online*. As conflict between different cultural groups develops, there is additional pressure on the individual to incorporate into the greater group identity, and one key method of doing that is through the use of language (Cerulo 1997). In the particular case of TEST

Alliance and Goonswarm, that they emerged out of online web forums that rely heavily on the principle of anonymity only helped encourage this cultural understanding of "offensive" language. Online conversations in anonymous places tend to be far more insensitive in a general sense, but also adopting the linguistic practices of a group online is an easier way not to reveal personal identity (Attrill and Jalil 2011). Over the course of their existence, these particular organizations have incorporated the use of such language as part of their collective identity and then have solidified it as a means by which they can differentiate themselves from other groups who play the game.

## Turning the Individual into Virtual Labor Power

*EVE Online* is at its core meant to be a simulator of absolute capitalism. All major game-play events are player driven, the market is manipulated freely, and piracy (a pure form of capitalist exchange—"I take your stuff and you get nothing") is accepted and even admired by some players of the game. This particular use of capitalistic ideology is referred to by players most often as "free-marker" or "neoliberal." The nature of this simulation means that many of the consequences of capitalistic systems extend into the sociality and culture of players in the game. One consequence is the incorporation of globalized definitions of time, which are addressed more deeply later. A second concept is that of turning individuals into labor. Even as players participate in the game willingly, ostensibly to find enjoyment, many of the actions taken by these same players are described as being "not fun." One leader explains that the stress of organizing the logistics efforts for TEST Alliance was so intense that the alliance was "burning through logistics directors like, you know, every two to three months." These processes that are least fun, however, can be crucially important to the success of the alliance. As such, there is a strong effort on the part of leaders to redefine membership in terms that equate participation and results (classic metrics of employment) to rewards and privileges within the game.

The goal of leaders in conceptualizing players as hours of participation is linked to the "camping" strategy seen earlier. To effectively use players in these sorts of conflicts, all 23.5 hours of server up-time need to be covered, and individuals need to be on location and paying attention throughout. This, at its core, is turning the individual into labor power. This creates an interesting conflict for the player. The player receives no physical gain but is expected to perform joblike duties. This "immaterial labor" (Terranova 2013, 40) creates a self-identity within the player of being a drone within her corporation and in many ways can cause tension in the player. In one battle, TEST players were forming up to enter together. Their voice system did not allow them to speak; only fleet commanders (FCs) have that right. They were not allowed to move or execute commands of their own. Any action by a pilot deviating from orders will have them yelled at, removed from the fleet, or, owing to the nature of combat, destroyed. The response by the players was acceptance of the rules, albeit with every effort to show their independence at the same time. The response to all commands was a mass of public statements of "Hodor," a servant from the *Game of Thrones* series who obeys all commands unquestioningly, replying only with his own name, Hodor. This outward obedience mixed with sarcasm and defiance shows how the nature of labor for *EVE Online* players in TEST Alliance creates an ambivalent attitude toward the structure of null-sec combat.

The ambivalence seen in these players may be irrelevant, however, because they are still willing to submit themselves to higher levels of control in exchange for the ability to participate in null-sec warfare. In socioeconomic terms, this means that players are willing to accept the role of an employee of the alliance in exchange for the ability to participate and potentially gain assets within the game world. The particular nature of this employment, however, would be best compared to neoliberal jobs such as customer service work. Much as in a common job, the key aspect of time that matters to both the organization (alliance) and the employee (player) is the way people and actions are tracked. In the nonvirtual world, the key means of knowing if an employee attends work is through hourly tracking or submission of work documentation in some form. This particular system of tracking compliance would not work directly in *EVE Online*: in-game objectives are fluid (owing to the PVP nature of the game), and as seen in other chapters, trust of membership by leaders is not rewarded by the mechanics of the game. Leadership of large alliances, then, needs to establish a different means of tracking player attendance and of marking how valuable a player is to the group.

The solution to this tracking problem is typically the use of the "kill-mails" mechanic. Every time a player's ship is destroyed, an automatic in-game message is generated to the player that lists all those who participated in the killing. In the interest of tracking player involvement in military operations, leaders adopted this mechanic to create "kill-boards" on their established web services that consolidate all these data to see who was active within a conflict. In tracking these particular kills, the alliance leader is able to look at certain members who should be congratulated and others who should be punished. Alliances or corporations may be given territory for performing well, and a lack of participation may be the basis for termination from the alliance. In a speech threatening to remove certain allies (essentially declaring war on them), one leader states, "If you're in a member corp and you don't bother showing up at a situation where we're having our territory invaded, what the hell are you doing with us anyway?" This particular threat would be pointless without some means of tracking attendance. The kill-board, then, acts as a time sheet for the *EVE Online* universe manager, tracking participation and acting as a means of establishing pay, which in this case takes the form of null-sec participation.

Because organizations such as TEST Alliance rely so heavily on the labor of newer players with relatively fewer skill points in the game, kill-mails get an important secondary function. Players are able to use these references as a means of distinguishing themselves from other players. Groups that are able to get large numbers of kills while defending the territory of the alliance are given greater leeway and responsibilities. This is tied with the ability to get other players involved and excited to participate. One member of TEST Alliance, for instance, was often given a pass for a poor attitude because "he's our most reliable FC right now. He's getting players out there. We're not going to drive him out 'til we have to." Owing to these types of interpretations, kill-board numbers can be very important. In no cases seen, however, were kill-board numbers used to determine if an individual would be promoted or moved into a leadership position, as they are used more as indicators of individual piloting skill than as demonstrating officer qualities. In typical TEST Alliance ambivalence, the use of such metrics has a mixed reception among players, and some of the most commonly retweeted and shared forum comments revolve around kill-mails of TEST Alliance players that show how poorly they equipped or piloted their vessels when they got killed. The importance of being seen as a superior player is simply not as central to the TEST Alliance player's experience as many studies in meritocracy have found, such as in *World of Warcraft* (Taylor 2008).

Players of many MMOGs have commented that the games they play feel like a second job to them, sometimes described as "playbor" (Kucklich 2009). In *EVE Online,* as seen in the case of kill-boards, certain real connections can be made in this game. Like time sheets, non-virtual-world managers have to schedule the times of many individuals to ensure tasks get completed effectively. In *EVE Online,* this task is primarily done by arranging the players into subgroups. For TEST Alliance, these groups are called squads and are focused on particular tasks that are undertaken at certain times. The primary role of this distribution of resources is to assist with territorial defense. Another type of camping, "gate camps," are a means of defending alliance gates within a region, because these are the only means of entry for a small enemy force intent on stopping player versus environment game play, which offer players a way to earn ISK inside null-sec. To have as close to a twenty-four-hour defense as possible, a leader needs to arrange people who have different play times to be active so there won't be any breaches. These types of camps also show the level of cohesion among the alliance members. Individuals are willing to sacrifice their time so allies can safely gain resources. In addition, they also mean that there is an emphasis among the leaders on ensuring that members who are assigned to certain tasks accomplish them. Of course, time restrictions are a reality that all players are allowed, but the pressures of the online world, due to the lack of a formal temporal structure, cause a greater disconnect between home and work (offline and online) than seen in the standard world. Even in customer service work, an individual is expected by her boss to take the time when she is not scheduled to do anything she pleases and not to be accountable for anything that occurs at the workplace until her shift begins again. The online player, however, can always be asked to participate in the case of an emergency, and the fact that he is off work only makes him a better candidate to participate in online activity.

## Time and War in *EVE Online*

In the military histories of Goonswarm and TEST Alliance, the key factors of their success have been tied to the organizational systems described earlier. By using their collective labor power, particularly their ability to use time, these groups have been able to completely change the nature of conflict in null-sec space. To explain how important time is, a quick explanation of the mechanics of territorial control in the universe of *EVE Online* is required. To destroy any player owned structures, an attack must occur in multiple stages. The first stage places the structure into a defensive mode, after which a certain amount of time needs to pass, after which the structure can actually be destroyed in a second-stage attack. This mechanic is used by players in war to control the time of conflict because controlling these "timers" may force players to play during times that they otherwise wouldn't. This chapter's digital ethnographic study (Boellstorff et al. 2012) of certain wars and conflicts shows that the reconceptualization of time as a weapon with which to wear down one's enemies is part of a successful strategy.

As the eventual victors of all of their military engagements (some of which can last many months), Goonswarm has established that the use of time serves one particularly key role in its military strategy. This role is to create burnout within the ranks of the opposition. In the First Great War, this could be easily seen in the way assaults were organized. At the start of the war, the Goon fleets and the other alliances trying to defeat Band of Brothers (BoB) arranged to have a multiple-front attack that spanned the different time zones in order to take space. This was primarily done through a coalition created with the Red Alliance (named RedSwarm), which has a prominent number of Russian and Eastern European members (more on Eastern European alliances in *EVE* can be found in chapter 6). By forcing BoB to defend on two different fronts, once in a U.S. time, and once in a Russian time, the plan was to destroy the willingness of BoB to fight. One forum post, for instance, argues that a large part of BoB's defeat was due to the alliance "suffering from low participation and . . . being assaulted on multiple fronts." Eventually, this strategy forced BoB to drop defense of one part of the map to be able to consolidate a singular front against Red Alliance, allowing use of uniform timers to force them into retreat.

This strategy of wearing down an opponent is not accidental; it is a very purposeful approach taken by the leaders of these alliances. As seen earlier, this strategy is widely and famously used by members of the Goons. By ensuring their opposition fails to get much enjoyment from the combat that they face, the Goons attempt to create a situation where their opponents do not even bother to enter the conflict, creating a win by default. The particular details of such a strategy can be extremely labor intensive on the part of the players in an organization. One leader gives this tactic the unfortunate name of a "rapecage." In this particular war, the opponents had found a safe location within the battle zone and refused to go outside it. The leader established teams of people to guard for any enemies attempting to leave that station at any time, regardless of the hour. He stated, "What we're going to do, is we're going to rapecage all their towers, we're going to park a thousand people in these systems. . . . We're basically going to rapecage them and kill everything. We've done this before . . . there's really nothing that they can do about it." The goal is to apply pressure directly on the ability of players to engage in the game at any point in time. This strategy of "camping" an enemy is slow, but quite effective, as it prevents the enemy from ever forming a cohesive fighting force. This tactic has become a cornerstone approach for military engagements undertaken by the Goonswarm.

This is also referenced heavily in the propaganda for these groups. Figure 5.2 portrays the dinosaur of TEST Alliance, the bees of Goonswarm, and the virus of Pandemic Legion watching over the "undock" of a region, to ensure no player can exit out to engage in the game, or otherwise have fun.

Figure 5.2. The TEST Alliance dinosaur, the Goonswarm bees, and the Pandemic Legion virus defending an "undock."

The use of Russian forces in this particular war reveals the mixed feelings that many players have regarding this segment of the *EVE Online* population. In many cases, these organizations are seen to be extremely insular (in no small part because of their use of a different language and alphabet) and dangerous. Much of this perceived danger, however, comes from the Russians' willingness to project forces at odd hours. One Russian-language alliance operating out of W-space (a special area of the game with only randomly generated entrances called wormholes) was known for having significant forces at every single moment in time guarding the entrances. As such, most players feared entering their territory because of the risk to their resources. This same projection ability, however, is what made the Russian bloc so particularly useful in the war against a large organization such as BoB.

The effectiveness of destroying the enjoyment of one's enemies can be seen in the way that the stress of "no fun" can affect specific players. For instance, one BoB director who had stopped fighting because of the hours required of him in the war was convinced by a Goon diplomat to dissolve the entire BoB alliance. This move, blamed on the director's burnout and general lack of interest, shows that manipulating interactions so that they revolve around time zones that they otherwise would avoid can cause serious problems for an alliance, in terms of logistics but also in terms of loyalty. This example also shows the level to which the time dedicated to politics in the game is important. As is explained in chapter 11, players willing to spend much of their time on diplomacy and other political exchanges are regarded as extremely valuable, even if they do not necessarily partake in battle often. At the same time, in this example, the stress of this time commitment can cause players to act in ways contrary to the interests of their alliance.

The multiple time zones of *EVE Online* have been used as a weapon in multiple conflicts, not just in the First Great War.[4] In the most recent war between TEST Alliance and Goonswarm, many of the timers set by the TEST Alliance fleets were done in Australian time zones, while much of the Goon fleet set timers for American time zones. TEST Alliance's strategy in this was to use the higher numbers they had in Europe and Australia to force their opponents into "alarm-clocking," which is to get up at uncomfortable hours to fight on a timer. The success of this strategy is described in one officer's post, where he states, "You guys in AU time are amazing. We're having great success in knocking down their towers." The organizational focus on this strategy is emphasized in the way the forums are arranged in TEST Alliance, to create a separate timing and scheduling system for different time zones, focusing on European and American time. This strategy is also effective in controlling image for the organization. Even though the actual progress of battles was turning against the TEST Alliance during this war, there was no real impact on territorial claims because of the use of these timers. The ability to have timers set at convenient times is just as important as setting up ones inconvenient for the enemy. In a speech to his alliance, a leader stated, "We got lucky, in terms of the timers. We have solid US time zone timers, generally from

2:00–5:00 EVE time." The ability to coordinate individuals to match these timers is crucial, either in terms of attacking or being able to defend adequately.

At the end of this war, TEST Alliance had decided to abandon its territorial claims and arranged to set up one last great battle to create a place for itself in *EVE* history before leaving null-sec space. This was the Battle of 6VDT. In an effort to create the numbers that could make such an event possible, both sides arranged to have the event occur at a prescheduled time. The arranged time, however, was based on an American time zone. This strategy did end up panning out for gaining the attendance. Under normal server strain conditions, this battle would have never been able to take place or would have crashed minutes into the engagement because of the amount of information being processed at once. To allow the battle to occur, CCP Games implemented its Time Dilation (TiDi) system, a process that makes player actions in Asakai occur more slowly than in the rest of the game. Because of this process, the battle actually took six hours. This meant that many players in European time zones started in the evening but were in the battle past four in the morning. This particular battle shows that there is a relative bias toward treating certain time zones, primarily those in the Americas, as being the most important to play. This concept is addressed more fully later in the chapter, in a discussion of how trends of globalization are re-created in the online sphere.

## Time as Fluid in *EVE Online*

Regardless of their feelings about labor in a virtual world, the size and complexity of organizations in *EVE Online*, such as TEST Alliance, show a dedication and willingness to work on the part of the players of the game. Rather than endlessly pursuing small-scale battles for instant gratification, sufficient numbers of players are willing to utilize their time and effort to create the framework and logistical foundations for large alliances, large fleets, and large battles. The difficulty inherent in maintaining order in *EVE Online* should not be underestimated; trust is not something players can rely on, and the spirit of the game is focused entirely on capitalistic greed. At its very core, this particular problem faced by leaders can be collected under a single category: encouraging contact. Maintaining consistent social connections between leaders and members of an alliance leads to far higher levels of group-focused effort (Butler et al. 2002) and also increases the loyalty the leader gains from the group (Kelly et al. 2008). For an organization that operates on a twenty-four-hour game clock, this means having systems to communicate between players when they are not online.

It should come as no surprise, then, that both Goonswarm and TEST Alliance, two of the largest alliances in the game for a vast majority of the game's recent history, were based off of forum websites. Players who are used to discussing topics in threads that span multiple days are much more willing to engage in asynchronous communication. What this means is that they are willing to listen to speeches after they have been given or to follow battle orders drafted a week in advance. Owing to the difficulty in maintaining constant communication between multiple different time zones, the comfort players have with using asynchronous systems manages to create a social space where large alliances may arise. In a similar vein, many players make themselves (or, after receiving particularly expensive ships, find themselves forced to be) accountable to their alliance outside of normal operating hours. Many pilots of the largest ships in *EVE Online* will get text messages and warnings from their alliance if their assistance is needed in a battle. Much like a doctor can remain on call even when she is not actively in the hospital, so does an *EVE Online* pilot remain on call in response to major in-game events.

Groups that are most successful in *EVE Online* tend to use time very effectively, particularly as a weapon. Earlier, reference was made to fights for sov (or sovereignty) in null-sec space. This type of control of territory requires the placement of special towers and the ability to prevent them from being destroyed. In the early days of BoB and Goonswarm fighting for space, one side would place towers in European time, and the other would destroy them in American time, setting up their own towers. The territory would then exchange space every day for weeks, leading to a stalemate and an eventual change by CCP to the entire dynamic of how sov worked in-game. In a similar application of time, the decision by Goonswarm to invade TEST Alliance at the very start of the summer months was also purposeful. With attendance for their alliance being strong, but with many TEST Alliance players taking time away from the game during the summer months, the leaders of Goonswarm felt comfortable that they would have an advantage entering war at this time. A leader acknowledged this when he stated that "just because the sun is out and about doesn't mean we shouldn't be playing with other nerds online fighting [enemies] off. Log in for fleets; try to at least participate and become a true internet nerd for 1 day." The focus given to players who are willing to join in combat during the summer months shows how important this tactic was in establishing victory conditions. The practicality exemplified by groups of players using time in as efficient a manner as possible shows that players of *EVE Online* are comfortable conceptualizing time as a specific tool rather than as an overarching framework for standard world action.

By the time this research was done, leaders in large organizations were knowledgeable about what kinds of systems worked and used them in that way very consistently. Widely distributed official speeches, for instance, are common among the leadership of all large null-sec alliances. The leader giving the speech knows that because of a relative interest in participating in *EVE* history, members will be much more likely to appear to a military action if it directly follows a speech that is given at a prepared time. As such, leaders create a military plan in secret and then reveal it and activate it during the speech itself, so that participants who are listening are able to engage immediately with the plan. On the part of both the leadership and the members, there is a dedication to these aspects of time. For instance, if a forum post states that a meeting will take place at 8:00 server (UTC), players will congregate early, and the leader is expected to have his communications programs running before the start time. If a server error affects a speech start time, the leader feels the obligation to explain his tardiness and apologize to the listeners for the breach.

What this use of time in discussions of conflicts indicates is that time is in many ways used as a resource. The success of RedSwarm, for instance, came from its ability to project force at many different moments in time. Similarly, the camping strategy of war can only be effective if there is enough time (in terms of labor hours) to devote to the task. A leader who is interested in the maintenance of his organization will be sure to incorporate the use of these resources of labor and time along with the typical considerations of logistics and politics. This is why directorships in charge of propaganda and HR are usually centrally important positions in an alliance (The Mittani's role as central propagandist for the Goonswarm being a prime example).

The use of forums as a means to create these organized activities is important as well. Owing to membership in an alliance living in many different time zones, there is a very small chance that players will be able to meet up at a certain time without prior planning. As such, even smaller groups, such as the Tournament Alliance team of TEST Alliance, need to have their own special forums to create agreed-on times to practice. By using asynchronous communication, these organizations show that there is a dedication to the group greater than a reliance on "comfortable" timetables, such as those that are expected of a nine-to-five job. In fact, in many ways, players in null-sec space of *EVE Online* are more willing than most people to see time as a fluid construct, one that can be used as a tool or a weapon. Rather than relying on preordained concepts of when events should occur, the *EVE* player is far more willing to challenge a classical concept of time and instead see it as a means toward an end.

This is not to imply that members of groups won't have standard events that occur regularly. Players tend to view *EVE Online* as a unique MMOG, but certain actions are incorporated from the standard world. These types of organizational scheduling techniques have been consistent in these games. In fact, even in the early days of *Ultima Online*, standard times for guild events were established to encourage higher rates of participation (Taxén 2002). In many ways, the processes accepted by the player base are based on a practical understanding of what needs to be done. For players that need to arrange times for Alliance Tournament training, the ability to maximize attendance is a priority (more on eSports in *EVE Online* can be found in Carter and Gibbs 2013). The leadership of the group, however, was split into separate time zones. In an effort to maximize the effectiveness of the group, the training was organized to begin in the early weekend morning in Pacific Standard Time (PST), which correlates to a late afternoon start in England (GMT). This was actually a change from previous years; prior training was earlier in European time, but that prevented certain leaders from being able to participate, so the time was changed to create greater participation and representation of the multi-time-zone alliance. This pragmatic scheduling is indicative of two recurrent points in this chapter: first, that the playing of *EVE Online* and the pursuit of specific in-game goals (success in the tournament) are so important that they are arranged and scheduled similar to the way a person would arrange her life around a job; second, how time zones that contain leaders of organized groups are given precedence in terms of scheduling, which in many ways seems to replicate the way in which globalization has occurred in the standard world.

## A Western Time

As stated previously, the official server time for *EVE Online* is UTC, a time zone established because of the game being produced in Iceland. Despite this, as seen in the last section, there is a consistent tendency on the part of alliances and leaders to focus on certain time zones, specifically American ones (UTC − 7 to − 4), while disregarding most others. One primary reason for this is simply a matter of resource management. If the majority of an organization's labor power works a typical job in the United States, then events are most likely scheduled after hours for that time zone, which for Eastern European and Asian players would coincide with a time of 4:00 A.M. or even later the following day.

As mentioned earlier, massive battles, prearranged speeches, and other propaganda pieces are important for large alliances in drumming up support (in the form of participation) or encouraging greater recruitment. To get the necessary numbers, a leader will need to set these events at points in time that coincide with player play time. Most TEST Alliance speeches, for instance, were arranged to be early in the evening for American players, which is late in the evening for most of Europe. Although this meant that the players in the alliance were more able to participate, it also affected applications by players who saw or participated in these events, and those who tended to get involved in these events were in the same time zone. As time goes on, then, focus and priority will be given to Western players and, by extension, Western conceptions of time and culture.

As with all social occurrences, however, there is more to a decision besides merely economic rationality. The avoidance of Eastern European or Asian time zones, for instance, is sometimes explained through a fear of the Russians or a desire to avoid Asian "botters" or "farmers." This perception of players from certain time zones shows that these stereotypes, which are consistent in many MMOGs, can create an unfair dynamic based on Western perceptions of players (Nakamura 2009). This particular tendency of individuals to ascribe meanings to others based on these sorts of factors is not atypical, but the way in which they are formalized through the use of time structures in organizations shows how similar this process in *EVE Online* is to the process of globalization in the standard world.

Ostensibly, the globalized world is one where equal opportunity creates a worldwide market, a perfect form of free-market capitalism. In reality, however, the interests of people from certain regions, primarily those from the Western world, are favored (Korzeniewicz 2004). The universe of *EVE Online* exhibits this particular feature of the standard world very well. Although the game is created to have the perfect laissez-faire economy, completely free of regulation, people who are even suspected of botting (using automated processes to generate income) get banned with little need for extensive proof (TheMittani 2013), and the vitriol expressed toward them in game forums shows that what kind of economic action is considered "fair" comes from Western understandings of the concept.

As with many situations where a dominant culture safely dominates a majority of social interactions, there are many occasions in which individuals will incorporate aspects of other cultures into their interactions. These incorporations, however, are often based on stereotypical understandings of these cultures.

As such, *EVE Online* offers many circumstances when non-Western culture is incorporated into propaganda made by alliances for a Western audience. One common approach is to incorporate communist-era Soviet imagery into pictures posted online. As another example, Figure 5.3 shows how Goonswarm incorporated a style adopted from Middle Eastern books to release a pamphlet titled *The Great War* to explain its

Figure 5.3. Goonswarm incorporating Indian and Middle Eastern art styles in a document explaining some history and reasoning for a major war.

reasons for attacking a certain enemy. It contains a history, an artistic style reminiscent of Indian and Middle Eastern books, and the bees representing Goonswarm players on the bottom. This incorporation of certain imageries is only made more pertinent (and potentially offensive to some) as the campaign was named a "jihad" by the leader in charge of the operation.

What this discussion of globalization shows is that the social structure created in the universe of *EVE Online* is based in Western conceptualizations and in many ways helps reinforce these ideals. In terms of how this affects the use of time, it can be seen that many of the ways that time has been described in this chapter reinforces the way it is used in capitalist, market-driven societies. Although this may be explained by the relative effectiveness of such processes in a free-market game, it also shows that these norms are deeply ingrained in the minds of the players of *EVE Online* and that no amount of futurism or virtual freedom can change that.

## Conclusion: The Resource of Time

By looking at typical uses of time in-game, this chapter has shown how time is seen by the players and alliances of *EVE Online,* particularly in null-sec space. Even as they are heavily limited by the code of the game (de Zwart and Humphreys 2014), the players use the single-server universe of *EVE Online* to form a dynamic that creates large logistical difficulties for an alliance, forcing the alliance to undertake complex time-management strategies reminiscent of neoliberal (focused on capitalist efficiency) customer service jobs, much like a call center. These contexts, taken from the nonvirtual world, show that players are willing to innovate and reanalyze things that commonly aren't seen as tools (such as time) and use them in a manner that benefits them. This can be seen in cases where these alliances wield time as a weapon with which they can strengthen assaults or weaken the resolve of their opponents.

These players are not, however, immune from nonvirtual influences in their everyday lives. The many ways in which globalization has shaped our mental structures seem to be replicated in *EVE Online* as they are in everyday contexts. Inequalities can easily be seen in the way time is used, for instance, and, as seen in the relatively offensive culture and language, in sexual and gender inequalities as well. Focus is placed on players and regions that occupy American and European time zones, with a far greater emphasis being placed on players who are based in the Americas. Similar biases can be seen in the acceptance of sexist and racist attitudes and language during fleet maneuvers and on Jabber.

This attitude of acceptance is a significant problem. This is a phenomenon that has been documented throughout the gaming world for both women (Bergstrom 2012; Kerr 2003) and people of different nationalities (Nakamura 2009). Understanding the reasons behind the formation of these linguistic patterns—solidarity, external threats, generation of propaganda—offers an opportunity to attempt to encourage a better community. In new games as well as in *EVE Online,* it is possible to use in-game processes to encourage greater levels of inclusivity.

Most important, players and leaders who engage in the universe of *EVE* have established their own conceptualizations of their world, particularly of time. The example of American TEST Alliance pilots volunteering to work in special squads to cooperate with individuals in Australian time zones shows that these players are more than happy to reconceptualize time in their own individual interests. This gives us hope that, even in the standard world, the tendency will be for people to be more willing to change, whether by adopting operating times that fit their own preferences and social networks, rather than relying on the consistent nine-to-five existence that has been propagated throughout most of recent history, or by adopting a new understanding of the limits of acceptable action.

## NOTES

1　The Battle of Asakai occurred on January 27, 2013, in the system of Asakai. It was a territorial battle between the HoneyBadger Coalition (headed by TEST and Pandemic Legion) and the ClusterFuck Coalition (headed by Goonswarm). The battle occurred when a pilot in the ClusterFuck coalition accidentally moved a valuable asset into the middle of Pandemic Legion's forces. As additional reinforcements arrived on both sides, eventually more than three thousand players were involved, with more than US$20,000 worth of resources lost. Of this, the vast majority was lost by Goonswarm, who retreated after approximately six hours of combat.

2　http://mmodata.net/.

3　https://wiki.pleaseignore.com/wiki/Dreddit_Corporation_History.

4　The First Great War began in March 2007 after RedSwarm (a combination of Goonswarm and RED Alliance) attacked an ally of BoB. This conflict triggered many treaties and eventually led to more than thirty thousand players being involved in the war. By the time the RedSwarm withdrew in April 2008, a large number of alliances had broken apart, leaving BoB in control of its home territory in Delve. It was only after a treasonous director in BoB disbanded the alliance in February 2009 (triggering the Second Great War) that BoB lost its control of the area.

## BIBLIOGRAPHY

Attrill, Alison, and Rahul Jalil. 2011. "Revealing Only the Superficial Me: Exploring Categorical Self-Disclosure Online." *Computers in Human Behavior* 27, no. 5: 1634–42.

BBC. 2013. "Eve Players Stage Giant Online Space Battle." http://www.bbc.com/news/technology-23489293.

Bergstrom, Kelly. 2012. "Virtual Inequality: A Woman's Place in Cyberspace." Paper presented at FDG 2012, Raleigh, N.C., May 29–June 1.

———. 2013. "Constructing the Ideal EVE Online Player." Paper presented at DeFragging Games Studies, Atlanta, Ga., August.

Boellstorff, Tom, Bonnie Nardi, Celia Pearce, and T. L. Taylor. 2012. *Ethnography and Virtual Worlds: A Handbook on Methods.* Princeton, N.J.: Princeton University Press.

Butler, Brian, Lee Sproull, Sara Kiesler, and Robert Kraut. 2002. "Community Effort in Online Groups: Who Does the Work and Why?" http://repository.cmu.edu/hcii/90.

Carter, Marcus, and Martin Gibbs. 2013. "eSports in EVE Online: Skullduggery, Fair Play and Acceptability in an Unbounded Competition." Paper presented at FDG 2013, Crete, May.

Cerulo, Karen. 1997. "Identity Construction: New Issues, New Directions." *Annual Review of Sociology* 23: 385–409.

Charmaz, Kathy. 2006. *Constructing Grounded Theory: A Practical Guide through Qualitative Analysis.* London: Sage.

de Zwart, Melissa, and Sal Humphreys. 2014. "The Lawless Frontier of Deep Space: Code as Law in EVE Online." *Cultural Studies Review* 20: 77–99.

Foster, Mike. 2013. "Unfortunate Capsuleer Learns Not to Move EVE Online PLEX in Starter Ships." *Massively by Joystick* (blog), November 8. http://massively.joystiq.com/2013/11/08/unfortunate-capsuleer-learns-not-to-move-eve-online-plex-in-shut/.

Garfinkel, Harold. 1967. *Studies in Ethnomethodology.* Englewood Cliffs, N.J.: Prentice Hall.

Geere, Duncan. 2010. "EVE Online Fraud Nets 'Bad Bobby' £42,000." *Wired Magazine,* September 14. http://www.wired.co.uk/news/archive/2010–09/14/eve-online-heist.

Goffman, Erving. 1959. *The Presentation of Self in Everyday Life.* New York: Anchor Books.

Jester. 2014. "Something Real." *Jester's Trek* (blog), March 7. http://jestertrek.blogspot.com.au/2014/03/something-real.html.

Kelly, Erika, Blake Davis, Jessica Nelson, and Jorge Mendoza. 2008. "Leader Emergence in an Internet Environment." *Computers in Human Behavior* 24: 2372–83.

Kerr, Aphra. 2003. "Girls/Women Just Want to Have Fun: A Study of Adult Female Players of Digital Games." In *Level Up: Proceedings from the First International Conference of the International Digital Games Research Association,* 270–85. Utrecht, Netherlands: University of Utrecht.

Khaw, Cassandra. 2013. "Meet Tranquility, the Military-Grade 2,500GHZ Monster That Powers *EVE Online.*" *PC Gamer,* June 15. http://www.pcgamer.com/au/2013/06/15/eve-online/.

Korzeniewicz, Miguel. 2004. "Commodity Chains and Marketing Strategies: Nike and the Global Athletic Footwear Industry." In *The Globalization Reader,* edited by Frank Lechner, 175–85. West Sussex, U.K.: Wiley-Blackwell.

Kucklich, Julian. 2009. "Virtual Worlds and Their Discontents: Precarious Sovereignty, Govern Mentality, and the Ideology of Play." *Games and Culture* 4, no. 4: 340–52.

Lofland, John, David A. Snow, Leon Anderson, and Lyn H. Lofland. 2006. *Analyzing Social Settings: A Guide to Qualitative Observation and Analysis.* 4th ed. Belmont, Calif.: Wadsworth/Thomson Learning.

Milik, Oskar. 2012. "Studying Identity and Control in Online Worlds: Ethnomethodology and Categorization Analysis and Its Applicability to Virtual Space." MA thesis, Boston University.

Nakamura, Lisa. 2009. "Don't Hate the Player, Hate the Game: The Racialization of Labor in World of Warcraft." *Critical Studies in Media Communication* 26, no. 2: 128–44.

Purchese, Robert. 2013. "EVE Online: When 3000 Players Collide." January 28. http://www.eurogamer.net/articles/2013-01-28-eve-online-when-3000-players-collide .

Taxén, Gustav. 2002. "Guilds: Communities in Ultima Online." Retrieved from http://www.nada.kth.se/~gustavt.

Taylor, T. L. 2008. "Does World of Warcraft Change Everything? How a PvP Server, Multinational Playerbase, and Surveillance Mod Scene Caused Me Pause." In *Digital Culture, Play, and Identity: A World of Warcraft Reader,* edited by Hilde G. Corneliussen and Jill Walker Rettberg, 187–201. Cambridge, Mass.: MIT Press.

Terranova, Tiziana. 2013. "Free Labor." In *Digital Labor: The Internet as Playground and Factory,* edited by Trebor Scholz, 33–57. New York: Routledge.

TheMittani. 2013. "The EVE–Uni Botting Controversy." February 12. http://themittani.com/news/eve-uni-botting-controversy.

Woodford, Darryl. 2012. "Hanging Out Is Hard to Do: Methodology in Non-avatar Environments." *Journal of Gaming and Virtual Worlds* 4, no. 3: 275–88. doi:10.1386/jgvw.4.3.275_1.

# The Russians Are Coming!

## Stereotypes and Perceptions of "Russianness" in *EVE Online*

*Catherine Goodfellow*

Funny, I thought the whole point of EVE was to get absurdly rich and powerful to the point where no one could stop you from taking over the whole galaxy. Oh wait, no that's not it. It's a "sandbox." And the Russians just backed a dumptruck up to it.
—Hermosa Diosas

In the context of *EVE Online,* Russian players are considered particularly aggressive and disruptive to game order. *EVE* has a fairly small Russian population: the last official data, from 2008, showed 6.4 percent of *EVE* players to be Russian (Kogh Ayon 2010). Despite this, their in-game reputation leads to much discussion and many complaints on both the official forums and more generally in the community. In this chapter, I categorize and analyze some typical themes in English- and Russian-language blogs, forums, and metagame reportage; points raised by PhD survey respondents; and observations from my own time as a bilingual *EVE* player. I also undertake a visual analysis of propaganda images from English- and Russian-language corporations to demonstrate and unpack the prevalent characterizations of Russian players in the game. How are Russian players characterized in the wider *EVE Online* community? What are the roots of these characterizations and stereotypes? How does the unique political history of *EVE Online* shape behavior toward Russian players? What can this case study contribute to literature on conflict in online gaming and intercultural play?

This case study highlights the effect of a single-shard (or server, sometimes known as a realm or shard) game environment on the development of the game's culture. I argue that *EVE*'s single-shard game space brings players from different cultures into direct contact, and direct competition, with one another to a far greater extent than most other massively multiplayer online games (MMOGs) do. The kinds of fears outlined here are exacerbated in *EVE* because, rather than separating players from different regions onto their own servers, CCP Games chooses to maintain one server for all players. Any player can therefore potentially interact with any other player;

the immediacy of the "Red Threat" in *EVE* is heightened by the cyberproximity of the players to one another.

Scholarly literature tends to view conflict in games as the result of Western players pushing back against nonnormative, or non-Western, modes of play. Sometimes, as in the case of Jacobs's (2008) work, this can imply Eastern "deviance" versus "normal" Western play. International or interethnic conflict in these examples is often perceived as being one way, and we rarely hear the voices of those who are targeted by the majority of players. This framing can obscure tactics and behaviors used by players to push back against Western hostility and limit discussion about the agency these players can wield. Furthermore, the focus on economic activities (such as gold farming) draws attention away from details about modes of play, common understandings of what is "fair" or "acceptable," and other subtle social behaviors. In *EVE,* in-game activities considered to be acceptable, such as aggressive, nonconsensual player versus player (PVP) combat and scamming, are deemed game ruining when perpetrated by Russian players. Conversely, ethnic and national slurs that are explicitly prohibited by the terms of service are common when discussing the place of Russian players in New Eden.

I begin by outlining some related work on national tensions and conflicts in video games. Next, I explore the facets of real-world and in-game history that have shaped *EVE* players' views about their Russian counterparts. I argue that lingering Cold War–era stereotypes have an effect on player attitudes toward Russians in the game, leading to a kind of virtual "Red Scare." I then present some of the dominant narratives about Russian players within the game, drawing on player commentary and discourse from various forums and *EVE* news sites Finally, I discuss the controversy surrounding Russian players from other angles, showing how Russians sometimes seek to enhance their reputation in-game by associating themselves with these stereotypes and discussing the use of Russian cultural material in the recruitment propaganda of primarily non-Russian corporations. It will become clear that in the *EVE* community, notoriety is not always universally negative; with traits such as aggressive play often valorized by players, the common stereotypes named here can work in favor of Russian pilots.

## Literature on Conflict in Online Games

Fictional conflict is a powerful narrative device throughout the MMO genre, which often pits two or more opposing factions against one another, but in *EVE,* conflict becomes a defining game mechanic. Ever-shifting player alliances, betrayals, ambushes, mass battles, and dogfights are widely considered to be more entertaining and more challenging than the fictitious backdrop of the game. As the *EVE* wiki EVElodepia (n.d.) says, "there is no such thing as 'a fair fight' or 'an unfair fight.' . . . Circumstances are irrelevant." Unlike, say, *World of Warcraft, EVE* does not guide a player through quests and story arcs; instead, after a brief tutorial, mission running is relegated to a sideline, while players are left to design their own amusement in a sandbox universe.

However, the *EVE* universe of New Eden is not entirely unmoderated, although it allows for a wider spectrum of play, especially hostile play, than other MMOGs.

*EVE Online*'s terms of service, or end user license agreement (EULA), lay out a number of violations for which players can be suspended or banned from the game. As with the majority of games that include an element of user interaction, the rules do not allow players to "abuse, harass or threaten another player or authorized representative of CCP" or use "abusive, defamatory, ethnically or racially offensive, harassing, harmful, hateful, obscene, offensive, sexually explicit, threatening or vulgar language" (CCP 2013). Related to the rule on offensive and hate speech, players "may not organize nor be a member of any corporation or group within *EVE Online* that is based on or advocates any anti-ethnic, anti-gay, anti-religious, racist, sexist or other hate-mongering philosophies" (CCP 2013). The terms of service specify that role-playing cannot be used as a way around these rules; CCP acknowledges here the line between "real" and "virtual" identities in play and clearly prohibits players from crossing it where abusive speech is concerned. Although limits of speech are defined, there seems to be little consensus on exactly what defines "improper" play in *EVE*. With the exception of a narrow range of behaviors, such as can baiting and harassment based on real-life attributes, players' behavior in-game is rarely restricted. The tasks of this section are, first, to outline broader literature on conflict in online games and, second, to discuss how players and scholars draw lines between acceptable and unacceptable conflict within games.

Most work on national or ethnic conflict in games discusses hostility toward gold farmers in MMOGs like *World of Warcraft* and *Lineage*. Gold farmers are players who spend their time repetitively collecting in-game currency, which they then sell to other players (often Western players) for real-world currency. Typically, these players are presumed to be Chinese. A number of scholars have identified that stereotypes about gold farmers often echo stereotypes about Chinese people. Lisa Nakamura argues that certain styles of play have been racialized as "Chinese" in nature, and fan-produced content that discusses gold farming constitutes an "overtly racist narrative space" (Nakamura 2009, 136). Nick Yee, Bonnie Nardi, and others have concluded that such antipathy stems from a kind of economic Sinophobia. Nardi (2010, 176) writes that "the [gold farmer] meme belies an inchoate sense of disturbance; far away, Chinese people have found a way to intrude into the North American economy by slipping into a virtual world." Similarly, Nick Dyer-Witheford and Greg de Peuter (2009, 146) cite and expand on Nick Yee's conclusion that the "virulent distaste" for gold farmers echoes "a historically familiar pattern of Sinophobia and, more broadly, of Western racism against mobile, precarious foreign labor." As many games maintain separate servers or shards for players in different geographical regions, we might also surmise that gold farmers are met with hostility because they violate these norms of virtual territory.

Melinda Jacobs (2008, 324) describes a game environment in *Omerta* in which "players of Turkish nationality are being refused admission into families [player groups] due to the perception that their primary loyalties are to other members of their own real-life nationality, rather than members of their current family." She attributes the perceptions surrounding Turkish players in the wider community to "the nature of traditional Turkish culture in general, and perhaps the mismatch of the Eastern culture with the majority of Western cultures that participate in the international game" (324). As in *EVE*, players react to "the perceived aggressive nature of the Turkish community while playing the game" (324). Jacobs argues that dislike for Turkish players is rooted in distaste for "honor-based" game play.

Nick Lalone (2013) reports similar dynamics in *Age of Wushu* on the English-language Blue Dragon server. A large concentration of Vietnamese players, often allied together, are accused of perpetrating "all manner of hacks, cheats, and dirty deeds," including block voting to acquire political power and unfairly distributing game items to one another. Lalone points out that the behaviors attributed to Vietnamese players on Blue Dragon are hardly unique to players of one ethnicity or nationality but that they have "become the bad guys" because they are "winning" in a different language (Lalone 2013).

## Complex Allegiances within New Eden: Real and Virtual Histories

Allegations of particularly aggressive play, and broader themes of resentment about Russian players, are more complex to understand and unravel. *EVE Online* is a game that prizes cutthroat PVP skill, but as in other MMOGs, the community has very definite ideas about what constitutes appropriate play. In this section, I argue that stereotypes about the aggression displayed by Russian players are built on a combination of game history and real-world history. I begin by outlining some elements of game mechanics and history that exacerbate national tensions, before showing how the ways Russians are depicted in metagame reporting and by community figureheads echo Cold War–era Red Scare rhetoric.

*EVE Online* is unusual among MMOGs because it affords its players a remarkably high level of agency in shaping the politics and economy of the gameworld. The game's politics, economy, alliances, and character activity are almost entirely driven by the players. Many blogs and websites are devoted to reporting the events inside *EVE*, the differing alliances, conflicts, economic events, and dramas that players write as they move through the star systems and pursue their game goals. Generally the game developers prefer to moderate with a light touch and allow the players to enact their own political and economic dramas inside the gameworld. Indeed, during a recent player-organized event to lock down a regional trading hub, the developers reinforced their servers to account for the extra game load and gleefully encouraged their clientele to lay waste to one another. A staff member blogged after the event that it "sure feels good to be the hosts of such massive amounts of spaceship carnage" (CCP Explorer 2012). The game therefore has a demonstrably low level of

moderation compared with other MMOGs and a development team who actively encourage emergent play.

Owing to this minimally moderated atmosphere in *EVE,* players cannot rely
on outside help when they are gaming, except where the terms of service are clearly
violated. With the majority of items in *EVE* being player crafted, and with much of
the game based in treacherous "low-security" star systems, players must group up in
corporations to fight for sovereignty and resources. These groups and larger alliances
fuel metagame discussion and dramatization of game events on the official and unofficial forums, on blogs and fan sites, and in between players on a more personal
level. Naturally, language barriers and national loyalties have led to the proliferation
of corporations and alliances whose pilots hail from the same region. Trustworthiness,
loyalty, and communication are vital for fostering a sense of small-group identity, and
linguistic and cultural differences can be a hindrance. Among the ultrasuspicious
denizens of New Eden, unknown quantities are frequently perceived as hostile; the
ways in which players perceive Russians in-game show that cultural differences fuel
the already prevalent in-game paranoia and political machinations that have come
to characterize *EVE Online.*

Red Alliance (a large, predominantly Russian collection of corporations) has
been associated with the Goonswarm alliance, a large group based in the Something
Awful forums, because the latter alliance entered *EVE* in late 2005 (Smith 2011). This is
a stretch of time that covers most of the history of the game and renders the histories
of the two corporations almost legendary among players. The association of Red Alliance and Goonswarm is noteworthy for the bitterness it engendered and for its brutal
effectiveness. Goons are often depicted as an organized group of griefers, a label that
many identify with and exploit and that others reframe as a commitment to delivering
excitement into the lives of the *EVE* population. They are a remarkably successful in-
game group, benefiting from a well-established organizational structure, compelling
recruitment drives, and a great deal of advice and support for players new to the game.
However, the entry of Goons into New Eden was surrounded by dissent and complaints from "old guard" players. The group pioneered a number of new PVP tactics,
in particular "blobbing," a strategy whereby large numbers of small, cheap ships that
require little training to pilot are used to bring down much bigger and more valuable
vessels. Players armed with these new tactics partnered with the tenacious and more
experienced Red Alliance pilots to great effect.

Goonswarm spymaster The Mittani (a powerful and divisive figure in the *EVE*
community) discussed the hostility toward both Red Alliance and Goonswarm in a
*Rock Paper Shotgun* interview, pointing out that both groups were "similarly vilified"
and that an alliance therefore made sense (Smith 2011). Backed into a corner by the
populous and powerful Southern Coalition, the Russian players were also subject to
abuse from their in-game enemies. Comments ran along themes of "selling ISK to
feed their children," employing "dishonorable" tactics such as logging off rather than

fighting, and "not granting the enemy fights when the enemy wanted fights" (Smith 2011). *Shacknews* similarly reports that the in-game hostility led to "a steady verbal attack by their enemies" (Breckon 2007). In this source, The Mittani elaborates on the kinds of stereotypes aimed at Russian players, noting that their enemies "would basically fling every racist stereotype about Russians onto the forums that you could imagine," such as "jokes about buying Russian brides, calling them Russian dogs" (Breckon 2007). Partly as a result of this campaign, Russian players have been marked out within the *EVE* community. Despite the fact that the old alliances have shifted myriad times since 2005, many of the slurs leveled at Red Alliance continue to be commonly used on the official forums and in everyday game interactions to represent the wider Russian community. Game history greatly contributes to the negative portrayal of many Russian *EVE* players, and the fact that hostility occurs in the game does not make it more easily forgiven or forgotten. "RA [Red Alliance] gets very offended about attacks on their ethnicity," explains The Mittani in an interview. "Even today, RA leaders will be able to tell you which LV [Lotka Volterra] individual pilots smack-talked them in local and made racist jokes. They'll drop anything to go kill them or hurt them in-game" (Breckon 2007). The author's interview with a prominent Red Alliance member sees the player tell him (apparently without being prompted), "Russian dogs. Feed our children. I still have those screenshots" (Breckon 2007).

However, it is the form that the hostility takes that is fascinating to a student of Russian history. The criticisms directed at Russian players run parallel to American political rhetoric during the Red Scare periods of 1920–21 and 1947–57. During this time, strong anti-Communist and wider anti-Russian sentiment were common, and many of the stereotypes about Russia and the Russians that were popularized during the Red Scare are still in evidence today. Cooperation between the two groups was described in a *Shacknews* article using terminology that clearly draws on Cold War rhetoric to color the in-game drama. "For the first time," writes the author, "the traditionally straightforward Russians were using the olive branch, actively seeking a major ally through diplomatic means—and Westerners at that. Of course, it's not surprising that the American leadership of GoonSwarm rejected the initial offer. Separated by both practical and cultural divisions, the two organizations had never before spoken—and in a throwback to the Cold War, it would take some convincing before the Americans could trust an alliance known for being even more ruthless than they" (Breckon 2007). The Mittani characterizes his alliance with the Russian corporations in similarly rhetorical style: "The Reds have lost all their territory and still come back with disciplined, vicious, and effective assaults against innumerable foes, and they've been in nonstop combat for almost three full years now. It's just insane" (Smith 2011). Note that he collectively names Red Alliance not as "Red" or with the common abbreviation "RA" but as "the Reds," a common descriptor for the Soviet bloc.

In *EVE*, then, Russians are viewed as secretive, economically powerful, and militarily aggressive; during the Red Scare, the "Soviets" were characterized as masters of espionage, ready to influence American society through bribes and propaganda and possessing a fearsome nuclear and military armory. In this case, game and world history map onto one another almost perfectly; hostility toward Russian players is amplified because the ways in which they seem to behave in-game are irresistibly similar to stereotypes about how Russians behave in the real world. Unlike Jacobs's vague delineation of "Eastern" and "Western" modes of play, the tensions between Russian players and others shows identifiable stereotypes of "Russian," or more accurately "Soviet," behavior, which make Russian pilots ideal community scapegoats.

## Tropes of "Russianness" in *EVE Online*

There is a remarkably cohesive set of perceptions of Russian players in *EVE*, which displays consistency across the official forums, in-game chat, and (putatively) objective coverage of game events by observers. Russians are considered to employ particularly aggressive PVP tactics; to be especially cliquish and secretive, refusing to speak English in local game chat channels; and to be deeply involved in (and, to some players, almost exclusively responsible for) real-money trading and botting activities. Complaints about the inability or unwillingness of Russian players to speak English are frequent, with some players suggesting that English should be the lingua franca in public chat channels. Discussions about the integration of the Russian community in *EVE* invariably lead to players suggesting that Russians be confined to their own server.

Editorials about the game's open hostility are rare, but the same stereotypes are constantly reiterated and reinforced. The intricate political interactions in *EVE* lend themselves to long-form analysis as well as more immediate news bulletin–type reportage. *Shacknews* and *Rock Paper Shotgun* in particular have published extensive articles about the game as well as interviews with key community figures. In one such piece, *Shacknews* author Nick Breckon portrays the Russian-speaking Red Alliance as the "bear" to Goonswarm's "rat" (Breckon 2007). In a lengthy analysis of the relationship between the two groups, he draws a broad (and rather inappropriate) comparison between the Siege of Leningrad and the long in-game war between Red Alliance and its opponents. For Breckon (2007), the three-year game conflict between Red Alliance and its enemies, and its eventual, cautious negotiations with Goonswarm, are an irresistible echo of Cold War–era history. "Resurgence in the face of destruction is par for the course when it comes to Russian history," he writes, "whether the nation's indefatigable people are under attack by Hitler, Napoleon, or a fleet of enemy spaceships."

## Aggression

Forum posters suggest that the Russians are not playing according to the social rules of the game, having different—and sometimes incomprehensible—game priorities, and are trying to "take over." The game population at large complains about "our new overlords" (Phugoid 2011) both in terms of broad, detrimental effects on game play and in terms of personal quibbles about how Russians seem to act toward non-Russian players. Russians, it is suggested, "don't integrate with the community" and "go beyond PvP pirating and . . . are just total ganking griefers," and that they display an in-game attitude that is "aggressive, pack like, abusive, nihilistic, hate filled" (Alexander Bor 2010). The characterization of Russians as "ganking griefers" seems a contradiction when the rules of the game specifically state that nonconsensual PVP is an acceptable facet of game play. "Ganking" in other MMOGs generally refers to a group of players ambushing another or to a high-level character attacking a much lower level character. In *EVE*, there are no level distinctions. Many multiplayer games reward players with experience points for completing tasks and killing enemies; at a certain point total, the player will gain a level, becoming more powerful and gaining access to better items and weapons. As the community wiki EVElopedia (n.d.) warns, there is no such thing as "a fair fight" in *EVE* because newer, less experienced players are in no way protected from veterans, as they are in other games. When players complain of Russians "taking over" the game, they may be referring to this sense of unfairness in individual fights or to the endless sovereignty battles for valuable areas of null-sec space (areas of space with no security; imagine a kind of lawless frontier space).

## Botting and Real-Money Trading

"Taking over" the game can also refer to a sense of economic incursion that echoes complaints about gold farming in other games. In *EVE*, it is sometimes suggested that market trading is a form of PVP. Indeed, alliances and corporations can use economic sanctions against one other, the market for certain materials or items can be crashed, hoarding materials or ordnance can limit availability outside of one's own alliance, or a player able to produce an item even fractionally cheaper than another seller can rake in large sums of money at the expense of other traders. More insidiously, Russian players are accused of exploiting the game mechanics in forbidden ways to gain a strategic edge or, as is sometimes suggested, earn real-world currency. The suggested reasons for this real-money trading vary, but commonly players posit that Russian players live in poverty and therefore use *EVE* as a source of income. The impetus is therefore not generally perceived to be greed but rather a strategy by which (poor, non-Western) Russians earn a living wage. There are no publicly available data about the instances of botting and real-money trading by Russians as compared to other national groups in *EVE*; however, the stereotype is pervasive and may stem in part from the high incidence of financial fraud and malware on the Russian-language Internet. Russian players are persistently described as ruining the game with "their RMT/botting empire" and "their EULA breaking habits" (Phugoid 2011).

## Language/Secrecy

*EVE* is available in three language localizations in addition to the original English: German, Russian, and Japanese. Although all players are interacting on the same server, player-facing game text such as menu items, player biography text, nonplayer character (NPC) dialogue, and voice acting are translated. A Russian player may therefore log in, scroll through a menu in Russian, type a profile message about himself in Cyrillic, chat with his friends in his native language, and hear his ship AI speaking in Russian. However, when in public chat and flying through space, he may see other players typing and leaving messages in other languages and respond in the same languages if he chooses. Note that CCP does not require players to communicate in English in all public channels; the only language restrictions in place are on the official forum, where the lingua franca is English, and the help channel in-game. There are separate subforums for Russian-, German-, and Japanese-language discussions.

An overview of several forum threads on this topic shows that, generally, at least one poster will note the irony of English speakers insisting on English-language interactions in an Icelandic game. However, it is significant that aside from rare comments about "kamikaze" tactics from Japanese players, the presence of German or Japanese speakers in chat is barely noted by the player base. Instead, players complain that "no one else spams their native language as much as Russians do" (Alexander Bor 2010) and that they "can't stand monkeys speaking Klingon in local" (Hermosa Diosas 2011). The language barrier, coupled with the existence of a handful of popular and well-known Russian-language corporations, has also led to accusations of insularity on the part of the Russians.

## Playing with Stereotypes

In the earlier literature review, the tendency to view in-game ethnic and national conflicts as a Western reaction to incursion was criticized for its one-dimensionality. Here an examination of some of the other visible dynamics between Russian and non-Russian players in *EVE* will show the complexity of international relations in this game space and move away from one-way models where traits of the vilified group are universally portrayed as negative. Particularly in a game like *EVE*, where PVP prowess is sought after, The Mittani's characterization of Russian corporations as "disciplined, vicious, and effective" reads more like a compliment than a criticism. He is not alone in this view; forum members frequently remark with admiration upon the efficiency and ruthlessness of Russian fleet operations and wider in-game geopolitics. "This is why I respect the russians," writes one player, "they know there [*sic*] game. they stick together and play to win" (Hermosa Diosas 2011). Other players have noted that while the Russian contingent of the game may be formidable, it is due more to their cohesive corporations and national unity than to any EULA-breaching behavior.

Moreover, non-Russian players and corporations may mimic Russian names as a way of aligning themselves with the vicious, PVP-oriented stereotype surrounding Russian players. On a simple level, this can involve giving a character a Russian name or, as one forum user explained, setting up a corporation that "looked Russian" to dissuade attacks. In the latter situation, a player describes how he and four friends set up a small corporation with the public description stating in Russian that they were a null-sec Russian logistics corporation. "Needless to say," writes the player, "we were neither Russian nor had any of our 5 corp members ever lived in null. . . . We went untouched for six months" (Strike Severasse 2012). In my own travels through New Eden, I saw several such examples, marked out by misspelled names, male nicknames like "Sasha" applied to female characters in Cyrillic, or an inability to respond in Russian when messaged in that language.

Such a reputation is useful for Russian players, although searching through Russian-language discussions on the topic yields conflicting opinions. Russian players also freely associate themselves with many of these traits, mockingly employing stereotypes about their nationality into the bargain. Some players, such as Master and UAxDeath, will draw on stereotypes about Russians to lend an ironic twist to their interview responses. In discussion with *Shacknews,* Master answers a question about recreation with the proclamation that "from time to time we organize corp meetings, to drink vodka and to kill a few bears" (Breckon 2007). Later, he discusses the fortitude required to win against overwhelming odds, saying, "Tell you the truth, it was scary—when you want to kill your enemy and you have nothing. But we had a spirit like all other Russian—never surrender" (Breckon 2007). Elsewhere, Russian players seem to be unaware of the stereotypes that surround them or, at least, feel they contain no hostility. In the *Rock Paper Shotgun* interview with CCP's Hilmar Pétursson mentioned earlier in the chapter, Pétursson was asked about "national divides" in the game and, in particular, about the case of the Russians, who supposedly "originally only communicated in Cyrillic" (Griliopoulos 2012). Pétursson's response focused not on conflict but on the "context and excitement" of having multiple national alliances in the game, and he suggested the international element to be "spoken very positively of by players" (Griliopoulos 2012). A Russian-language discussion thread about this piece (translated for *EVE* fan site Skoli.ru and from there disseminated to the official forums) initially seemed to agree with Pétursson and questioned the interviewer's assertion that any significant national divides exist. "There were problems with national stereotypes in *EVE*?" asks one commenter. "How come? And when was this?" (ISD Grossvogel 2012). He reports, "I personally don't remember any problems with 'Nobody understands the Russians, they write in Cyrillic.' The game is English-speaking" (ISD Grossvogel 2012). Lower down in the thread, another player argues, "Actually, there really is a problem now . . . usually it stops at the boundary of allied chat, but sometimes it goes from allied to local" (ISD Grossvogel 2012).

Finally, a handful of Russian-speaking players can be seen pushing back against complaints about Russians and the Russian language in-game. After one player posted a thread calling on CCP to launch a separate server for Russian players, one Russian pilot responded, "How about CCP puts every racist/nationalistic douche like you on a separate server and charges whatever subscription fee to keep the server running" (Mel0veyou Longtime 2013). Similarly, in a discussion about the prevalence of the Russian language in local chat channels, one Russian speaker asked, "How do i report americans who think they can impose what language i speak in Local? You have a problem with me speaking occasional russian in a unfied Local channel? What you gona do about it? Come at me bro, see how far you get" (Detritus Newton 2013).

In the data gathered for this overview, the responses of Russian players to both positive and negative stereotypes about them depend on two factors: first, the ability to understand the English-language material on the official forums and in interviews and articles and, second, their reactions often seem linked to their own experiences in-game and in the community. Many posts in Russian-language threads and forums were relatively apathetic about whether national conflict and hostility toward Russian players were widespread problems. Often, forum posters would express the opinion that probably some players had xenophobic views but that they had never been a victim of hostility. Another common strategy when posting was to list a number of national stereotypes and suggest that anyone could express negative opinions about people of any nationality or ethnicity. "Russians can be called illiterate serfs . . . Germans the Nazis . . . Americans oppressors," writes one poster. "It's possible to stick many labels on any nation, the only thing such labels have in common is that they bear no relation to living people, who have not committed anything that history ascribes to their people" (ISD Grossvogel 2012).

There is often a pragmatism about Russian-language responses to this debate; personal experiences, individual enjoyment of the game, and a tendency to cite the anonymity of the Internet as a contributing factor to hostility were overwhelmingly common in metadiscourse. The exception to this approach is in discussions with English-speaking players, where other pilots may be openly expressing negative opinions about their Russian counterparts. In these cases, Russian players defend themselves and other Russian players as a matter of course.

## Russo-Soviet Imagery in English-Language Corporation Propaganda

Corporations and alliances have drawn on Soviet-era imagery and rhetorical flourishes in their recruitment and propaganda material, most notably Razor Alliance and Goonswarm. Razor's propagandists exhort their players to seek out "glorious victory" and annihilate "imperialistic" enemies (Razor Alliance n.d.). Razor Alliance's propaganda pages imitate the breathless fervor of early Soviet political messages:

> RAZOR LEADERSHIP, tiring of endless provocations from the RAIDEN(dot) imperialist aggressor colonialist MONSTER, order GLORIOUS INVASION! (Razor Alliance n.d.)

Here I analyze a selection of propaganda images that employ a Socialist Realist style or that adapt existing Russo-Soviet imagery or posters to promote the corporation or alliance. These images all promote a concept of "Russianness" that emphasizes military strength, organization, and industrial power. Although neither Razor Alliance nor Goonswarm is Russian speaking, they strategically deploy these mock-Soviet images to associate themselves with the positive aspects of Russianness as defined by the *EVE* community: cohesion, power, and military success.

The official Razor Alliance website hosts an array of propaganda images impressive in their detail and consistency. Razor refers to itself in these images as the "People's Democratic Dictatorship of Razor" and titles its propaganda page "Ministry of Propaganda and Morale," imitating the convoluted and sometimes euphemistic naming conventions of Soviet bureaus. Each image listed on the page is available in a

Figure 6.1. A typical example of Russian- and Soviet-inspired propaganda images.

newsletter form, outlining recent game events, whereas smaller images are available as mini-posters.

The red-and-white color theme and squared-off font in Figure 6.1 are typical of Russian- and Soviet-inspired propaganda images. Although many of Razor's propaganda newsletters draw on World War II images from other nations, the red-and-white theme is common to almost all images. In contrast to the usual focus on piloting ships and participating in fleet battles, this poster addresses the economic side of the game. "Supercap," short for "supercapital," describes the largest ships in *EVE*. These vessels require a time, skill, and resource commitment prohibitive for all but larger corporations; the exhortation on the poster calls alliance members with the requisite skills to participate in their creation and operation. The line "X for glory" refers to the practice in *EVE* of typing an "x" in chat to request an invitation to a fleet (a battle group). In the *EVE* community, it is most usually used in this context, but here it is employed as a more general call to arms. The stylized male face on the left possesses the hallmarks of the Socialist Realist style: it depicts a worker in the role of the "positive hero" and adheres to the pseudo-Soviet ethos Razor has adopted. A good comparison between this image and a Soviet classic is the 1985 Alexei Stakhanov postage stamp, depicting a black-and-white portrait of the hero of the productivity movement against a red-and-yellow background with the enthusiastic slogan "Yesterday—a foreign innovator. Today—a working norm!"

Figure 6.2 marks the alliance between Goonswarm and Red Alliance. The bee is Goonswarm's symbol, in line with its philosophy of training new pilots early and encouraging them to take a part, no matter how small, in corporation life and fleet battles. Here it wears a Russian military *ushanka* emblazoned with a red star.

Figure 6.2. Modified Goonswarm mascot wearing a Russian military *ushanka* with a red star.

Now note the swarm of bees in Figure 6.3. Revolutionary Soviet leader Vladimir Ilyich Lenin is removed from the original context (Aleksandr Gerasimov's 1929–30 painting *Lenin on the Rostrum*) and is instead depicted calling forth the combined might of Goonswarm and its Russian allies, overlain by the Goon's winged grenade symbol in—naturally—red. The style of the latter two images is a natural fit for Goonswarm, allied as they are with Russian player groups. Although their executor, The Mittani, describes his style of leadership as autocratic, Goons maintain a collectivist attitude toward integrating new players and present themselves as close-knit and well defended against espionage. Conversely, Razor Alliance's rhetoric of glory, power, and victory draws on the perception that Russian *EVE* players are more aggressive and militaristic than others.

Figure 6.3. Modified painting of Soviet leader Vladimir Ilyich Lenin transformed with Goonswarm imagery and logos.

## Conclusion

The game mechanics, history, and culture of *EVE Online* encourage, and in some cases require, that players work closely together and adopt tactics that would be considered cheating in other games. To play on a single server is to enter a diverse sea of pilots from around the world, interacting in an ever-shifting and interlinked set of alliances, friendships, enmities, and random acts of (highly satisfying) in-game violence. As the culture surrounding the game has developed and a history of key events has been recorded, many players have adopted a kind of semi-role-playing attitude toward their time in the game. They cannot, however, entirely leave their real selves behind, and so their behaviors in and around the game are always jointly influenced by virtual and real-world histories, perceptions, and stereotypes. Depictions of Russian players in-game draw on both existing cultural stereotypes and mythologized narratives. Successful Russian corporations are frequently seen as representative of *all* Russian players, a presumption that leads to conflict but also to a begrudging level of respect. Russian pilots therefore have a place in the game community that is both shaped by stereotype and viewed as aspirational in terms of game success. In *EVE Online,* the tendency to approve of cutthroat play and innovative tactics means that hostility toward Russians players is often tinged with respect, a fact of which Russians themselves are acutely aware. Other groups may attempt to capitalize on the reputation of Russian players by adopting Russian names and propaganda. Non-Russian players may perform Russianness, because the potential benefits of pretending to be Russian seem to outweigh the possibility of harassment (although note that in this case, the player can always revert back to non-Russianness, a much harder proposition for Russians in the game).

The attitudes toward *EVE Online*'s Russian player base from the game population as a whole initially seem to follow the pattern of Western reactions to Eastern economic incursion. However, a deeper look at some of the specific stereotypes and complaints shows that hostility toward Russian players is rooted in a set of more complex cultural stereotypes that are echoed in both game and real-world history. I have suggested here that national or ethnic stereotypes can map on to modes of play and in-game behaviors, leading to the creation of a scapegoat group who becomes responsible for any element of the game that players dislike. However, it is hard to think of another game in which a collective reputation for being aggressive and secretive can also be viewed as beneficial. This is a sharp contrast to dynamics between Western *World of Warcraft* players and their (allegedly) Chinese counterparts: few English-speaking players have any social capital to gain by pretending to be a gold farmer, for example. Instead, the *EVE Online* community, despite myriad complaints, begrudgingly note that "this is just like the Cold War except Russia winz in *EVE*" (Hermosa Diosas 2011).

## BIBLIOGRAPHY

Alexander Bor. 2010. "Russians in EVE" (online forum thread). *EVE Online forums.* March 3. http://oldforums.eveonline.com/?a=topic&threadID=1278700.

Breckon, Nick. 2007. "EVE Online: The Bears and the Rat." *Shacknews,* September 13. http://www.shacknews.com/article/48917/eve-online-the-bears-and.

CCP. 2013. "Terms of Service." *EVE Online,* September 9. http://community.eveonline.com/support/policies/eve-tos/.

CCP Explorer. 2012. "Observing the 'Burn Jita' Player Event." *EVE Online developer's blog,* May 2. http://community.eveonline.com/devblog.asp?a=blog&nbid=28640.

Detritus Newton. 2013. "Russian Takeover of English Channels" (online forum thread). *EVE Online forums,* December 12. https://forums.eveonline.com/default.aspx?g=posts&m=3995946.

Dyer-Witheford, Nick, and Greig de Peuter. 2009. *Games of Empire: Global Capitalism and Video Games.* Minneapolis: University of Minnesota Press.

EVElopedia. n.d. "Golden Rules." https://wiki.eveonline.com/en/wiki/Golden_Rules.

Griliopoulos, Dan. 2012. "The MMOnitor: CCP and Eve." *Rock Paper Shotgun* (blog), February 26. http://www.rockpapershotgun.com/2012/02/26/the-mmonitor-ccp-and-eve/.

Hermosa Diosas. 2011. "Welcome to the New Russian Server . . . ! ENOUGH IS ENOUGH!" (online forum thread). *EVE Online forums,* June 1. http://oldforums.eveonline.com/?a=topic&threadID=1520581.

ISD Grossvogel. 2012. "Interview with Hilmar on *Rock Paper Shotgun*" (online forum thread). *EVE*

*Online forums,* February 26. https://forums.eveonline.com/default.aspx?g=posts&m =864305.

Jacobs, Melinda. 2008. "Multiculturalism and Cultural Issues in Online Gaming Communities." *Journal for Cultural Research* 12, no. 4: 317–34.

Kogh Ayon. 2010. "Subscription % by Country—When Can We See It Again?" (online forum thread). *EVE Online forums,* March 22. https://forums.eveonline.com/default .aspx?g=posts&t=84490.

Lalone, Nick. 2013. "*Age of Wushu* Culture Clashes." *Warcry* (blog), August 8. http://www.warcry .com/news/view/126635-Age-of-Wushu-Culture-Clashes.

Mel0veyou Longtime. 2013. "Is There a Russian Only Server?" (online forum thread). *EVE Online forums,* December 18. https://forums.eveonline.com/default.aspx?g=posts&t=305941.

Nakamura, Lisa. 2009. "Don't Hate the Player, Hate the Game: The Racialization of Labor in World of Warcraft." *Critical Studies in Media Communication* 26, no. 2: 128–44.

Nardi, Bonnie. 2010. *My Life as a Night Elf Priest: An Anthropological Account of World of Warcraft.* Ann Arbor: University of Michigan Press.

Phugoid. 2011. "Russians?" (online forum thread). *EVE Online forums,* August 18. http://oldfor ums.eveonline.com/?a=topic&threadID=1567166.

Razor Alliance. n.d. "Official Archive of Glorious RAZOR Alliance Propaganda." http://propaganda .eve-razor.com/index.html.

Smith, Quintin. 2011. "EVE Online: Audience with the King of Space." *Rock Paper Shotgun* (blog), April 7. http://www.rockpapershotgun.com/2011/04/07/eve-online-audience -with-the-king-of-space/.

Strike Severasse. 2012. "Changes Are Coming: High, Low, and Null Will Be Mixing More" (online forum thread). *EVE Online forums,* July 21. https://forums.eveonline.com/default. aspx?g=posts&t=135314.

# The Art of Selling Trust

_Chribba (Christer Enberg)_

**For years now,** one of many pieces of advice new pilots have received about playing *EVE Online* has been that "you cannot trust anyone, except Chribba"—something that has always made me smile and feel proud. I started playing *EVE* in 2003, sort of by accident. At the time, I was playing the old Elite game series, when I happened to come by an article in a PC magazine showcasing something that looked like Elite but with fancier graphics, set in this online world together with hundreds of other gamers. I quickly became hooked.

In a world where there was very little help (the manual that came with the boxed game provided next to nothing about how to start playing the game), I slowly started to learn more and more about the game by interacting with other pilots, even though I mostly kept to myself. It never appealed to me to fight and shoot others—I like to think that I'm a nice person in real life—but my mistake may have been that I brought that persona to my virtual character as well.

For a time I flew alone, doing my own thing while interacting with the community, both in-game and on the forums. Over my first two years, the memory I have of the community is that it was small but very engaged. We had a close relationship with CCP Games and the developers, suggesting and discussing ideas and improvements on the forums. As I started to feel more and more a part of this special group of people (thousands, by this stage), I became even more engaged in seeing the community grow. I noticed ways the community could be improved. At a time when sites like YouTube and Imgur did not exist on the scale they do today, the first thing to make my name known in the *EVE* community was my release of an image- and video-hosting site dedicated to *EVE* (EVE-Files.com). Thinking back, I most likely would not have ended up where I am today if it weren't for that site.

Seeing the success of EVE-Files and the appreciation from the community, I created more *EVE*-themed websites, such as EVE-Search (a forum mirror) and EVE-Offline (which monitors the growth and online numbers of *EVE*). The more popular

93

these websites became, the more my name became known. This proved very important when CCP introduced supercaptials to the game.

Up until the introduction of supercapitals, all ships could be bought and sold
via the in-game market and safely accessed within stations. Supercapitals changed
that; too big to dock or to be built in stations, they could not (and still cannot) be sold
on the in-game market. Thus selling one of these ships was an enormous risk—a risk
that a real-life friend did not want to take. At the time, many pilots were trying left and
right to scam supercapital pilots of their ISK or ships. As my friend knew that others
knew of my name and my love for the community, he approached me asking if I would
be willing to help him out acquiring his first Hel supercarrier (a ship class known as
motherships at the time); the idea was that if the seller was OK with me helping out, I
would hold the money until my friend had warped safely away.

With some hesitation, the seller agreed. He took a leap of faith that I would not
run with the money—he faced just as much risk as my friend did. The rumor of a safer
way of trading a supercapital spread quite quickly, and more people started to ask for
my assistance, still not without some hesitation, because a lot of ISK was involved—
especially for the titans, which are worth approximately 120 billion ISK, or roughly
US$7,600 in PLEX (using 2010 figures).

For the first few months, I didn't think of this as a business but just enjoyed
helping people out and feeling appreciated. At one of these trades, a trader suggested
that I should offer my services to everyone, in a public way, as up until that point, news
of my offerings had spread by word of mouth. I took his advice and posted on the forums, offering my services to anyone in need of "trust"—I thought, why not? Let's give
it a try. Worst case, no one needs it, and I'll mine asteroids full-time instead.

This proved to be a wise choice, because people had more need of trustful
oversight than I had imagined, not only for tricky ship trades but also for just about
any situation in which a seller or buyer wants to avoid getting scammed—and I get to
do one of the things I like most: help out and get paid for it.

With the growth of my reputation, pilots started to call me a celebrity, something that I don't see myself as, at least not in the way of, say, some famous movie star.
I do enjoy people greeting me, wanting to say hi just for the fact to have said hi to me,
or offering me a beer at a player meet-up—I know I wouldn't be where I am today if it
weren't for everyone in the community. I feel I didn't do anything special; it was just
a good idea at the right time, with the help of friends placed in even better situations
that allowed me to offer a needed service.

Pilots have often asked me if I've ever been tempted to take the money and
run at a titan trade, for example. Strangely enough, I never have felt tempted at all.
Of course, in the beginning, the thought crossed my mind, but I never saw the point
in doing so; looking at my financial data, I have made far more ISK being legitimate
and honest than I could ever have stolen, and as long as CCP Games does not change
things up, there should be a solid ground for more income. To date, I have brokered a

little more than 100 trillion ISK, which is approximately US$6.3 million in PLEX, with quite an OK cut in the process.

The sandbox world CCP created truly feels like a sandbox. Thinking back, I'd never imagined that I would be in this position today. If I had told the 2003 Chribba that in ten years or so, he would be a key pilot to some of New Eden's most high-stake, high-profile transactions, I would have laughed and sarcastically said I was going to win the lottery too—and in a way, I have. Lots of players say that *EVE* is "spreadsheets in space"; although I somewhat agree with this sentiment, it is only if you make it like that. You can take help from analyzing the market, for example, but just as you use that spreadsheet to set up the

Figure 7.1. Chribba card in the fan-made *EVE Online* trading card game.

optimal trade route, the guy looking at the market screen will have snagged that item that someone drunkenly sold by mistake. A spreadsheet most likely will not save you when you get pinned down by pirates, but you could always try to bargain your way out with fancy calculations and formulas.

Sometimes when I come across articles of about celebrities in other games, for example, in *World of Warcraft (WoW)*, I reflect back to the single-shard universe we have in New Eden. Compared to a game like *WoW*, with millions of subscribers, but on a ton of different servers, what we have in *EVE* is amazing. Being on the same server means events and players affect everyone—something that for me feels like we have a bigger community than others—and community is key (at least, I wouldn't be around if the community weren't as awesome as it is). As a developer of *EVE* resources, CCP's assistance has been crucial. Providing us with tools (such as the application programming interface [API]) to vastly improve and interact with both game and community has been a major step, and allowing developers to access *EVE* data, some even in real time, has created all sorts of useful resources—and, of course, taken the metagame to a whole different level.

Resources like the API also allow driven people with good ideas to develop tools and make a name for themselves, beyond being the most ruthless pirate or most evil scammer, even if most probably aim more for these—but it's your choice, sandbox style!

Players have told me that I'm not playing the game correctly, and I've always asked them what the correct way is. It's amusing how many different "right ways"

Figure 7.2. Chribba's four titans—ships each worth approximately US$7,600—mining veldspar, *EVE Online*'s cheapest mineral.

there are in *EVE Online*; opinions vary from person to person. Needless to say, CCP did a piss-poor job of telling us the "right way"—but I am glad they didn't, and I hope that was also the point! Many players' jaws have dropped when they've learned that I don't engage in player versus player (PVP) combat, nor ever did. In a game so PVP oriented, many feel I'm simply doing it "wrong"—but this has paid off for me. I think my chosen play style is something that has greatly benefited from the single-shard universe; events happening in-game simply would not have as much of an impact on sharded servers, because a player feels much more involved in events that occur on her own server.

The right way, for me, to play *EVE* is to do what a player wants, with his own personal goals, regardless of whether his goal is to be the leader of a huge alliance or simply to corner the shield booster market in the largest trade hub. I've had many goals during the years, some small and some large. They have kept me driven and enjoying things, so who is to say that that is not the right way?

An example of this occurred back in 2005, when CCP first introduced formal alliances, something that caught my interest, but in a much different way than for other players. This was one of the earliest times I was told that I wasn't "playing the game right." My goal was to train the skills needed and collect the ISK to create an alliance for myself on my own (not a simple task, seeing as the 1 billion ISK alliance fee

was a lot more money than it is today). I happily created the alliance using almost all my money, only to get told by other players that alliances are for big groups of people and not for a single pilot like myself—I was playing "wrong." To this date, I am still the only pilot in my alliance—because I can be. It was the right way for me.

The same happened when supercapitals were introduced into the game—these monstrous ships were (supposedly) for the biggest alliances. So valuable and powerful, investing 120 billion ISK, or US$7,600 in PLEX, any alliance with a titan was a force to be reckoned with. So I set a new goal: to acquire all four racial titans for my alliance and use them to mine asteroids.

Nowadays, I'm the standing joke (in a good way) when it comes to pilots having goals to own and fly a titan, because regardless of the specific reason for that pilot to want to do so, he can never do it worse than the carebear Chribba, who turned an alliance warship into the most expensive mining ship. Yet again, for me, that was the right way to use a titan; for others, it would be wiping out an entire battlefield of ships using the titan's doomsday device. This brings me back to what playing *EVE* really comes down to: it is a player's choice to do the things she does. Thanks to the choices everyone makes that shape the New Eden universe, the content we see and read about is created by the players; CCP has given us the tools to shape it, but it is up to us to use these tools: the right way or the wrong way, there's no such way—there's only your way.

My journey since 2003 has shown me many views and aspects of the gaming community and its people, some bad, most good, but it is all those encounters that have shaped things, even in real life. Although I still am not fully up to par with the celebrity thing, I have pride that people appreciate the things I've done, which has evolved me as a person, and for that, I am forever grateful; it has been an honor to experience.

# We Play Something Awful

## Goon Projects and Pervasive Practice on Online Games

*Richard Page*

One of *EVE Online*'s most notorious corporations, Goonwaffe, leaders of the Goonswarm Federation, is made up of members of the Something Awful forums (SA forums), a long-established Internet community founded by comedy website Something Awful (SA). They have gone by many different names and been led by a number of charismatic leaders, but *EVE* players from the SA forums have always shared a particular culture, and they have always been known commonly as "goons." Goons have had a profound impact on the world of *EVE*. They have changed the way wars are fought by introducing swarm tactics, they founded the game's first espionage and diplomatic corps, and they have encouraged ruthless play, such as griefing and scamming. Goons have been major players in all the galaxy-spanning conflicts of *EVE* since they instigated the First Great War with Band of Brothers. They have always had a representative on the Council of Stellar Management (CSM), and a goon has often been its president. Although they have frequently been one of the major powers in null-sec, the goons of SA have also been fond of saying that *EVE* is boring and a bad game, but that "playing Something Awful" in *EVE* is fun. If goons dislike *EVE*, how did they become one of the most powerful and influential groups in the game? Understanding why goons play *EVE*, and play it so successfully, tells us a great deal about how online communities create meaning.

Building on Alex Golub's phenomenological approach to raiding in *World of Warcraft*, this chapter shows that is the projects that players bring to *EVE*, rather than what is inherent in the design of the game itself, that make the game meaningful. We know that games are not bounded "worlds" (Lehdonvirta 2010). Not only does playing a game involve making use of material from outside sources but communities formed in a game can continue to flourish outside of the coded world (Consalvo 2007; Pearce 2009). This chapter expands on that view by showing how meaning does not only travel out from the game but is brought into it from preexisting cultures, whether broad national or ethnic cultures (Page 2012; Golub and Lingley 2008) or smaller subcultures such as SA. Furthermore, much research has focused on the practices that appear unexpectedly from within game systems. Though there are *emergent* practices that arise from these systems, I argue that there are also *pervasive* practices that originate in communities outside of the game. Pervasive practice is a kind of emergent practice in that it is an unpredicted result of people interacting with a complex system. It is worth distinguishing because it is not the result of "bottom-up individual actions" but of the culture of a large group with preexisting social norms (Pearce 2009, 40).

Through participant observation among the goons of SA in *EVE*, interviews with players, and analysis of existing forum posts and other online texts, the chapter shows how goons express SA culture in *EVE* through their activities and ideologies. Members of the forums see themselves first as a social group, second as gamers, and the SA forums are perhaps most succinctly described at the top of the forum rules: "We here on the Something Awful Forums are very elitist and strict assholes." Three key elements to goon culture are outlined here. First, goons see themselves as "elitists" and as separated from the masses of the Internet. Compared to famously liberal forums like Reddit and 4chan, goons are more willing to accept strict moderation in exchange for removing undesirable elements from their group. Goons are also self-described assholes, which in this context means they refuse to take others seriously. Finally, by using the Burn Jita events in *EVE* as an example of pervasive practice, we will see how goons make use of the affordances of *EVE* to engage in practices that would not exist without the influence of their unique external culture. This culture drives the "goon project," an attempt to write their own values onto the virtual world.

The objective of this chapter is to demonstrate that approaching online games and other virtual worlds as projects rather than as worlds is a fruitful way of understanding the meanings players draw from them. Furthermore, it shows how meaningful play can emerge, not from game design alone, but also from the meanings that players bring to the game themselves. While limiting itself to a very small Internet subculture, this chapter demonstrates the importance of considering the impact of external cultures on game play, such as national or ethnic cultures and the various subject positions within these.

## Emergent Play

The concept of "emergence" comes from complex systems theory and describes behavior within complex systems that cannot be predicted by the structure of the system or by individual actions. With regard to online games, Celia Pearce (2009) writes of emergence as a result of the interactions between individual players and the game system. Emergence is the unpredictable result of agents within systems (42). Broadly, this includes the ways people make use of systems like roadways, but in online games and virtual worlds, it includes emergent markets in real money (gold farming) or in-game protest (Dibbell 2006; Pearce 2009, 40).

*EVE* itself features countless examples of emergent game play, many of them cataloged in this volume, such as the spontaneous memorials created for the dead (see chapter 11). In *EVE*, a Ponzi scheme fleeced investors of more than 1 trillion ISK (Martuk 2011). Trusted player Chribba operates an escrow service to facilitate the sale of massive ships (see chapter 7). Players protested prices for cosmetic items by mass-shooting an invincible station (Edwards 2011).

*EVE* is designed to support emergence, and emergent game play is part of what makes the game popular with many players. "The game is about extremely complex player interactions instead of the game mainly being about struggling against something the devs set up like is the case in most MMOs and games in general," said one goon in a personal interview in 2014. Whereas other games focus on challenges that are planned by developers, *EVE* provides systems like contracts, alliances, and sovereignty that allow players to direct their own projects.

This research builds on Pearce's work by providing an example of emergent game play (in that is an unexpected outcome of the design of the game) that did not "emerge" from the interaction of independent people with the game system but rather was imposed on the game from the outside by a preexisting external culture. This is what I am terming a *pervasive practice*. A pervasive practice is emergent in the sense that it arises from the interaction between a system and its environment but is unusual in that it is an already-coherent system imposed on the game from outside. Whereas Pearce's *Uru* players formed their society from play of *Uru* and then exported it to other play worlds, goons arrived in *EVE* with an existing community based around discussion forums. Goon behavior in *EVE* can in several ways be traced back to the structure of the SA forums and the expectations of those who post there.

Goons have often been equated with griefers, not only among Internet communities but also in academic literature. Bakioglu (2009) and Dibbell (2008) name SA as the origin of organized griefer communities in *Second Life* (*SL*). Bakioglu observed groups in *SL* that disrupted social groups or economic activity with extreme humor. Normal play of *SL* consists of using elaborate tools to create objects in the world that can then be sold on a market. Griefers in *SL* have driven down real estate prices with models of the burning towers of the World Trade Center and disrupted serious interviews with virtual entrepreneurs with dancing penises. At their most disruptive, SA goons tried to bring down *SL* itself with a self-replicating "gray goo" attack. While others make money or role-play, goons refuse to take the virtual environment seriously.

Bakioglu says grief play in *SL* has value because it disrupts the signification systems of that world, ultimately serving as an almost revolutionary critique of the creative capitalist system of *SL*. But she also argues that this works because *SL* is not a game in the true sense, and so the boundary between game play and the normal world is thinner so that "grief play" can become "griefing," the latter being a disruptive social act. Does goon play in *EVE*, which some would call griefing, likewise have subversive value? Goons tried to destroy *SL* with gray goo, but they have become one of the most powerful and influential factions in *EVE*. How does the subversion of one world become success in another? I argue that by looking at *EVE* as a project rather than as a world, we can see how the systems of *EVE* meet the values of SA goons and how goons then subvert *EVE* into their own project.

## Worlds Are Projects

In his treatment of *World of Warcraft* (*WoW*) raiders, Alex Golub (2010, 20) argued that virtual worlds such as massively multiplayer online games (MMOGs) would be best treated as "systems of meaning and commitment which spread across multiple locations" rather than discrete locations. In that case, Golub was working against those who argue that virtual worlds are unique places that can be studied without reference to the real world (Boellstorff 2008)—but his phenomenological approach can be fruitfully applied to the analysis of other cultures of online worlds.

Golub argues that theorists and designers of virtual worlds have implicit assumptions about what people value. These values arise from Western notions of expressive individualism. As a result, worlds like *SL* are considered more real than mere games because they allow people to express themselves individually through their creations (Boellstorff 2008). Player characters in virtual worlds are assumed to be individual free actors without commitments, and this is what makes the virtual world so real: you can do anything, be anyone. Player-run free-market economic systems are a common feature of these individualistic games (particularly in *EVE*), and it has been argued that the complexity of these systems proves the reality of the game worlds (Castronova 2001). Linden Labs viewed its creation of *SL* as a free world for individual creativity, where people could collaborate without commitment to geographical boundaries, so much so that even its internal corporate structure lacked authority (Ondrejka 2007; Malaby 2011). David Myers (2007) considered play in *City of Heroes* to be fundamentally selfish, as players sought to maximize their own characters' abilities, and he argued that this established the formal reality of the game. *WoW* guilds are organizations of free association that W. S. Bainbridge (2012) has argued serve as a model for the real future of human society.

Golub showed that the project of raiding extends far beyond the virtual world and in fact undermines some aspects of its "worldliness." Successfully completing raids requires players to decompose the visual world presented to them and rebuild it into something more useful. They remove graphical flourishes and replace them with useful information that helps them to coordinate their attacks. The "world" of *Warcraft* is defined not by its graphical fidelity but by the projects that its players undertake. Virtual worlds don't have value because they accurately simulate a libertarian utopia; they have value because they allow players to carry out the projects to which they are already committed. We should approach players not as uncommitted individuals but as people with previously existing commitments to groups larger than themselves. Understanding how *EVE* is different for goons means understanding the goon project.

In this study, I approach the emergent practices of a social group of griefers. These emergent practices can be understood by approaching them, not as aspects of the design of the game world, but as expressions of the players' projects. Four key elements of goon sociality are explored here: (1) the fact that goons see themselves first as a social group, second as gamers; (2) SA's exclusivity and insularity; (3) goon acceptance of authoritarian social structures; and (4) goons' self-described "assholery," a refusal to take the systems of the game and its common players seriously that leads to conflicts with developers and other players.

## Goons Are Social

The key difference between goons and other communities of play is that goons have a primary identity that is not based in play. The SA forums are meant to be a social group. The activity that makes someone a goon is participating in conversations on the forums. As a result, goons in *EVE* see themselves as primarily a social group. Gaming comes second.

The SA forums are now more popular than the main site, with more than 180,000 registered users and 150 million total posts. The forums are divided into various topical subforums—occasionally changing but currently more than fifty in number. Topical forums cover games, gadgets, computers, fitness, cooking, cars, pets, guns, drugs, film, books, music, television, comics, anime, and many other topics. Because the topics covered are so broad, membership is driven by affinity to the SA culture, not interest in a particular topic. There are also private forums for organizing real-world goon meets, buying and selling items, and organizing private game servers.

Goons frequently play games online together, forming groups collectively called "goon squads." Several subforums on SA are devoted to goons getting together to play games. Being an active member of the SA forums is usually a requirement for joining these groups. This is not simply a matter of sharing a sense of humor but of actually joining the SA community. For *EVE,* being an actively posting member for at least three months is a listed requirement to be accepted into the corp in-game. Players who join the SA forums for the purpose of joining Goonwaffe or any other goon squad guild are termed "J4G"—"Join for Game/Guild"—and, once detected, are trolled out of the community. Goons in games are not interested in people joining the forums who do not intend to become part of the community.

Goons in *EVE* take pride in being social outside of the game. They emphasize that these social events are relatively "normal" compared to real-life events other organizations might hold. According to corporation CEO The Mittani,

> goonmeets have been a thing two to three times a year since the beginning . . . as best as I can tell we're the hardest partiers in *EVE*. Goons are by nature more social than random Internet denizens, and especially your average *EVE* nerd. . . . So, Iceswarm, good example. Everyone meets up at the host's house in Chicago, eats food, gets drunk, and

smokes weed. Goes to a gay bar, invades gay bar with a horde of drunk and high goons. Sings show tunes/torch songs with perplexed regulars. Hits a few more bars, then goes to a goth/industrial club. We end up eating at Five Guys at 5:00 A.M. to sober up/get burgers. Good times. That's a party. Not sitting around folding tables talking about *EVE Online*. This is with a crew of like, fifty or more people. Mass chaos. (personal interview, 2014)

Furthermore, goons distinguish their online community as active and social compared to others. The Mittani compares the SA forums to Reddit:

Compare [SA] to Reddit, where you can "be a redditor" by passive-aggressively upvoting/ downvoting and never need to comment/participate in a community. That's why the TEST [a corporation of redditors] meet-ups were like autism conventions with a bunch of wallflowers and nerds sitting around folding tables talking about *EVE Online*. Goon-meets folks almost never talk about spaceships, it's kind of taboo. (personal interview, 2014; cf. chapter 5)

Reddit allows comments on articles to be voted up or down by users, creating a system where the most popular comments rise to the top of a thread. Posts in an SA thread are listed chronologically, and threads are sorted by most recent comment. As a result, SA threads are structured more like a conversation. Participating in an SA thread means reading the comments that came before. Posters will be disparaged if they post something that was already discussed within the last few pages. The Mittani, and other goons, see this as fostering an active social community. This community is what draws them together and is seen as more authentic than Reddit's "passive-aggressive" voting. Goons don't talk about *EVE* outside the game, because *EVE* was not what brought them together.

But it is not only outside of *EVE* that goons prioritize socializing over gaming. "Slosh ops" occur regularly, where the primary goal is not to accomplish anything in-game but to get drunk playing *EVE*. Even strategically important ops have an emphasis on fun. Goons make jokes and post funny images in fleet chat. "Goon radio" plays music for all participants to listen to during lulls in ops. Within Goonwaffe, players organize into like-minded "squads" with private chats, in-jokes, and signatures. Goons often say that the most fun comes from helping other goons have a good time. "The thing that gives me the greatest satisfaction in *EVE* is making sure my corp members are having a good time and getting sweet kills and going on cool fleets" (personal interview, 2014). New players in particular are offered free ships, training, and mentoring. "Goons are really friendly and helpful to newbees. They have great attitudes about things in general. . . . Wherever a one-week-old guy in a slasher gets a point, there we all point with him" (personal interview, 2014).

Elements of the SA forums help foster the community. Goons broadly support the membership fee and the strict moderation because they believe these foster a stronger, funnier, and more troll-free community:

> [To join SA] you have to be a risk taker, be willing to pay to hang out with people of like minds, etc. Ten bucks is a huge psychological barrier for most people for some reason. "Why should I pay to join a forum?" So people who do pay *want* to be a goon, and are willing to get hazed/adapt to the culture to do so. A lot of SA forumgoers just lurk, but to be in GSF [Goonswarm Federation] in particular you need a long posting history to prove yourself, going back three months before you ask to join GSF. (The Mittani, personal interview, 2014)

Having to pay and having real consequences for not fitting in result in a community with consistent values. And although it's certainly possible never to post in SA, joining goons in *EVE* requires active participation.

The social aspect of goons is a key part of how goons avoid ever being totally removed from *EVE*. The Mittani explained how goons avoid the "failure cascade" that ends in-game groups—perhaps most notably Band of Brothers (BoB):

> The genius of Goonfleet was to make such a large group of goons by using advertising to point to the megathread that it became an institution impervious to drama. Human groups below a certain critical mass always implode in drama eventually, but if you put 1k people into an org, suddenly you have an Institution and it's too big for the drama of any one person. (The Mittani, personal interview, 2014)

Goon groups prior to Goonfleet had indeed imploded in internal drama. According to Goonfleet founder Remedial, "the cause of death was drama caused by a small handful of goons that resulted in the entire corp being torn apart by strife and everyone becoming disgusted and quitting for better things" (quoted in Goonfleet internal wiki). Remedial's solution in founding Goonfleet was to draw on the population of the SA forums with a recruitment thread and to support new players with ships and training to reduce *EVE*'s learning curve. This was possible thanks to the new tactic of using masses of cheap, low-skill frigates to "tackle" larger ships and hold them while larger ships destroyed them. At this time, Remedial advertised *EVE* as a bad game but playing *EVE* with goons as fun. The history of goons in *EVE* began from a fundamental alliance between goon sociality and pushing the boundaries of the game mechanics—something that we further explore later.

The most recent internal trouble with goons was when former CEO Karttoon disbanded the alliance:

> After the Delve sov welp [when Goonswarm lost sovereignty in Delve over an administrative error], Karttoon got blamed for being a shitty AFK CEO and disbanded the alliance/went fuckgoons. Ebrryone just moved to Goonwaffe. So there wasn't a schism there, just him being assmad that he got called out by everyone insisting he resign. (The Mittani, personal interview, 2014)

The technical disbanding of the alliance had no real effect on goon unity and led to no failure cascade, as it did with BoB during the Great Wars. Goon players joined a different, already existing corporation called Goonwaffe, and their alliance was re-constituted as Goonswarm Federation. One factor was that goons in *EVE* were at that point numerous enough that the actions of one player were not enough to upset the whole organization. Additionally, because goons had strong social ties to one another outside of the game, loss of the in-game organization was no real loss. Goons in *EVE* continued, and the only challenge was keeping the names straight—the executive corp of the alliance was now Goonwaffe, and the Goonfleet corp as well as the Goonswarm alliance were now hostile. They even had the opportunity to retroactively expel Kart-toon from goon society. One non-*EVE* player posted on the SA forums,

> Karttoon as you know him isn't even a J4G, he's a straight up pubbie. The real Karttoon
> joined SA when we played Travian together, just to get in our Travian alliance. He's an
> OK guy. he later gave someone else in our non-SA, non-*EVE* clan his SA + *EVE* accounts.
> i don't think any goons actually knew the original owner when he played *EVE*. (Straker
> 2010)

As a result, Karttoon had never been a real goon. The veracity of this story is ques-tioned, but it has the funny effect of maintaining the continuity of the goon community in *EVE*, supporting the idea that the real source of trouble is outsiders.

## Goons Are Insular

The key feature of the SA forums is the membership fee, unusual when first implemented in 2001 and unheard of today. At times, limited access may be granted to unregistered visitors, but only people willing to pay US$10 can access the full forums. Additional forum perks, such as the ability to private message, search, and access the archives, carry additional charges. It is extremely unusual for an Internet forum to charge a membership fee, and this barrier keeps many from registering. This is the whole idea. It keeps out "folks not serious about adhering to the rules" and protects the forums from trolls (Something Awful n.d.). There are real costs to being banned from the forums for breaking rules, because reregistering will cost the user another US$10, plus the cost of any add-ons she wants to restore. The site is also deliberately not advertised, because Lowtax would rather people find out about the site from like-minded friends than have a lot of people with different senses of humor register. An interview of one of the site's writers on American cable television—perhaps the most public exposure SA has ever had—deliberately misrepresented the site in an elaborate prank, claiming it was covered in ads and charged US$80 to access the forums (Kasik and Walsh 2005).

Goons see the membership fee and strict moderation as necessary to creating a worthwhile community and content-filled, junk-free forum. This is fairly unusual among Internet communities. In contrast, Reddit prides itself on being open to all peo-ple and topics, which has led to a proliferation of popular and interesting subreddits as well as subreddits on a variety of borderline topics. Many goons are also redditors, but it is common to disparage the lack of moderation on Reddit. In fact, it was a goon effort to bring attention to Reddit's tolerance of pedophilia that led to that site's recent closure of several subreddits. Similarly, the imageboard 4chan, home of the notorious Anonymous movement and founded by a former goon, allows members to post entirely anonymously on its /b/ "random" board. This feature is considered by many goons to result in repetitive, uninteresting content and constant trolling on 4chan, because it cannot be strictly moderated. This has led to 4chan occasionally being termed "our retarded little brother" by goons (Dibbell 2008).

In *EVE,* prior success in-game is not a requirement to join goons. When new players join an *EVE* corporation through the SA forums, the first instruction is to kill themselves. Players are expected to podjump into goon space, abandoning any assets in Empire. In fact, they prefer players who have no experience in *EVE* but long histories of participation in the SA forums.

Goons also define their uniqueness by their difference. Players who are not goons are called "pubbies" and are roundly disparaged by goons. Pubbies are considered to be boring, asocial, and overly concerned with making ISK:

> [Playing with pubbies was] just boring as fuck. They mined and didn't work as a group. A corp of people doing their own thing, chasing ISK, ISK, ISK. In Lordless [a goon corp preceding Goonfleet], we wreaked havoc and played pranks and did crazy shit. (The Mittani, personal interview, 2014)

Recruitment propaganda emphasizes the difference between goons and pubbies. One popular image claims that the "old guard" of *EVE* was right to call goons a "cancer." It encourages players to join and "spread the infection." Goons were more than a threat; they were a disease, implying that goons weren't just practical enemies but ideological or emotional threats. The propaganda image subverts this by claiming that the old guard was right. The image implies a fundamental difference between goons and other players that would lead others to call goons a disease and goons to claim the term as their own. In the next section, I show that one of the key differences separating goons and pubbies is that goons are very accepting of authoritarian structures.

## Goons Are Authoritarian

The SA forums broadly, and goons in *EVE* in particular, are in many ways authoritarian organizations. There is an atmosphere of subversion among goons, but it operates by its own internal structure, which tends to be organized top-down rather than bottom-up. Although SA allows offensive or tasteless humor, it does not allow things that are unfunny. Moderators and administrators are equipped with arbitrary power to probate or ban bad posters. Similarly, among goons in *EVE,* being an asshole to pubbies is encouraged, whereas internal drama is quashed from above. Leaders, though popularly selected, are autocrats followed by a cult of personality. Resources are required to be shared, allowing reimbursement for lost ships, but only on approved ops and with approved fittings. "It's an amusing irony that GSF is a socialist autocracy," said The Mittani, "and is so effective due to suffocating redistribution" (personal interview, 2014).

The authoritarianism is part of what makes goon organizations in *EVE* functional and highly successful. It is a selling point for members. "It's actually an insanely functional organization" (personal interview, 2014). Goons use *EVE*'s tax mechanic, which automatically deducts a percentage of any member's earnings for the corporation wallet. In addition to maintaining sovereignty and other corporation tasks, this helps provide funds to give free ships and implants to new players, encouraging them to stick with the game. Authoritarianism not only organizes ops efficiently but also prevents drama. In a way, this is another functional use of the authoritarian organization, because it helps prevent internal schisms from destroying the corp. Goons use *EVE*'s wallet access tools to prevent any one player from having access to the complete funds, even as all important decisions are deferred to one autocratic CEO.

Leaders of goons have often held cults of personality, in a somewhat tongue-in-cheek way (it's only Internet spaceships, after all). Soviet-style propaganda is common, posted side by side with edits of American World War II posters. Goons often draw on Communist rhetoric in speech, referring to The Mittani as "dear leader." Asked what culture goons share, one goon in an interview said, "Long live the cultural revolution, glory to Mittani thought, etc." Goons' current home base in Deklein has long been known as Mittanigrad, and though other outposts undergo frequent name changes to fresher jokes, Mittanigrad has been consistently named such since July 2011 (DOT-LAN n.d.).

Goons offer a complementary case study to Pearce's migratory *Uru* players. Like *Uru* players, goons have migrated their culture into many different contexts, especially online games. However, goons migrated to *EVE* from a milieu that was not based on play. The SA forums are a social space. Pearce contrasts the emergent, bottom-up play of the users of virtual worlds with the authoritarian, top-down actions of the developers of these online games. In-game protests in *WoW*, for example, were cracked down on by Blizzard by shutting down the mechanical systems behind the game. Goons, however, have a culture that is insular and authoritarian. As a result, their practices are less an example of emergence from independent actors and more the expression of a unified and top-down culture. Because this culture is at odds with those that have emerged from online games, it is perceived as comprising anarchic griefers but in fact displays a unique internal set of values, which I call *asshole culture*.

## Goons Are Assholes

The goon project in *EVE* is more than griefing and is more accurately termed among goons as being a "space asshole." This word has provenance in SA, beginning with SA front page articles on "asshole physics." For goons, being an asshole means refusing to take anything seriously and subverting the systems that other people take seriously. This attitude originates in the foundation of SA, runs through the culture of the SA forums, and can be seen in the ways that goons play online games, including *EVE* Online.

The original "Asshole Physics" article by SA founder Lowtax shows how the realistic physics engine behind *Max Payne 2* allows him to live out his "fantasies of being a giant asshole" (Kyanka 2003). While the realistic physics were designed to make the gunfights central to the game more immersive, Lowtax finds he can knock over everything in an office without any of the nonplayer characters reacting. Given a set of tools meant to enhance immersion in the game world, the behavior that emerges is a desire to push the boundaries of the rules set by the game and expose their limitations.

Goons in *EVE* often describe themselves as assholes, or "space assholes." They have set up dedicated forums and channels for scamming, including a fake web page to farm application programming interface (APIs). "Newbees" are encouraged to make fast money by running recruitment scams. Many players who want to join goon corps are not aware that membership is limited to those who are already members of the SA forums. Other marks are players who want to move from Empire space to null-sec. Goons are serious about scamming and serious about getting new players in on the action. An entire subforum in the corp private forums is dedicated to scamming. A fake recruitment page that looks identical to the real goon alliance home page has been set up to support scamming, particularly by new players. Marks sent to this page can enter their APIs to apply to join goons, allowing the scammer to see if the mark has any valuable assets. The page can then be set to return messages indicating an application fee is required to join or that the Directorate is considering the application. Dedicated chat channels offer scammers additional support in landing difficult marks. Of course, in keeping with their us versus them mentality, goons are told not to scam allies.

In this volume, Martin R. Gibbs, Marcus Carter, and Joji Mori have written about the spontaneous shrines that appeared following the death of Vile Rat (chapter 11). The goon spirit is best exposed in the spontaneous memorial to Vile Rat: shooting "blues." Because Vile Rat was the head diplomat, any time a player accidentally killed an allied ship (shot a "blue"), the player was meant to alert Vile Rat so he could smooth over relations with allies. After his death, a thread appeared organizing goons to go out and deliberately shoot allied ships, then return to the thread to post reports of their kills to an absent Vile Rat. This frankly touching tribute relied on treating the built-in alliance tools like an asshole.

Being assholes in *EVE* could also be seen as the origin of the First Great War with BoB. BoB was seen by goons as an alliance of "poopsockers"—arrogant, elite players who supposedly would not even get up from the game to use the toilet. BoB players, particularly the founding corporation Evolution, were perceived by goons to be taking the game far too seriously. Conversely, goons were accused of not taking it seriously enough.

If a single event could be said to have sparked the war, it was a signature used by goon Tetsujin on the corporation's private forums referring to the death of well-liked *EVE* player Smoske. In the thread in which the signature was revealed to the wider public, BoB CEO SirMolle responded that he found it incredibly tasteless. Shortly thereafter, SirMolle made his infamous "there are no goons" post on the *EVE* forums, declaring that goons would be driven out of *EVE* and that it was now "personal." It is widely believed among goons that Tetsujin's signature was the flash point for the conflict.

More broadly, the two groups had opposed ideologies. According to SirMolle, the point of *EVE* was to control as much of space as possible. Goons saw the game as mostly just fun:

> [Goon commander Isaiah] Houston says the Goon motivation was more about carrying out their general mandate as the gaming world's most excellent griefers, than simply revenge: "It was about griefing the oldest and most established players in the game, making them eat their own words just happened to be the best way of doing that. We've had some scores to settle along the way, it's true, but really the impetus has just been us staying true to our roots as Goons." (Dibbell 2008)

Essentially, goons believed BoB took the game far too seriously—and this was ultimately also their downfall. BoB was betrayed by one player who was sick of its internal culture. He used his director privileges to disband the alliance, resulting in the loss of sovereignty throughout BoB space. On an internal wiki, the reason he gave was that he was sick of BoB being arrogant and "OMG WE ARE BETTER THAN YOU," and that he'd had more fun in three days with an alt in goons than he'd had in three years as a director of BoB.

## Burn Jita as Pervasive Practice

The Burn Jita events are the perfect example of how *EVE* affords its players the tools to make their own game and how player blocs like goons can use these tools to remake the game in their own image. The system Jita is the major trading hub in Empire space. It has an ideal location and has long been the most populated player system. Although Jita is safely within high-sec space, more than once, goons have set it on fire. How and why they did this will show how goons have worked with *EVE*'s system and developers to remake the game in their own image.

"Ganking" is a method for destroying a target in Empire space despite the presence of CONCORD nonplayer police ships. Typically, an unprovoked attack in Empire space will bring an overwhelming force of CONCORD to instantly destroy the offending vessel. However, even in the most secure areas, CONCORD's reaction time will allow at least one attack to hit. Ganking, or "suicide ganking," is when a group of players band together in cheap ships with a high "alpha strike"—ships that do the most amount of damage in a single hit. Targets will typically be slow-moving and undefended freighters, particularly those using autopilot, who assume that CONCORD will be protecting them. One ship is tasked with "bumping" the target ship by directly running into it. This knocks the target ship off course and interrupts its warp sequence, allowing time for the target to be called and the ganking ships to warp in and make the alpha strike. Almost instantaneously after the missiles hit, CONCORD will appear and destroy the ganking ships. If the gankers have estimated their strike capability and the target's defenses correctly, the target will also be destroyed. The bumping ship, which did not get marked as an aggressor simply for running into another ship, can pick up any loot dropped by the target, or other ships may warp in to collect the loot.

During the Burn Jita events, the goon ganking organization Ministry of Love organized mass groups of suicide gankers in the Jita system. The events were heavily advertised on both the official *EVE* forums and on the corporation's forums—the first advertisement was a warning, the second was recruitment. All members of Goonswarm and its allies were encouraged to participate, even if they had no experience in ganking. Fittings were recommended beforehand. Enterprising players provided set contracts of several ships for ganking players. Many experienced gankers served as bumpers. Goons and allies set up several ganking teams on each gate into Jita. Any ship entering Jita space could be a target, but in practice haulers using autopilot were the primary targets.

Goons saw the first Burn Jita event as a way to shake up Empire space. They wanted to teach a lesson to players who flew freighters on autopilot—that you are not playing *EVE* alone, that you are not safe. Carebear haulers in high-sec are the antithesis of goons; they don't interact with others much at all, much less attempt to harass them. Goons sought to teach players what kind of game they were playing. This is why they posted a warning on the *EVE* forums. Players who read the forums would be those who were engaged in the community, not just playing a boring game of "watch-the-numbers-go-up." One participant said, "You can burn Jita with, gosh, maybe a couple weeks of training? There's a very democratic sentiment about it" (personal interview, 2014).

CCP Games also had warning of the first Burn Jita event and thoroughly supported it from the server end: it moved Jita to its strongest server. The event also allowed CCP to test the performance of its Time Dilation (TiDi) system in high-sec space, because the TiDi system was designed to slow time for massive fleet fights in null-sec. CCP was proud of the Burn Jita event, as it showed off its "unrestricted player movement and limitless player choice in a single, shared game universe" (*EVE* Community 2013). It was "amazed" at what its players were doing in the world they had made and encouraged them to "make your stories happen!"

The second Burn Jita event took place in a far different context, although unexpectedly. Goons had already been planning Burn Jita 2 prior to the *EVE* Fanfest in Reykjavik. At the Fanfest, a scandal enveloped The Mittani, goons, and CCP. As part of his planned presentation, The Mittani made fun of a mail he'd received from a player who had been ganked and scammed by goons, in which the player claimed to be contemplating suicide. Off the cuff, he added the character's name, suggesting that other players harass him into killing himself. In an apology, The Mittani said that he went over the line in saying that anyone should try to make the player kill himself in real life. As a result, The Mittani was booted from the CSM and banned from the game for thirty days.

The Mittani made a State of the Goonion address before Burn Jita 2, affirming that the event would occur as planned, on the day his ban was lifted. He saw CCP's reaction as being influenced by the higher profile of the event. CCP was promoting Dust and had many journalists in attendance who might not have been covering such an event normally. As a result, there was some concern that the scandal would represent a sea change for CCP, which would begin to crack down on bad behavior in-game. The Mittani said in the State of the Goonion, "We must wait and see, when I am banned, whether *EVE* is the *EVE* we know and love." In that context, Burn Jita became less of a fun experiment in griefing and more of a test of whether goons could still be goons in *EVE*:

> We are going to go to the heart of high-sec, the beating heart of *EVE Online*, and we are going to stab it repeatedly. And, if CCP is still the old CCP, this will be heralded as an amazing in-game event, a "Free Mittani" event, as it were, my first day out of the box. . . . If there is some kind of crackdown on Goonswarm being Goonswarm, then we will have more information and can make an informed decision on how we proceed. I know that after we have had conflicts in the past with CCP . . . we basically went to war with CCP. It was a disaster. We are not going to do that this time. . . . You can't shoot CCP with a laser.

In the conflict with BoB, Goonswarm had led a campaign against developer influence in the game that was ultimately seen as futile. Now, goons see themselves as co-creators of *EVE* with a CCP that shares some of their values. High-sec is designed to be safe, and ganking is a difficult work-around. CCP didn't imagine an event like Burn Jita in its original design for the game—but it was willing to adapt its systems to handle it. In the second Burn Jita, goons wanted to know if CCP was still willing to work with them to create a fun version of *EVE*. Thus goons co-create the world of *EVE* not through official petitions and the CSM (although they have always had a seat) but through being assholes and pushing against the system to play the game they want.

Burn Jita is more than an emergent behavior between players and games. It is the result of a particular group of players attempting to enact their own project onto the systems of *EVE*. Burn Jita occurs because goons want *EVE* to be social, because they see themselves as separate from pubbies, and because they treat constructed systems like assholes. This makes Burn Jita a perfect example of how the goon project is enacted through pervasive practice.

## Conclusion

Why have goons been so successful in enacting the goon project in *EVE* Online in particular? *EVE* is built in a way that appeals to goon culture. Even though "*EVE* is a terrible-ass game with terrible mechanics, [it has] enough leeway on how you can choose to play your own game that it's fun with the right people" (personal interview, 2014). Like the physics objects in the office in *Max Payne 2* that Lowtax could knock down to fulfill his dream of being a giant asshole, *EVE* is full of complex structures built by players and developers that goons can knock down as they refuse to take seriously the business of Internet spaceships.

But the structures CCP set up are not the whole game. Burn Jita is not an event that emerged spontaneously from the code, nor did it arise from the emergent behavior of freely acting individuals—it could not have happened without the pervasive practice of goons and their values. Understanding Burn Jita and other projects enacted in complex games means seeing emergent behavior as more than the result of individual agency; it is also the result of social values that are enacted as a group.

Furthermore, this chapter shows that considering online games as projects rather than worlds helps explain the ways that players use them. Burn Jita is only one example of a major in-game event that did not emerge from the formal properties of the game but from the project that goons undertook within it. Recruitment scams, the "Shoot blues, tell Vile Rat" memorial, and even the First Great War with BoB also could not have happened from individuals acting with *EVE*'s systems alone. The examples here show that some players' projects will be pervasive, entering from a social world outside the game and interacting with the systems set up in the game so that new practices emerge.

More broadly, this research challenges the idea of games as things with formal properties. Goons don't play *EVE* to get the strongest character or the biggest ship. They don't enjoy ratting, mining, or industry in and of itself. This is why they say that "*EVE* is a bad game." In its formal aspects, *EVE* has often been a bad game. It's unintuitive, difficult, unbalanced, and often dull. That's why goons don't play *EVE*; they play Something Awful.

## BIBLIOGRAPHY

Bainbridge, W. S. 2012. *The Warcraft Civilization*. Cambridge, Mass.: MIT Press.

Bakioglu, B. S. 2009. "Spectacular Interventions of Second Life: Goon Culture, Griefing, and Disruption in Virtual Spaces." *Journal of Virtual Worlds Research* 1, no. 3. https://journals.tdl.org/jvwr/index.php/jvwr/article/view/348.

Boellstorff, Tom. 2008. *Coming of Age in Second Life: An Anthropologist Explores the Virtually Human*. Princeton, N.J.: Princeton University Press.

Castronova, E. 2001. "Virtual Worlds: A First-Hand Account of Market and Society on the Cyberian

Frontier." *The Gruter Institute Working Papers on Law, Economics, and Evolutionary Biology* 2, no. 1. http://papers.ssrn.com/sol3/Papers.cfm?abstract_id=294828.

Consalvo, M. 2007. *Cheating: Gaining Advantage in Videogames.* Cambridge, Mass.: MIT Press.

Dibbell, J. 2006. *Play Money, or, How I Quit My Day Job and Made Millions Trading Virtual Loot.* Reprint ed. New York: Basic Books.

———. 2008. "Mutilated Furries, Flying Phalluses: Put the Blame on Griefers, the Sociopaths of the Virtual World." *Wired Magazine,* January 18.

DOTLAN. n.d. "EveMaps. VFK-IV VI—Moon 1—Mittanigrad—Outpost." http://evemaps.dotlan.net/outpost/VFK-IV.

Edwards, T. 2011. "*Eve Online* Players Protest against Monocle Prices/Microtransactions. Lasers Involved." *PC Gamer,* June 25. http://www.pcgamer.com/2011/06/25/eve-online-players-protest-against-monocle-pricesmicrotransactions-lasers-involved/.

*EVE* Community. 2013. "Observing the Burn Jita Player Event." May 2. http://community.eveonline.com/news/dev-blogs/28640.

Golub, A. 2010. "Being in the World (of Warcraft): Raiding, Realism, and Knowledge Production in a Massively Multiplayer Online Game." *Anthropological Quarterly* 83, no. 1: 17–45.

Golub, A., and K. Lingley. 2008. "'Just Like the Qing Empire': Internet Addiction, MMOGs, and Moral Crisis in Contemporary China." *Games and Culture* 3, no. 1: 59–75.

Kasik, Chris, and John Walsh, writers. 2005. *Attack of the Show!* Season 1, episode 123, aired July 6. United States: G4 Television.

Kyanka, Rich "Lowtax." 2003. "M*ax Payne 2* and Asshole Physics." Something Awful, October 21. http://www.somethingawful.com/news/max-payne-asshole/.

Lehdonvirta, V. 2010. "Virtual Worlds Don't Exist: Questioning the Dichotomous Approach in MMO Studies." *Game Studies* 10, no. 1. http://gamestudies.org/1001/articles/lehdonvirta.

Malaby, T. M. 2011. *Making Virtual Worlds: Linden Lab and Second Life.* Ithaca, N.Y.: Cornell University Press.

Martuk. 2011. "*EVE Online* Ponzi Scheme Claims over 1 Trillion ISK from Players." Ten Ton Hammer, August 12. http://www.tentonhammer.com/eve/news/eve-online-ponzi-scheme-claims-over-1-trillion-isk-from-players.

Myers, D. 2007. "Self and Selfishness in Online Social Play." Paper presented at Situated Play, Digital Games Research Association Conference, Tokyo, September.

Ondrejka, C. 2007. "Collapsing Geography (Second Life, Innovation, and the Future of National Power)." *Innovations: Technology, Governance, Globalization* 2, no. 3: 27–54.

Page, R. 2012. "Leveling Up: Playerkilling as Ethical Self-Cultivation." *Games and Culture* 7, no. 3: 238–57.

Pearce, C. 2009. *Communities of Play: Emergent Cultures in Multiplayer Games and Virtual Worlds.* Illustrated ed. Cambridge, Mass.: MIT Press.

Something Awful. n.d. "Forum Rules." http://www.somethingawful.com/forum-rules/forum-rules/.

Straker. 2010. "Re: *EVE* ONLINE—Laugh Even More at *EVE* Goons Who Can't Keep Things from Being Stolen" (online forum thread). Something Awful Forums, February 3. http://forums.somethingawful.com/showthread.php?threadid=3210674&pagenumber=243.

## The Accidental Spymaster

*Keith Harrison*

In my early twenties, I accidentally applied to become a spy. Having graduated with a degree in law—and having firmly decided that a lifetime spent conveyancing houses in Auchtermuchty was not for me—I found myself perilously close to having to go out and get a real job. Determined not to do so until every last, plausible alternative had been exhausted, I applied to St. Andrews University to study in its Department of International Relations. The course was run by Professor Paul Wilkinson, sadly now deceased, but then a specialist in terrorist studies who would go on to become a fixture on television news in the aftermath of 9/11. Shortly after the course began, Professor Wilkinson took small groups of us aside and mentioned in an offhand manner that, should any of us be interested, the British domestic intelligence services did take a keen interest in graduates from the course, and further contacts could be arranged should we wish to avail ourselves of this job opportunity. A politically active Scottish nationalist, I gratefully declined, never suspecting that the lectures and lessons my parents were generously funding would eventually prepare me to be head of an entire (if somewhat imaginary) intelligence agency, using many of the techniques and methods learned during that year.

For many years, I have played the game *EVE Online* as a member of Goonswarm Alliance, a group of approximately twelve thousand in-game characters drawn primarily from the Something Awful discussion boards and the leading force in a coalition involving some thirty thousand players, the largest in *EVE*'s history. For about half a decade, I have been head of the Goonswarm Intelligence Agency (GIA), under the somewhat underwhelming *nom d'espionnage* "Endie." Still, as code names go, it surely beats "M."

If I suggest that the core of what the GIA does is, at least in abstract, broadly similar to the functionality of any modern, Western state (or even nonstate) intelligence-gathering structure, then the reader may experience the insistently strident sound of alarm bells ringing: the suspicion would be that I am at best rather too involved in the task to look at it dispassionately and at worst so immersed in role-playing a far-future, spacefaring spylord that I am incapable of rational discernment.

Of course, the apparent, surface similarities between our activities in the GIA and those of real-world intelligence agencies lead to a quite conscious mapping of those tasks, and of the methodology involved, onto the ground of conventional intelligence work. This is encouraged and accelerated because generations of both factual and fictional representations of the intelligence community have lent the role of "spy" many apparently aspirational aspects: why would I *not* want to be a "spymaster," after all? And, given the setting, it is quite fitting that we often use a traditional, quite le Carréian term to describe this aspect of *EVE Online*: "the intelligence *game.*"

It is perhaps even more fitting that this difficulty of unpicking the map of our created, in-game structures from the ground of traditional intelligence work occurs in the virtual reality of a game. Baudrillard would be quite comfortable with the ultimate unreality of all of the resulting, in-game structures and goals. All of this activity, work, and technique are mere simulations of intelligence work carried out in pursuit of goals and aims within a game which is itself a simulacrum of a science fiction universe necessarily utterly without reality.

More mundanely, what the GIA does is use a combination of social engineering and technical methodology to gather and analyze information on friendly, neutral, and hostile groups in *EVE Online* to identify risks and opportunities and to allow our leadership to make informed decisions. It is, at the risk of putting you off, an overwhelmingly dull task. To persuade you to keep reading, I shall employ heavy-handed foreshadowing: down through the years, it has also involved brushes with honey-traps and borderline domestic terrorism.

## An Imaginary War

To understand the purpose of intelligence gathering in *EVE*, it is necessary to understand only one key facet of *EVE* game play: *EVE* involves vast amounts of effort. Many wars in *EVE* involve tens of thousands of people, and each player will at a minimum require virtual spaceships, a supply of ammunition and fuel for those ships, and defended staging locations for that matériel. To provide all this for a major offensive can easily take a week or more of preparation and thousands of hours of preparatory logistical effort. For the defender to respond will take a similar degree of effort, all of which will occur under the pressure of an attack.

The ability to know in advance where an enemy will attack, and what doctrinal choices he has made, is therefore extremely valuable: defending fleet commanders can choose counters to the hostile ship doctrines and can hamper logistical efforts, while agents can ensure that vital fuel goes missing or defensive bases fail. The job of intelligence agencies in *EVE* is to provide just such information to leaders and inflict such disruption on enemies.

As with traditional intelligence agencies, the key methods of gaining information about the intentions of enemies in *EVE* divide fairly neatly into human intelligence and signals intelligence. The former involves information gleaned from placed agents, turned informers, and reported chatter. The latter involves the (largely automated) interception of communications.

## Signals Intelligence

Each character in *EVE* has something called an application programming interface (API) key attached to it. This lengthy string of numbers and letters grants access to information about that character: its location, its possessions, the amount of money in its wallet, and so forth. It also allows access to any e-mails that that character has sent or received. Historically, this was extremely valuable: alliances and corporations in *EVE* used *EVE*'s built-in mail system to send orders and to communicate plans. Possession of these keys was much sought after, and the GIA possessed thousands of them, gleaned via various methods, often involving misdirection and deceit. At one time, we regularly read the personal EveMails of the leadership of those with whom we were at war and were able to use the resulting information in a manner that was highly destructive of hostile morale.

The key to effectively using the deluge of information—most of it irrelevant—that this method provided was based in software: analysts would learn to skim the hundreds of EveMails that were flagged for interest each day, but without bespoke software that we wrote and maintained, the task would have been overwhelming.

We, however, no longer make much use of API keys. Partly, this is because our enemies are wise to the use that we and others have made of them. Indeed, sites such as EveSkunk, which publicly post the mailbox contents of those whose API keys they have acquired, have raised awareness of the insecurity of EveMail, and most people now use external communications clients (some of which, with the use of further bespoke software and the help of inserted agents, we are also able to relay and monitor).

Partly, however, we have discontinued the use of stolen APIs because of the untested but potentially problematic legal issues involving the use of private information without the explicit consent of the party granting access. CCP Games has, for many years, *tacitly* accepted this use of the API key. That said, the web of relationships here is a complex one involving the player who pays for the character with which the API is associated; her in-game corporation and alliance; the out-of-game web presence of those same groups, which will often require explicit confirmation that a key is not "stolen"; CCP as game developers and key providers; and the agency using the API key for implicitly malicious purposes. My first degree having been in law, I am extremely averse to empirically testing the legal virtues of the defense that "it was only a game!"

This argument that "it's only a game" frequently leads individuals from other intelligence agencies in *EVE* to walk what we view as being some very risky lines, however. Other agencies, often lacking the numbers to adopt our brute-force approach to inserting agents wherever they are needed, use purloined API keys to "prove" their identity and register on the websites, team communication services, and forums of their enemies to glean information, cause damage, and so forth.

## Human Intelligence

Far superior to signals intelligence, in any case, is the use of agents. The ideal is to place someone you know is loyal in a low-level position in a hostile alliance and have that person work his way into a leadership position over a matter of months or years. Indeed, I started in the *EVE* intelligence game as such an agent myself, and in one tasking eventually became head of counterintelligence for a hostile group, allowing me merrily to burn innocent members while giving clean bills of health to our own spies.

We do this on a substantial scale in the GIA: periodically, we will recruit and train new agents in basic fieldcraft before sending them out to infiltrate targets. Although carried out individually so that no new agent can burn any others, this will usually involve us training ten to fifteen new agents over a period of a couple of weeks, of whom four or five at most will ever feed back actionable intelligence.

This training and preparation will usually involve the use of remote proxies and virtual private networks to mask their online identities, but in some cases, it will go as far as creating fictional, out-of-game identities—"legends"—involving Facebook and Twitter accounts that will stand up to a degree of investigation by hostile counterintelligence teams often run by more than just hobbyists. Goonswarm's own counterintel team, quite separate from the GIA, is run by an experienced information security professional—a state of affairs that is far from unusual.

Handling these agents is by far the most onerous and time-consuming aspect of our work, and agent handlers burn out frequently. Each agent will, on average, require several hours of conversation per week, and we often have several dozen agents active in the field. This can amount to hundreds of hours of conversation per week—fortunately with each handler able to carry on simultaneous conversations with several agents, owing to the nature of text-based communication—spread across all major time zones. Even when not providing intelligence, agents isolated from their "home" group require this attention to persuade them that what they are doing is valuable. They are, after all, playing what is often a fairly joyless online game with people they do not like, while putting in the hours and hard work to persuade those same people that the agent is worthy of promotion and trust. Where we have planted an agent on the pretext of her being a turncoat, the handler is often her only link to Goonswarm, most of whose members believe that they have betrayed the alliance.

Inserting agents takes time and work and cannot be done in time to provide valuable intelligence (or to carry out useful sabotage) when a conflict begins. Therefore agents have to spend time spying on a target, which often seems pointless, harmless, and even irrelevant. As a result, many burn out, and a few get caught before we can ever use them to gain useful intelligence in an *EVE* conflict. One agent even "went native" (although he was detected as having done so before he could do any serious harm).

Volunteer agents from hostile alliances—"walk-ins"—shortcut this issue and can decide wars: in the Fountain War of 2013, the head of hostile reconnaissance worked for us, and we were able to use streaming technology to provide a real-time audio feed from our enemies' voice command channels. However, as with any intelligence agency faced with a walk-in, it can take a great deal of time to ensure that we are not the target of a hostile insertion effort, and such an agent is rarely fully trusted until after that particular conflict is complete.

There is also what we call the "Enigma problem," referring to the limited use that the World War II Allies were able to make of Enigma decrypts: though they could have consistently steered convoys around U-boat wolf packs with great success, by doing so, they would have risked alerting the Germans to the existence and, ultimately, the source of that information. Similarly, the regular use of spy intel in *EVE*, especially on the tactical level, allows hostile counterintel teams to narrow down what fleets an agent was in and what intelligence she had access to, and eventually to burn her. The more valuable and highly placed the agent, the fewer the number of people who have access to the intelligence that the agent provides, and the easier it is, therefore, to identify her. Conversely, failing to use the intelligence provided by an agent discourages the agent and can lead to her burning out.

When one considers the thousands of hours of work, most of it dull and much of it fruitless, the question inevitably arises as to whether it really qualifies as play. Although the targets and goals are based in a fictionalized setting, has a line been crossed between game and work? The best I can confidently say is that, if it has assumed many of the aspects of an occupation, at least I enjoy my job.

## Fear and Loathing

On a conventional battlefield, one of the advantages of possessing biochemical or chemical weapons is that your opponent has to constantly bear that fact in mind: if your opponent believes that you might use those weapons, then your opponent's troops must fight (at greatly reduced efficiency) in suitable clothing, and their logistics chain must support the extra cost of their preparations.

Similarly, one of the most important functions of the GIA is to impose costs on our enemies, even when we have failed to penetrate them. By introducing paranoia and suspicion into their calculations, we degrade their efficiency. For instance, newer players are often among the most enthusiastic and will cheerily volunteer to perform boring, dull, repetitive, but vital logistical in-game tasks for their alliances. This takes much of the burden off the shoulders of an alliance's trusted cadre of veteran players and leaders, while bonding the newer players more closely to the group's identity.

It is thus a vital role of the GIA to ensure that our enemies cannot trust these younger characters and to deny them the ability to leverage their energy in this way. We can do this simply by making it clear that we are *attempting* to insert agents into them, meaning that any of these bright-eyed ingénues may, in fact, be a GIA mole feigning enthusiasm to inveigle themselves into the alliance and from there either to gather intel or to disable defenses at a vital moment.

*EVE* players regularly meet up in real life: this can provide a degree of perceived security, although nothing prevents agents attending such meet-ups to persuade targets of their bona fides. Indeed, the turned agent who destroyed Band of Brothers (an incident that dramatically changed the course of *EVE* history and was the turning point in a *five-year-long EVE* war) was well known to, and trusted by, those he betrayed. However, limiting those whom hostile targets' leadership can trust to such a geographically challenged inner circle or real-world associates would constitute a major limitation upon them.

Where we do have some penetration, one of the more ethically problematic aspects of *EVE* intelligence work is possible. One can judiciously use garnered intelligence to frame innocent leading individuals within a hostile alliance. This, in turn, can cause sufficient paranoia about fiendish infiltrators and fifth columnists to cause finger-pointing and suspicion between entirely loyal members. These "circular firing squads" have helped hasten the end of several of our enemies.

This latter approach, to someone not immersed in *EVE Online,* may seem actively distasteful. Norms of behavior within *EVE* are, however, substantially different from those in many other online games (and radically different from those outside of gaming): asked to describe the game, many players will at some point use the term "dark," and aspects of *EVE* game play involving theft, sabotage, and fraud are lionized. Those of us who become involved in the top levels of the "metagame"—those aspects of the game that occur outside of the game play mechanics of the *EVE* client and server software—tend to accept that our in-game relationships with other players may be targeted.

## The Wild Frontier

I have stressed the dull and repetitive nature of much of the work the GIA does to help Goonswarm "win" in *EVE*: endless hours of agent handling and information analysis, mixed with the use of software. I'll finish with some of the more colorful examples of when a somewhat overcompetitive approach has crept into the *EVE Online* intelligence milieu.

One of my predecessors, as head of the GIA, was once approached by members of a Russian group with whom our bloc shared interests: could he provide the home address of a certain hostile, U.K.-based player? When he inquired as to the reason for the request, the Russians' plan was at least simple: provided with the address, two of their London-based compatriots would, during a major fight, cut the power to the player's house, leaving his (strategically important) ship vulnerable in-game, where it could then be destroyed. We, of course, demurred: *EVE* is all fun and games, until someone wakes up at 5:30 A.M. to a visit from armed police.

On another occasion, and one that reflects less gloriously on the moral judgments made by leading players of *EVE Online*, the GIA was asked to find out whether any of the workers at CCP Games (*EVE*'s developers) happened to be "usefully homosexual," signaling an intended approach that would have sat easily in the context of the 1950s Cold War spy game but that was perhaps somewhat extreme when viewed through the frame of twenty-first-century Internet gaming. Naturally, the GIA politely declined this particular tasking.

Finally, in 2014, a Russian alliance was revealed as having asked its members to download an add-on for the audio-conferencing software Teamspeak, which many alliances use for online communication. For an alliance to ask members to install additional software on their PCs is a little unusual, and one individual decompiled the add-on to find out just what it was trying to do on the client computer. Screenshots were posted, bounties were paid, and accusations flew between various individuals regarding misinformation and malpractice, but the gist was that the plug-in searched through various disk locations to locate and upload user data, including logs of conversations and considerable nongame information. Given that this alliance contained both Russian and Ukrainian players, and that it occurred at around the peak of the crisis over the Crimea, this was a particularly troublesome blending of the real and the virtual.

## Make Straight in the Desert a Highway

Strip away the imaginary spaceships, the science fiction jargon, and the essentially arbitrary goals, and you are left with an organization whose aim is to gather and analyze data to advance the interests of that organization and of its parent group.

Though the language and methodology of what I have described clearly borrow heavily from traditional intelligence work, it is intriguing to wonder to what extent conventional intelligence agencies may already be encountering many of the same challenges we have met in dealing with gathering and analyzing data on potential threats in a purely online environment.

As with so many fledgling organizations on today's Internet, the real question is how to monetize it. You don't know of any small countries who need an established, if perhaps somewhat unconventional, intelligence agency, do you?

## The Evolution of Player Organizations

A Goonswarm Perspective

*The Mittani (Alexander Gianturco)*

When we talk about or play online games, there are online games, and then there is *EVE Online.* When a player or guild kills a raid boss in a standard fantasy massively multiplayer online game like *World of Warcraft,* no one cares—perhaps at most a hundred people have been affected by the event. When a devastating war or particularly catastrophic battle takes place in *EVE Online,* tens of thousands of players participate directly, hundreds of thousands more are impacted in tangible ways, and one must field calls from the BBC, the *New York Times, Wired,* and the *Wall Street Journal.*

These player conflicts—the Great Wars, the Battle of Asakai, and, most recently, the titanic slaughter in BR-5—revolve around pixelated spaceships blowing one another up on the Internet in a computer game. The nuances of the attributes of the spaceships and the warfleets they comprise is of only specialized interest; what captures the imagination about *EVE Online* among both the wider nonplaying public and the mainstream media is the sheer scale at which these forces clash. The largest player organization in an online game outside of *EVE* may have perhaps a thousand members; typical games limit organization size to five hundred members or fewer, and most games also have sharded server environments with a total population of three thousand people or fewer per shard. *EVE Online,* with no sharding, places all of its players together like rats trapped in a cage, a sandbox with barely any rules except force of arms.

For several years now, I have been the simultaneous leader of a corporation, an alliance, and a coalition in *EVE Online*; I lead the corporation Goonwaffe, the alliance Goonswarm Federation (GSF), and a coalition of alliances called the Clusterfuck Coalition, known as the CFC in polite company. In practice, this means that I am in direct command of approximately forty thousand human beings. My daily play revolves around making sure that our membership is protected against our many enemies, supplied with the best material available, led in battle by the best fleet commanders, supported by generous reimbursement programs, and mentored in the arcane yet critical nuances of this extraordinarily complicated game.

Almost none of this involves actually playing *EVE Online*. Between 2005 and the present day, I have logged in to the *EVE Online* client on my computer—that is, "played *EVE Online*" as most would conceive of it—a relative handful of times. For most players, *EVE Online* is about spaceships flying around in a piece of software; however, for me and a few other "pure-metagame" players, *EVE Online* is a chat program, a kanban board, and a network of connections, institutions, organizations, and cultures that my compatriots and I have worked to create, defend, and strengthen.

What has kept me fascinated and engaged with *EVE*—despite finding the client itself rather tiresome—is the people within the game and how they behave in large organizations in an environment with very few rules. In *EVE Online*, the scale of player groups means that one can witness the evolution of player organizations from small, loosely organized tribal entities through a clearly demarcated feudal era toward what we see today—the creations of coalitions and blocs that mirror the functions and institutions of modern nation-states, complete with bureaucratic departments, communications networks, and extensive social programs. While this has happened, the sandbox of *EVE* has provided an opportunity for players to experiment with a number of governmental systems and test them in no-holds-barred warfare against one another.

To give the academic reader an idea of what makes *EVE* wildly different from other games, I'm going to give an example of how I "play" *EVE* on a typical day and a picture of how GSF, the alliance I lead, operates and interacts with its allies within the CFC bloc. Then we'll discuss the evolution of player organizations in *EVE*, from tribal to feudal to modern federated states, and the proliferation of squads and microtribes under the banner of these massive institutions. We'll cover player governments in *EVE* and whether they are an example of a nightmarish autocracy right out of Fromm or an example of radical postscarcity democracy.

Most days, my playing *EVE* involves a real-time chat program called Jabber, a secured forum (Goonfleet.com), a task management system called Trello to monitor the projects of our various directorate departments, and a whole host of custom-designed software to manage our in-game infrastructure and social programs. Depending on how you choose to define *play*, one could argue that I almost never play *EVE* or that—so long as I am communicating with someone about the game or contemplating it—I am incessantly playing *EVE*. My Jabber client usually has approximately thirty chat rooms open, each with secured access to a particular organization in Goonswarm Federation—the logistics group, the diplomatic corps, the military coordination war room, our real-time intel relay, and, of course, Illuminati, the infamous GSF directorate channel.

The tempo and style of play depend largely on whether we are at war or peace; during peacetime, I play *EVE* by chatting with directors or my chiefs of staff to focus on projects to improve the alliance. One example is an attempt to restructure the in-centives in our peacetime reimbursement program, through which the alliance re-funds line members the costs of losing combat ships outside of strategic-level fleets to nudge those players toward recreational player versus player combat to improve their skills. Another common example involves fixing a malfunctioning organization within the alliance, where we need to replace an inactive or incompetent director and change the structure of that organization to ensure that it doesn't break down in the same way in the future. This is all rather dull if you prefer Internet spaceship violence and primarily involves chatting—lots of chatting—but I have become convinced over the years that it is the relentless institutional tinkering and obsession with best prac-tices during peacetime that has allowed GSF to succeed and develop such resilience compared to our competitors.

Wartime is very different. I distinguish idle messing about—fleets blowing one another up in low-stakes conflicts for fun—from serious warfare, which is any conflict with substantial stakes for the survival of one's alliance or one's allies: usually an attempt to capture or defend a region of sovereign space in null-sec. During war, I still don't log in to *EVE,* unless it's a situation where I absolutely need to "wave the flag" to fill up fleets, but I'm constantly on call: the directorate has my phone number, and if a crisis erupts when I'm asleep, I'm shaken out of bed to deal with it. This was how B-R5, the famous Battle of the Titans, began for me; on barely two hours of sleep, my phone exploded with our lead fleet commander informing me that he wanted to drop on our foes and go all-in, committing our entire supercapital fleet; I gave clear-ance, and the next twenty-one hours were a hellish blur of coordination, anxiety, and, finally, victory.

During these pivotal battles, I am usually perched in command channels on our coalition Mumble server, bouncing between fleets—each in its own segregated channel—relaying information from spies, ensuring that order is maintained, spin-ning up new fleets or merging existing ones, and trying to make life easier for our fleet commanders, all to ensure that thousands of players arrive at their objective in a coordinated way in the appropriate ships. The most extreme case of this type of task was the Battle of 6VDT, which involved some four thousand players engaged in a single system during the Fountain War. When we found ourselves confronted with twenty-four hundred players participating on our side, the organization of our own fleets on a deadline proved to be more of a challenge than actually defeating the foe. With a maximum of 250 players in any given fleet and multiple command roles re-quired for each (commander, backup commander, scout, intel relay, logistics anchor, etc.), it was a mad scramble to get every role filled as needed and the ships en route to the target on time, without losing a fleet in the shuffle. We managed—with some seventeen separate fleets, coordinated under a unified command with tight doctrinal discipline—and were victorious.

GSF has itself become such a large organization over the years that the leadership position almost necessitates a pure-metagame management style. To govern our approximately twelve thousand line members, we've learned the hard way that one cannot afford single-person dependencies in any aspect of the alliance, including my own position—should I be unavailable, there are two chiefs of staff who can speak for me. Each primary organization has a team of directors working in concert to maintain it. Logistics keeps our in-game infrastructure maintained, Finance levies taxes and manages investments and rental programs, Fleet Command handles war fighting, Reimbursement ensures that our pilots are able to fly and lose their warships without any personal cost, Corps Diplomatique works to smooth relations with allies and enemies alike, and the Recon and Intelligence teams provide our eyes and ears on the field and from within our foe's own ranks. Under each director team (between three and eight, depending on organization size and complexity) is a staff of subdirectors and line members working toward fulfilling their particular function in the alliance, networked via real-time chat on Jabber across every time zone, every day. The level of complexity comfortably dwarfs that of many real-world multinational corporations.

Beyond GSF itself are ten allied alliances that make up the CFC bloc, raising our total community size to approximately forty thousand players. These allied alliances have their own independent internal structures; though GSF may lead the bloc in times of war, in peacetime, each entity in the CFC enjoys total freedom to run its organizations how it sees fit within a loose federal structure.

These structures evolved out of necessity and competitive pressure as the social system of *EVE* has developed since the game's launch in 2003. In the early days, the first unit of social order was the corporation—like the guilds of any other online game. Bringing in allies to help swing the tide of a conflict is a time-honored strategy in warfare, and groups of corporations began working together regularly, whereupon CCP Games implemented the alliance mechanic to formalize these structures within the game itself. Smaller organizations don't need complex structures; like a tribal unit, everyone knows almost everyone else within the group, and the needs of the organization don't need a layer of management. However, organization and numbers win wars, so as time went by, alliances grew ever larger to become more militarily effective and, during their wars, would call on still more alliances to assist them—gradually forming the coalition and bloc system we see today, where a bloc war can easily see fifty thousand players on each side.

Perhaps the single most important innovation in the expanding size of *EVE*'s player organizations is the federated Jabber server, allowing members of multiple alliances to receive broadcast information from alliances within their own bloc. As an example, within the CFC, an alliance like Executive Outcomes hosts its own Jabber system for members, yet because of Jabber relays, its membership receives fleet announcements and alerts from the CFC as a whole. Perhaps more important, Jabber runs independently of the *EVE* servers, meaning that a player can be doing something else entirely—working or playing a different game—and still participate, socialize, and receive combat alerts from her alliance and coalition, and log into *EVE* to join a fleet if she so chooses. Instead of planning ahead and reading a forum post in hopes of remembering when a fleet will form sometime in the future, an alert pings the player on his desktop the moment a fleet commander or director sends a Jabber broadcast.

A notable trend counter to the ever-increasing size and organization of these player-created pseudo-states is the emergence of microcultures within the overarching umbrella of an alliance. As alliance sizes have grown far beyond Dunbar's number and developed their own institutions and bureaucracies, informal or semiformal player "squadrons" have become popular as social groups, the kind of tribal family where everyone knows your name. These are not military entities with any formal structure mandated by alliance leadership and tend to resemble neighborhood bowling leagues. Examples within GSF include Theta Squad (obsessed with making money), European Goonion (European-based players with a focus on high-skill combat), Hole Squad (living in and camping out in wormhole space), Space Violence (anything and everything to do with the region Syndicate), and TopGoon (a curious combination of scamming, hostile players, and "black ops hot drop" combat tactics). These squads give players who are part of a vast and possibly faceless organization an in-group to belong to as part of a greater whole.

The brutal Darwinian process of organizational conflict in *EVE* has given players the opportunity to competitively test the effectiveness of various alliance governments. Just as the size and complexity of these alliances have grown over time, so have systems of alliance government evolved along a continuum. Although the mechanics of the game itself render the CEO of each corporation in *EVE* a dictator of sorts, the fact that each player can leave and join another corporation with no consequence brings up a curious situation—one can say an alliance or corporation leader is an autocrat, but, unlike in the real world, where actual tyranny can be applied to keep a population obedient, in the postscarcity universe of New Eden, players have complete freedom (assuming they are allowed to join an organization) to choose how they are governed, and by whom. *EVE* player government—on the face of it—appears to be a paean to an ingrained authoritarian and hierarchical leaning within the player base but may actually represent a form of radical democracy.

Perhaps because the mechanical underpinnings of the game allow this freedom to choose one's alliance, formal democratic systems in managing player entities have been an unmitigated disaster throughout *EVE*'s history. Hailing primarily from Western democracies, players in the early days of *EVE* would set up organizations run on "fair" principles cribbed from their own real-world governments and promptly found themselves paralyzed with competing interests and factionalized. Simple council structures of alliances saw each corporate CEO with an equal voice in the direction of the alliance, and this was no better: at every turn, these council-led alliances were outmatched in battle by autocratic alliances. The landscape of modern *EVE* does still have a few council systems in place—someone is always trying to reinvent the wheel—but the vast majority of conquerable space is concentrated in the hands of autocratic governments supported by their own institutions and bureaucracies. Given the option of choosing a vote or choosing a strong leader, the player base has overwhelmingly adopted this unique form of alienable autocracy.

One possible side effect of the rise of autocracies in *EVE*, the scale of their institutions, and the ubiquity of the federated Jabber server may be that a form of peace and stability (some might say stagnation), or "controlled warfare," is becoming the norm. Several years ago in the aftermath of the Great War, the leaders of all null-sec alliances and entities throughout the game began communicating via a Jabber channel called "Jabberlon5," created by Vile Rat, a reference to the *Babylon 5* television program. The sheer amount of fraternization and communication that has taken place among *EVE*'s ruling class since then has created a system where nominally hostile leaders regularly trade favors between each other and devastating blows against one another are softened or turned aside. In several situations, an autocrat in this club has lost a war, only to have a friend in Jabberlon5 offer a couch in the form of space and territory—gratis. For example, in the aftermath of the famous Battle of BR-5, where the forces of the CFC routed the side of Pandemic Legion and trapped the Legion's entire staging system of assets in a captured, CFC-held station, instead of twisting the knife and denying those assets to the Legion forever, the CFC simply opened the station to the Legion and allowed them to evacuate unmolested.

My personal theory on how the escalating size and complexity of player entities in *EVE* have come to pass revolves around how a player conceives of his identity within the game. At first, the player is a solo pilot; then he joins a corporation, then an alliance, then a coalition. How the player sees himself (sadly, in *EVE*, it is almost always a he) determines both his loyalty and his behavior—and the strength of the entity he has joined. A healthy alliance is full of players who think of themselves as primarily members of that alliance; an alliance that will shatter under pressure is full of players who identify only as members of their corporations or, worse, as individuals involved in the group only for their self-interest. In GSF, we have consistently defeated our enemies by taking hostile line members and shifting them from thinking of themselves as "I am Johnny Spaceman, a member of Band of Brothers" toward "I am Johnny Spaceman, a member of Reikoku, and although that corp is in an alliance called BoB, I really only care about my corpmates." We now have relatively stable coalitions in *EVE* simply because players are willing to identify themselves as members of "the CFC" or "N3" or "the RUS," beyond their own alliance, corporate, and personal identifications.

A number of interesting parallels within *EVE* to real-world structures and behaviors merit academic study. *EVE* has a good old boys' club, complete with golden parachutes. The structures of large alliances increasingly mirror those of real governments; the impact of universal real-time communication seems to have brought about a controlled reduction in destructive conflict. I suspect that *EVE* is ripe for investigation from a background in behavioral finance and psychology—many of our most useful best practices have come from these sources—and a nightmare for rational choice theorists. Unlike in other games academics have studied, there is no question that *EVE* players will rapidly utilize anything of practical use revealed by these investigations—against one another, of course.

# 11

# RIP Vile Rat

## Makeshift Memorials in *EVE Online*

*Martin R. Gibbs, Marcus Carter, and Joji Mori*

On September 11, 2012, the American diplomatic mission in Benghazi, Libya, was attacked several times by a large number of armed militia. Four American personnel were killed in the attacks, including the U.S. ambassador to Libya, Christopher Stevens, and Sean Smith, a Foreign Services information management officer with ten years' experience, a husband, and the father of two young children (Clinton 2012a). Two Embassy security personnel, Tyrone Wood and Glen Doherty, also died (Clinton 2012b).[1]

Sean Smith, aka Vile Rat, was also a prominent figure in the game *EVE Online*. Vile Rat was a key senior member of the alliance Goonswarm Federation and its many incarnations.[2] He was regarded as the "chief diplomat" and negotiator for Goonswarm, most recently for the Clusterfuck Coalition, an informal null-sec coalition of alliances with more than twenty thousand members. He was a former elected member of the game's Council of Stellar Management (CSM) and was a moderator on Goonswarm's Internet "home," the Something Awful forums (see chapter 8 for more on Goonswarm).

Public announcements from the U.S. State Department and eulogies by Hillary Clinton emphasized his public service, his family, and his long involvement in online virtual worlds:

> Sean leaves behind a loving wife, Heather, two young children, Samantha and Nathan, and scores of grieving family, friends, and colleagues. And that's just in this world, because online, in the virtual worlds that Sean helped create, he is also being mourned by countless competitors, collaborators, and gamers who shared his passion. (CBS Interactive, 2012)

News of the Benghazi attacks and of the death of American personnel was reported widely. In the mass media, many obituaries and reports on Sean Smith's death rarely failed to mention his involvement in *EVE Online* alongside his career in the State Department and the wife and two children he left behind (e.g., Associated Press 2012; Beckhusen 2012; Kaufman and Hauser 2012; Kushner 2013; Thier 2012). Obituaries also followed from the U.S. State Department (Clinton 2012a); CCP Games (CCP Xhagen 2012); the CSM (Heard 2012); moderators on the Something Awful forums (Parsons 2012b); and The Mittani (2012a), leader of Goonswarm and former chairman of the *EVE Online* CSM. Commemorative and often heartfelt comments on various blog and forum threads dedicated to Vile Rat quickly ran to thousands of posts in length. A charitable fund for Sean's family was organized on the crowd-sourced fund-raiser site YouCaring.com and raised US$25,000 within twelve hours, eventually collecting US$127,001 from 2,634 supporters (Dicker 2012; Mittani 2012b; Parsons 2012a; Totilo 2013). A Wikipedia page dedicated to Sean Smith as a notable person was quickly established (Wikipedia 2012), and within *EVE Online*, pilots appropriated various game resources to construct and perform a range of commemorative acts in his honor.

In this chapter, we examine the mobilization of various game features, mechanics, and resources to create memorials and perform commemorative acts in Vile Rat's honor within the *EVE Online* game world. We argue that these practices resemble other forms of vernacular, or "grassroots" (Margry and Sánchez-Carretero 2011), commemorative practices that often follow deaths, tragedies, and disasters. Although the specific forms and materials used were idiosyncratic to the *EVE Online* universe, these commemorative acts drew on ritual forms and symbolic repertoires common to other forms of spontaneous and improvised memorializations. This suggests further possibilities for employing memorialization in game design. In the concluding section of this chapter, we reflect on the unique features of *EVE Online* that encourage a social world with such rich and meaningful community practices.

## Vernacular Commemoration, Spontaneous Shrines, and Makeshift Memorials

In recent years, scholars have studied emerging forms of mortuary, ritual, and commemorative practices that are less bound to institutions such as the church and more meaningfully connected with everyday experiences and activities (Margry and Sánchez-Carretero 2011; Wouters 2002). Examples of ritual practices of these kinds include roadside memorials (Clark and Franzmann 2006); memory fences such as those found at sites of national tragedy, such as the Oklahoma bombing or the World Trade Center (Doss 2002); and the AIDS quilt (Hawkins 1993).

Throughout the 1960s and 1970s, in the Anglophone world at least, mourning became an increasingly privatized and individualized practice, and traditional and formal rites that made mourning a public and community affair waned (Wouters 2002). As mourning became less of a formal social obligation, or duty, and became more private, less ritualized, and more personal, opportunities for public expression and acknowledgment of personal grief also declined (Jorgensen-Earp and Lanzilotti 1998). This waning, along with increasing emphasis placed on the expression of individual authenticity and personal identity, gave rise to new ritualized forms of public mourning and expressions of grief that were more informal, individualized, and varied (Wouters 2002) and that were increasingly disconnected from traditional sacred institutions. Makeshift memorials and spontaneous shrines are important forms of these new ritualized practices for public mourning.

*Makeshift memorials* and *spontaneous shrines* are two common terms used to refer to the practice of depositing and carefully arranging various kinds of materials and memorabilia in public spaces in response to someone's death or other tragic events (Margry and Sánchez-Carretero 2011; Santino 2006). These practices came into widespread public consciousness in the 1980s and 1990s, although examples have been documented that date back to 1865 and 1963, following the assassinations of Abraham Lincoln and John F. Kennedy, respectively (Margry and Sánchez-Carretero 2011). They reached their apogee in the global reaction to the death of Princess Diana in 1997, which included, in London alone, "50 million bouquets of flowers, weighing some 10,000 tons, that were laid outside Buckingham Place and Diana's London residence of Kensington Place" (Brennan 2008, 328–29). By the time of Princess Diana's death, and through the public response to it, these makeshift memorial practices had reached a relatively stabilized and commonly understood ritualized form. As Brennan suggests, this event, along with the Hillsborough stadium disaster, "appeared to mark the revival (and invention) of half-forgotten customs and traditions" (328). Both of these cases involved creating and signing condolence books; observing a minute of silence; communally occupying public space; and creating, and making pilgrimage to, temporary memorial sites to leave a ritual offering and witness what others had left (Brennan 2008).

These temporary, improvised memorials usually spring up at places of significance in the individual and/or collective memory of the death or tragic event. For example, a makeshift memorial may appear outside a person's place of residence; a roadside memorial will mark the place of a fatal road accident; a spontaneous shrine will appear at the place where a missing person was last seen; or, most commonly, memorabilia and tributes will be left at the site of a tragic event or disaster. Makeshift memorials typically occupy and appropriate public space and often appear and grow quickly without planning or institutional approval (Jorgensen-Earp and Lanzilotti 1998).

Although often referred to as makeshift, these memorials are carefully constructed acts of bricolage. Items are carefully placed and arranged by visitors and are often positioned to create and maintain pleasing aesthetic arrangements, repeating patterns, layering, and framing of objects. Care is also taken with the selection of items, and the choice is often imbued with significance. The artifacts placed at makeshift memorials vary but tend to be drawn from a common repertoire (Grider 2001): flowers, balloons, candles, teddy bears and stuffed animals, photographs and drawings, handwritten notes and banners, and poetry and missives are common. Memorabilia and materials drawing on religious symbolism and paraphernalia, such as angels and crosses, are usual. Item selection is typically not random but imbued with significance for the events being commemorated. For example, teddy bears and soft toys were common at the site of the Oklahoma City bombing (Grider 2001), and handwritten poems and drawings depicting themes of rebirth were prevalent at sites commemorating the Black Saturday bushfires (Mori, Howard, and Gibbs 2012). Furthermore, makeshift memorials are often an expression of community and solidarity (Wouters 2002), social discontent, and protest (Margry and Sánchez-Carretero 2011) as well as being public expressions of grief and condolence. Wouters (2002, 2) suggests that "these public expressions signal a rising need to find more public recognition of personal mourning and that, via these rituals, participants are seeking to assert membership of a larger symbolic or 'imagined' community."

These forms of mourning rituals have also been adapted and spread through the Internet and social media (Brubaker and Hayes 2011; Marwick and Ellison 2012; Walter et al. 2011; Gibbs et al. 2015). Given the rise and acceptance of these forms of vernacular commemoration, and given the amount of leisure time people devote to online video games, and as people form social relations associated with these media, it is perhaps unsurprising to find that these games also become vehicles for expressing grief and for commemorating the deceased (Wachowski 2008). Game developers have been known to place memorials within games (Gibbs et al. 2012), and numerous examples of player-driven funeral rites conducted within multiplayer games can be found posted to video-hosting sites such as YouTube, involving the reappropriation of in-game items and practices for public expressions of grief and mourning. These videos, and the process of sharing them, further document the funeral commemoration and act to memorialize the dead. The most (in)famous of these is depicted in the YouTube video "Serenity Now Bombs a World of Warcraft Funeral" (Gibbs, Carter, and Mori 2013; Hollingsworth 2006), which depicts a public virtual funeral under attack by other players. In the following section of this chapter, we describe and analyze how *EVE Online* players used various game mechanics and features to construct memorials for Vile Rat in the *EVE Online* game world.

## RIP Vile Rat

In the days following Sean Smith's death, many players of *EVE Online* began constructing memorials within the game using a variety of game resources and mechanics. Figure 11.1 shows a list of in-game items placed in a public space that have been named with missives to Vile Rat. Many featured a version of "RIP Vile Rat" or the leave-taking, conversation closer often used in the *EVE Online* community: "Fly safe VR." Others made public protests concerning the wars and civic unrest in the Middle East and North Africa that had led to Sean Smith's death. These costless and easily created cargo containers were deposited outside of the main station in VFK-IV, the principal home-based solar system of Vile Rat's Goonswarm alliance. Similar collections of cargo containers were also dropped in Jita, the main trading hub in New Eden. In this frequently traversed area of the vast and empty universe of *EVE*, pilots appropriated this public and visible space of community significance to create a temporary and public memorial outside Vile Rat's metaphorical home. Other pilots navigating through this community hub would see these items both as a cluster of objects floating in space and on the tablelike user interface depicted in Figure 11.1. Like many of the flowers and ephemera typically left at spontaneous shrines, which quickly weather and decay, these memorializations were also temporary: they disappeared in the daily reset of *EVE*'s servers.

In a similar fashion, pilots appropriated the game mechanic of cynosural beacons, or "cynos," to create a kind of candlelight vigil for Vile Rat in the days following his death. A large number of pilots gathered in their spaceships in the system UMI-KK and deployed a great number of cynosural beacons:

> We gathered in UMI-KK with tons of cynoships as well as some titans and carriers to light space-candles in honor of Vile "Sean Smith" Rat who died serving his country in Libya on 9/11/2012. RIP Vile Rat, you will be missed. (EnderCapitalG 2012)

Figure 11.1. Commemorative cargo containers observed outside Goonswarm's main station in VFK-IV, with missives such as "RIP Vile Rat."

Cynos are in-game items that enable pilots, even entire fleets of pilots, to make quick interstellar jumps to specific locations as long as another pilot has "lit" a cynosural beacon to guide them to its position (known as "bridging"). Tactically, this allows for the quick deployment of support in fleet battles or provides the survivors of a battle a quick route home. Consequently, the location and incidence of cynos is strategically useful information, and an in-game map exists that depicts the occurrence of cynos in each star system in the New Eden galaxy; the higher the occurrence of cynos, the brighter the star system appears. Figure 11.2 depicts the effect of lighting a huge number of cynosural fields on this map, something visible to any pilot in the game. In the comments on this image from Reddit, one pilot explained the aesthetic significance of this image: "The light shined over most of the galaxy as did Vile Rat's influence . . . sad day for EVE." The technical properties of the item within the game also had meaning, according to one Goonswarm member: "Cynos really were the perfect choice—they symbolized our wish: that VR would bridge home and come back to us. A wish so strong it dwarfed the rest of the galaxy."

While large numbers of beacons were lit in this vigil, pilots also artfully deployed warp disruptors to spell out the words "RIP Vile Rat." These objects appear in space as large, shimmering orbs, and owing to the technical process of deploying these beacons, arranging them to spell out "RIP Vile Rat" in open space would have been logistically difficult. Because of its size and location, this temporary monument also involved the appropriation of public space for a community's public expression of

Figure 11.2. Cynosural field map, displaying the volume of cynos lit at a memorial for Vile Rat. From Powers (2012).

grief. Images of this monument have been widely circulated by pilots, including being featured in commemorative YouTube videos with more than two hundred thousand total views. Close to a hundred pilots were captured in the video as they paid their respects in a virtual pilgrimage to this temporary monument. With a pilot populating each bubble, the YouTube video description explains that "the tiny dots of light inside the bubbles are individual players paying their respects by lighting a 'candle' using the in-game cynosural field item" (PinkyFeldman 2012).

Pilots also engaged in a more lasting form of commemoration by renaming player-owned stations in a similar dedicatory fashion. The main Goonswarm station was renamed "VFK-I Vile Rat Will Be Remembered" and remained so named until January 19, 2013. Numerous other stations were renamed, both by friends and enemies of Goonswarm. In total, 241 player-owned stations were renamed in some commemorative form, such as "6 Vile Rat Remembrance Station," "C-Can't Believe Vile Rat Is Gone," and "H-Never Forget Vile Rat." Some, such as "ZA0L-U VII–RIP Vile Rat," still remained at the time of writing several years later, as continuing player-created dedications. Poignantly, several stations remained as a memorial despite having been conquered by other player groups in the months following Sean Smith's death.

However, over time, these renamed stations slowly reverted to previous and other names. Although sometimes this was due to their capture by other player groups, we observed numerous instances when outposts were conquered but the missive to Vile Rat was left and several occasions when an outpost changed hands three, even

Figure 11.3. Candlelight vigil.

four times without being affected. Those renamed were often done in blocks, for example, RAZOR Alliance (an in-game opponent of Goonswarm) changed the names of sixteen of its outposts to commemorate Vile Rat, returning all of them to their earlier names two months later. Many of the other name changes occurred at times of no discernable significance to Vile Rat's passing; the names of outposts are often changed to reflect in-game events occurring around them, such as taunting invading players or referencing alliance members' mistakes and achievements. As seen in Figure 11.4, there has been a gradual decline in commemorative station names over the course of the past two years.

The notable cliffs in Figure 11.4 reflect alliance leadership decisions or significant in-game events. Midway through January 2013, Goonswarm (Vile Rat's own alliance) renamed the majority of its remaining stations for reasons of probity. The Mittani (2013), leader of the Goonswarm Federation, noted, "After a certain point I thought it was getting morbid, and had GSF's swapped back to their old names." The name changes had served their purpose, and for some, it was time to move on from that point. The notable declines in August and September 2013 were due to events surrounding the Fountain War (see Carter 2015; chapter 5). TEST Alliance Please Ignore, one of the largest holders of sovereignty in the game, which had been allied with Goonswarm at the time of the Benghazi attacks, lost all of its sovereignty to Goonswarm and its allies. Despite its changed relationship, TEST had not renamed its memorial

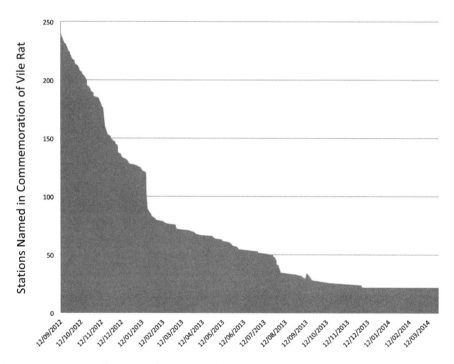

Figure 11.4. Number of player-owned stations with commemorative Vile Rat names.

stations, and the majority of these commemorative outposts were only renamed when Goonswarm took control.

Also of note is the reversal of the decline on the anniversary of Vile Rat's death. Ten stations were again renamed to commemorate Vile Rat at this time. In line with the widespread adoption of vernacular forms of commemoration following highly publicized deaths, we have since seen many outposts renamed to honor other deceased *EVE* players, though not nearly at the scale of the Vile Rat commemorations. We feel that the twenty-two stations that remain dedicated to Vile Rat have some persisting significance; for example, one of the six remaining Goonswarm memorial outposts is in UMI-KK, one of Goonswarm's historical homes and the site of the cyno lighting vigil. Others reflect the sole remaining commemorative outposts from allied (and enemy) alliances.

## Shoot Blues, Tell Vile Rat

Vile Rat was also highly regarded by many in the *EVE* community for his diplomatic skills. Many, like the prominent *EVE* personality The Mittani, credit his diplomacy skills and his artful and tenacious negotiations with other null-sec alliances with fundamentally shaping New Eden as it is known today:

> If you play this stupid game, you may not realize it, but you play in a galaxy created in large part by Vile Rat's talent as a diplomat. No one focused as relentlessly on using diplomacy as a strategic tool as VR. (The Mittani 2012a)

An important role Vile Rat played as the head of the Goonswarm's Corps Diplomatique was smoothing over trouble with and between allied corporations and alliances. This role was captured in an *EVE* meme showing a simple decision tree often referred to as "Shoot Blues, Tell Vile Rat" (see Figure 11.5):

> "Shoot Blues, Tell Vile Rat" is a phrase that has been a part of Goonswarm vernacular since time immemorial (2006), where a member of GSF would create a diplomatic incident (almost always on purpose), and then inform the head diplomat Vile Rat. (Mustache 2013)

In the *EVE Online* interface, the friend or foe status of other players is represented through color, moving through a spectrum from purple to red. Purple represents pilots in the same fleet, allied pilots and forces are represented with blue icons, and hostile pilots and forces are red. The simple meme captures the *EVE* null-sec ethos: if people are being assholes, blow them up—but if they are allies, talk to Vile Rat so he can sort out the resulting diplomatic issues.

On Saturday, September 15, a few days after Sean Smith's death, Goonswarm held an event it called "Vile Rat Memorial Not Purple Shoot It Diplomatic Disaster Op" as an ironic commemoration and celebration of Vile Rat's diplomatic contributions to

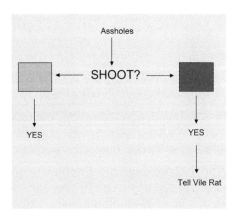

Figure 11.5. "Shoot Blues, Tell Vile Rat"
decision tree meme.

Goonswarm's alliance and to the game. The rules of the event were simple: "Bring whatever expensive stuff you can afford to loose [*sic*]. Rules are simple, form a fleet, whatever is not purple shoot. When your targets are all dead, just shoot everybody else!" All territory controlled by Goonswarm, and the territory of some of its allies who opted in to the event, was declared "Not Purple, Shoot It" (NPSI). That is, all pilots not in the same fleet were fair game to be attacked and destroyed throughout Goonswarm space. Furthermore, there would be no sanctions for any blue-on-blue destruction; pilots would not have to replace the spaceships they'd destroyed during the NPSI period. The event culminated in a "Thunderdome" in the UMI-KK system: a last-man-standing pitched battle that began with fleet-on-fleet combat and followed with an everyone-for-himself melee. At least twenty-four hundred ships were destroyed in the Thunderdome alone (EVSCO 2012), leading one participant to declare, "What commenced was surely the largest thunderdome (not to mention sheer waste of personal ISK) in all of *EVE* history" (millertime903 2012). The event was live-streamed by some participants, and the proceeds from views were donated to Sean Smith's family (CCP Navigator 2012).

The NPSI event was repeated a year later, with plans to make it an annual event. For eight hours on September 14–15, 2013, the space controlled by Goonswarm, and some of its allies who opted in to the event, was again declared NPSI. The NPSI Op culminated in another "megafight" at the warp-in point of the first planet in the EC-P8R system. It was estimated that more than twenty-five hundred ships were destroyed in the event (Mustache 2013).

A semipermanent player-created memorial to Vile Rat was built by the player Vnixx near the first moon of the sixth planet in the VKF system, the Goonswarm home system, using mobile small warp disruptors (MSWDs) to spell out the words "Never Forget Vile Rat." A MSWD is "a small deployable self powered unit that prevents warping within its area of effect" (EVElopedia n.d.) that can be anchored in space and persists until moved by the owner or destroyed. The warp disruption fields of MSWDs appear as shimmering bubbles in space (see Figure 11.6). Although we are unsure when this player-created memorial was constructed, we know that it was defaced on or around October 14, 2013. An unknown pilot destroyed the MSWDs in the word "Never" to leave the words "Forget Vile Rat."[3] Although outrage might have been the expected response to this kind of irreverent vandalism (as found in the case of similar harassment of commemorative rituals in games; see Gibbs et al. 2013), the general response

Figure 11.6. "Never Forget Vile Rat" tribute. From Mustache (2013).

from Goonswarm was unperturbed, amused, and even supportive of the defacement (Goonswarm member, personal communication, October 16, 2013). Comments on Reddit supported this view, with the top rated "the dude himself would have found it funny probably" (varoksa 2013) and reply "Not only would he have found it funny but after only a day or two would have asked 'why haven't any of you blown that up yet?'" (redworm 2013). In general, the view was one of support and that, given a suitable amount of time had passed, more than twelve months, such destruction was "in the spirit of eve" (Red_Oktoberfest 2013). Public outcry about the modification to the memorial was conspicuously absent, and the defacement was celebrated ironically as a further commemoration to the spirit and ethos Vile Rat brought to the *EVE* community.

## A Permanent Memorial

In the hours following Sean Smith's death, there were calls on the *EVE* forums for CCP Games to build some kind of permanent memorial in New Eden dedicated to Vile Rat. These calls echoed earlier requests for memorials to other individual *EVE* players who had died (e.g., Hrett 2012), requests that had previously been steadfastly refused by CCP. However, there were rumors that CCP was considering a monument, or graveyard, to collectively commemorate players who passed away. Proposals for both individual and collective, permanent monuments in New Eden were controversial, and remained so, among the player community.

Permanent monuments proposed by players included renaming a stellar system or star in honor of Vile Rat (ARMTEL 2012), such as renaming the Goonswarm staging system from VKF-IV to VR-RIP. Other suggestions for an individual, permanent memorial were smaller in scale and more localized. For example, Rashmika Clavain (2012) proposed "an Officer fit Titan wreck on a low-sec gate." Similar proposals for objects in space included permanent spaceship wrecks, structures, or containers with appropriate descriptions situated in significant or meaningful locations. Others proposed renaming an agent after Vile Rat (agents are nonplayer characters who give missions to pilots) and perhaps using his profile picture for the agent. Others proposed changing the "flavor text" (Gibbs et al. 2012) found in the "info tab" of an appropriate object, such as a spaceship or the Diplomacy Skill Book.

Proposals for a Vile Rat memorial restarted an ongoing conversation about a permanent memorial to collectively honor all the "fallen players" with an in-game monument of some kind. Ideas included a "graveyard" in or near one of the major trading hubs or the EVE gate. The EVE gate is a location with significant meaning in New Eden lore, as it was the location where humanity first arrived in New Eden, before being cut off from the rest of the galaxy. The EVE gate is the most tangible connection between the *EVE Online* universe and our own—the point where our universe was (or will be, chronologically) severed from the game universe:

> I like the thought of memorializing anyone who played *EVE* by giving them a virtual resting place just on the far side of the *EVE* gate—as if, in death, a small part of them passed on, and made it into the *EVE* universe itself. (Bizzaro Stormy MurphDog 2012)

Proposals for the graveyard suggested a variety of objects ranging from a large monument with listed names to spaceships or wrecked spaceships (again) or an orderly grid of container–tombstone objects each bearing the name and/or portrait of a deceased player, somewhat reminiscent of military sites such as Arlington Cemetery. Others suggested using the many in-game billboards located near stargates to cycle occasional commemorative messages. In making and responding to these suggestions, it appeared important for many commentators that all deceased players should be equally honored rather than some, such as Vile Rat, being singled out for special treatment by CCP.

However, among forum commentators, there was little consensus on what form these proposed permanent monuments created by CCP should take and, indeed, if they were appropriate and/or desirable in *EVE*. Objections ranged from the character of *EVE* as a game that offers escapism from real life to concerns about *EVE*'s sandbox properties: "EVE is a sandbox, if people want to memorialize someone within the game it should be on the players to do it, not CCP" (Paul Oliver 2012). Rather than CCP creating monuments, many players suggested that CCP should leverage *EVE*'s sandbox features and create the opportunity for players to purchase, construct, and/or maintain more permanent memorial objects. Again, these suggestions were somewhat contentious, with some players worried that, "*EVE* being *EVE*," with all the ruthlessness that entails, players would find some way to exploit memorial objects for tactical and strategic advantages or for disingenuous or offensive means. Others were concerned, within the context of *EVE* as a sandbox, that any objects players could create could also be defaced and destroyed by other players.

Although CCP has constructed a number of in-game memorials to celebrate major game events, such as large and destructive battles (CCP Dolan 2014), riddle (Drain 2011) and tournament competition winners (Carter and Gibbs 2013), and pilot riots and protests (Drain 2011), no memorials to deceased subscribers have been built to date that we are aware of. However, in early 2014, CCP announced that it would construct a monument dedicated to *EVE* subscribers to celebrate the first decade of

*EVE Online* (CCP Loktofeit 2014). Although the original plan for this monument was rumored to be a commemoration of deceased players, it has since evolved into a celebration all players of *EVE Online*. The Worlds within Worlds monument was constructed near Reykjavik Harbor and has been etched with the main character names of all players with active subscriptions on March 1, 2014. However, CCP did acknowledge the contributions and importance of players who have died in *EVE Online*'s first decade and consequently allowed leaders of *EVE* corporations to submit names of players who had passed away, to ensure they were also commemorated on the monument.

## Conclusion: Creative Appropriation of Game Resources in Commemorative Practices

Vernacular commemorative practices such as roadside memorials and the spontaneous shrines that appear in the wake of national tragedies have emerged in recent decades as valid and legitimate, expected and ritualized, public expressions of grief. These commemorative practices have hybridized tradition and modernity, religion and secularity, the old and the new, to create new rituals that connect meaningfully to the contemporary lived experiences of individuals and communities (Margry and Sánchez-Carretero 2011; Wouters 2002). In much the same way, the makeshift memorials created by *EVE Online* pilots through the creative appropriations of game mechanics that we have described in this chapter were also hybridizations that translated many of the traditional and contemporary tropes for grieving, commemorating, and memorializing to enact innovative mourning rituals that connected with the daily activities and practices of *EVE Online* communities.

Margry and Sánchez-Carretero (2007) have suggested seven characteristics common to makeshift memorials and spontaneous shrines. Each of these characteristics was evident in the Vile Rat commemorations:

1. *They involve bricolage.* Cargo containers, warp bubbles, cynosural beacons, and station names were the materials of choice appropriated for the commemorations.
2. *They are offerings both for the deceased and also for a wider audience.* Indeed, some comments were directed to Vile Rat, particularly those wishing him to "rest in peace" or "fly safe," but comments were also directed toward a broader audience, articulating his legacy for the *EVE* community. In addition, the NPSI events were a form of sacrifice, offering spaceships to Vile Rat's memory and creating events that could be consumed by a broader *EVE* audience through video streaming and humorous post hoc accounts of the events.
3. *Memorials convey meaning through narrative.* The lighting of many cynosural beacons symbolized Vile Rat's influence and the wish for his safe return from distance places. The NPSI events drew on established narratives about Vile Rat's place within New Eden's history.
4. *Memorials can reclaim a public space.* Many objects, such as cargo containers, were

renamed and deposited in Goonswarm's home system as well as in Jita, the most important trading hub in New Eden, claiming these spaces (albeit temporarily) as memorial sites. Similarly, the NPSI events laid temporary claim to vast swaths of space for commemorative activity.

5. *Memorials are unofficial and noninstitutionalized.* The game community (not the game developers) initiated and sustained the commemorative activities for Vile Rat. Interestingly, calls by pilots for CCP to permanently rename a star system or erect some kind of monument in Vile Rat's honor have not been fulfilled. This approach differs from other game developers' approaches to placing permanent memorials in game worlds, such as in *Dungeon and Dragons Online* and *World of Warcraft* (Gibbs et al. 2012).

6. *Sites are created in personal ways but also follow patterns learned and inscribed through the mass media.* Individuals could personalize individual contributions to the Vile Rat memorials but also used widely understood commemorative symbols, such as candles and RIP missives.

7. *Finally, shrines need not be religiously based.* The Vile Rat commemorations did not exhibit any overt religious influence.

These characteristics have helped us analyze the Vile Rat commemorations as an extension of existing practices into new media. They are novel in terms of their creative appropriation of game mechanics but also traditional or commonplace in their use of common tropes and motifs of contemporary mourning rituals.

Though memorializations and commemorative acts are not everyday events in game worlds, this analysis illustrates how the makeshift virtual memorials for Vile Rat in *EVE* closely replicate commonplace real practices. The considerable and meaningful outpouring of grief and mourning that occurred following Sean Smith's death was enabled by *EVE Online*'s unique single-server configuration, the ability of pilots to shape and influence the game universe, the persistent transmedia identity of *EVE* pilots, and player-driven governance. Having a persistent and single virtual world enabled the entire pilot community to participate in public commemorations that were, like many acts of public mourning, meaningful assertions of membership in the prominent and symbolic community of *EVE* pilots, a community enabled and enhanced by the presence of the player-elected councils and persistent identity systems. This further emphasizes the importance of *EVE*'s single-server configuration, explored in several chapters in this collection, in making *EVE* such a meaningful and real community.

Allowing public forms of mourning can be important to community formation and healing in the wake of tragedy. Thus consideration of how to design for these rituals in massively multiplayer online games and virtual worlds can be fruitful. However, care also needs to be taken before allowing (for example) permanent player-generated memorialization, particularly given the essentially spontaneous and temporary nature of many commemorative shrines and the manner in which they are meaningful appropriations. The sandbox character, or unstructured and open-ended game play (see chapter 1), of *EVE Online* also lends itself to memorialization far better than the more structured and directed play of "theme park" games such as *World of Warcraft*. As one pilot noted in response to pilot requests for CCP to create a permanent and official Vile Rat memorial, "in the Sandbox that is EVE, we can make our own memorials" (Zagdul 2012). The flexibility afforded by pilot-named items and the availability of player-created objects that persist publicly for periods of time in the game world enabled and facilitated spontaneous commemoration for Vile Rat.

"*EVE* is real" is a common *EVE* colloquialism, originally coined in an *EVE* advertisement but perpetuated by players as a catch-all phrase that captures both the real and meaningful impacts that *EVE Online* has on its players' lives, while also being used to (often simultaneously) poke fun at the seriousness that sometimes invades *EVE* play. As the other chapters in this collection indicate, *EVE is* real in that it is significant to its players, and the vernacular commemorative practices highlighted in this chapter further demonstrate the prominent and *real* culture that this virtual world has created and will continue to perpetuate, likely for many years to come. It will remain a question for CCP as curators, or janitors (see chapter 14), of New Eden to decide how deaths should be commemorated, memorialized, or noted within the virtual world of *EVE Online*. As Nick Webber suggests elsewhere in this volume (chapter 15), distinguishing between real and virtual in the case of *EVE Online* is meaningless and only causes conflict between CCP and its players when this finely granulated distinction with its many-layered allusions and contradictions is treated dichotomously and, as a result, is not successfully negotiated. Commemorative activities for Sean Smith, aka Vile Rat, were not limited to the *EVE Online* game world but blurred across a range of other media. Indeed, the rhetoric of the media and institutional responses to Sean Smith's involvement in the Something Awful and *EVE Online* communities further serves to legitimate involvement in *EVE Online* as a serious and *real* pastime.

## NOTES

1   We thank the Institute for a Broadband Enabled Society (IBES) and the Australian Communications Consumers Action Network (ACCAN) for their generous support. This research was supported under the Australian Research Council's Discovery Projects funding scheme ("Digital Commemoration," project DP140101871).

2   All Goonswarm Federation corporations, alliances, and their close associates are referred to as Goonswarm throughout the chapter.

3   http://imgur.com/a/4o61y.

## BIBLIOGRAPHY

ARMTEL. 2012. "Petition for System Name Change for Vile Rat" (online forum thread). *EVE Online* forums, September 12. https://forums.eveonline.com/default.aspx?g=posts&t=153153.

Associated Press. 2012. "Vile Rat Killed in Libya as Gamers Mourn Diplomatic Do-gooder." *Sydney Morning Herald*, September 13. http://www.smh.com.au/technology/technology-news /vile-rat-killed-in-libya-as-gamers-mourn-diplomatic-dogooder-20120913-25tu3 .html.

Beckhusen, Robert. 2012. "Diplomat Killed in Libya Told Fellow Gamers: Hope I 'Don't Die Tonight.'" *Wired Magazine*, September 12. http://www.wired/dangerroom/2012/09/vilerat.

Bizzaro Stormy MurphDog. 2012. "Petition for System Name Change for Vile Rat" (online forum thread). *EVE Online* forums, September 12. https://forums.eveonline.com/default. aspx?g=posts&t=153153&p=4.

Brennan, Michael. 2008. "Condolence Books: Language and Meaning in the Mourning for Hillsborough and Diana." *Death Studies* 32: 326–51.

Brubaker, Jed R., and Gillian R. Hayes. 2011. "We Will Never Forget You [Online]: An Empirical Investigation of Post-mortem MySpace Comments." In *Proceedings of the ACM 2011 Conference on Computer Supported Cooperative Work*, 123–32. New York: ACM Press.

Carter, Marcus. 2015. "Emitexts and Paratexts: Propaganda in EVE Online." *Games and Culture* 10, no. 4: 311–42.

Carter, Marcus, and Martin Gibbs. 2013. "eSports in EVE Online: Skullduggery, Fair Play and Acceptability in an Unbounded Competition." In *Proceedings of the Eighth International Foundations of Digital Games Conference*, 47–54. Chania, Greece: SASDG.

CBS Interactive Inc. 2012. "Special Report: Bodies of Americans Killed in Libya Return to U.S." *CBC News*, September 14. http://www.cbsnews.com/video/watch/?id=7421746n.

CCP Dolan. 2014. "The Bloodbath at B-R5RB, Gamings' Most Destructive Battle Ever." *EVE Community Developer's Blog*, February 1. http://community.eveonline.com/news/dev-blogs/ the-bloodbath-of-b-r5rb/.

CCP Loktofeit. 2014. "CCP to Erect Monument to EVE Online Players in Reykjavik, Iceland." *EVE Community News*, February 5. http://community.eveonline.com/news/news -channels/press-releases/ccp-to-erect-monument-to-eve-online-players-in-reykjavik -iceland-1/.

CCP Navigator. 2012. "EVE Player to Run a Fleet in Tribute of Vile Rat." *EVE Community News*, September 15. http://community.eveonline.com/news/news-channels/eve-online-news/ eve-players-to-run-a-fleet-in-tribute-of-vile-rat.

CCP Xhagen. 2012. "A Tribute to Sean 'Vile Rat' Smith." *EVE Online Developer's Blog*, September 13. https://community.eveonline.com/news/dev-blogs/73406.

Clark, Jennifer, and Majella Franzmann. 2006. "Authority from Grief: Presence and Place in the Making of Roadside Memorials." *Death Studies* 30, no. 6: 579–99.

Clinton, Hillary R. 2012a. "Statement on the Death of American Personnel in Benghazi, Libya." U.S. Department of State, September 12. http://www.state.gov/secretary/20092013clinton /rm/2012/09/197630.htm.

———. 2012b. "Statement on the Deaths of Tyrone S. Woods and Glen A. Doherty in Benghazi, Libya." U.S. Department of State, September 12. http://m.state.gov/md197732.htm.

Dicker, Ron. 2012. "Sean Smith Fundraiser: Donors Raise Nearly $70,000 for Family of Diplomat Killed in Libya." *Huffington Post*, September 18. http://www.huffingtonpost.com/2012/09 /18/fundraiser-for-sean-smith_n_1894060.html.

Doss, Erika. 2002. "Death, Art, and Memory in the Public Sphere: The Visual and Material Culture of Grief in Contemporary America." *Mortality* 7, no. 1: 63–82.

Drain, Brendan. 2011. "EVE Online Monument Commemorates the Summer Riots." *Massively* (blog), November 16. http://massively.joystiq.com/2011/11/16/eve-online-monument-commemorates-the-summer-riots/.

EnderCapitalG. 2012. "Vile Rat 'Candle Lighting' Ceremony." YouTube. http://www.youtube.com/watch?v=vnfHJGDC_xE.

EVElopedia. n.d. "Mobile Small Warp Disruptor I." https://wiki.eveonline.com/en/wiki/Mobile_Small_Warp_Disruptor_I.

EVSCO. 2012. "Related Kills and Losses: Battle Summary for UMI-KK, 2012–09–15 17:25–00:47." http://eve-kill.net/?a=kill_related&kll_id=14633235.

Gibbs, Martin, Marcus Carter, Michael Arnold, and Bjorn Nansen. 2013. "Serenity Now Bombs a World of Warcraft Funeral: Negotiating the Morality, Reality, and Taste of Online Gaming Practices." In *Selected Papers of Internet Research 14,* 23–26. Denver, Colo.: Association of Internet Researchers. http://spir.aoir.org/index.php/spir/article/view/761/350.

Gibbs, Martin, Marcus Carter, and Joji Mori. 2013. "Vile Rat: Spontaneous Shrines in EVE Online." In *Proceedings of the Eighth International Foundations of Digital Games Conference.* Chania, Greece: SASDG.

Gibbs, Martin, James Meese, Michael Arnold, Bjorn Nansen, and Marcus Carter. 2015. "#funeral and Instagram: Death, Social Media, and Platform Vernacular." *Information, Communication, and Society* 18, no. 3: 255–68.

Gibbs, Martin, Joji Mori, Michael Arnold, and Tamarah Kohn. 2012. "Tombstones, Uncanny Monuments, and Epic Quests: Memorials in World of Warcraft." *Game Studies* 12, no. 1. http://gamestudies.org/1201/articles/gibbs_martin.

Grider, Sylvia. 2001. "Spontaneous Shrines: A Modern Response to Tragedy and Disaster." *New Directions in Folklore* 5: 1–10.

Hawkins, Peter S. 1993. "The Art of Memory and the NAMES Project AIDS Quilt." *Critical Inquiry* 19, no. 4: 752–79.

Heard, Mark. 2012. "A Tribute to Sean 'Vile Rat' Smith." *EVE Online Developer's Blog,* September 12. http://community.eveonline.com/news/dev-blogs/csm-tribute-to-vile-rat/.

Hollingsworth, J. 2006. "Serenity Now Bombs a World of Warcraft Funeral." YouTube. http://www.youtube.com/watch?v=IHJVolaC8pw.

Hrett. 2012. "A New Star in the Sky" (online forum thread). *EVE Online* forums, May 13. https://forums.eveonline.com/default.aspx?g=posts&t=108404.

Jorgensen-Earp, Cheryl, and Lori Lanzilotti. 1998. "Public Memory and Private Grief: The Construction of Shrines at the Sites of Public Tragedy." *Quarterly Journal of Speech* 84, no. 2: 150–70.

Kaufman, Leslie, and Christine Hauser. 2012. "Attack Victim Shared His Fears in Messages." *New York Times,* September 12. http://www.nytimes.com/2012/09/13/world/middleeast/attack-victim-shared-his-fears-in-messages.html.

Kushner, D. 2013. "Vile Rat." *Playboy,* March 1. http://www.playboy.com/playground/view/vile-rat-virtual-world-of-eve-online.

Margry, Peter J., and Cristina Sánchez-Carretero. 2007. "Memorializing Traumatic Death." *Anthropology Today* 23, no. 3: 1–2.

———. 2011. "Rethinking Memorialization: The Concept of Grassroots Memorials." In *Grassroots Memorials: The Politics of Memorializing Traumatic Death,* edited by Peter J. Margry and Cristina Sánchez-Carretero, 1–48. New York: Berghahn Books.

Marwick, Alice, and Nicole Ellison. 2012. "'There Isn't WiFi in Heaven!' Negotiating Visibility on Facebook Memorial Pages." *Journal of Broadcasting and Electronic Media* 56, no. 3: 378–400.

millertime903. 2012. "Vile Rat Memorial Not Purple Shoot It Diplomatic Disaster OP." YouTube. http://www.youtube.com/watch?v=KJIUinAOhVk.

Mittani, The. 2012a. "RIP: Vile Rat." *The Mittani* (blog), September 12. http://themittani.com/news/rip-vile-rat.

———. 2012b. "Vile Rat Fundraiser Reaches $100,000." *The Mittani* (blog), September 24. http://themittani.com/news/vile-rat-fundraiser-reaches-100000.

———. 2013. "*Playboy* on Vile Rat." *The Mittani* (blog), March 21. http://themittani.com/news/playboy-vile-rat.

Mori, Joji, Steve Howard, and Martin Gibbs. 2011. "Poets and Blacksmiths: Implications for Global Memorialization Using Digital Technology." *Interactions* 18, no. 5: 48–54.

Mustache, Angry. 2013. "CFC Holds Vile Rat Memorial NPSI OP." *The Mittani* (blog), September 16. http://themittani.com/news/cfc-holds-vile-rat-memorial-npsi-op.

Parsons, Zack. 2012a. "Benefit for Sean Smith's Family." YouCaring. http://www.youcaring.com/tuition-fundraiser/benefit-for-sean-smith-s-family/306784.

———. 2012b. "Farewell to Vilerat." *Something Awful.* http://www.somethingawful.com/news/sean-smith-vilerat/.

Paul Oliver. 2012. "Eve Gate Graveyard for Player Memorials" (online forum thread). *EVE Online forums,* September 12. https://forums.eveonline.com/default.aspx?g=posts&t=153269.

PinkyFeldman. 2012. "EVE Online: Vile Rat Cyno Vigil Tribute (1080p)." YouTube. http://www.youtube.com/watch?v=pzBGHNzGi8M.

Powers. 2012. "Memento Mori: Candle Lighting in UMI-KK for VR." *The Mittani* (blog), September 13. http://themittani.com/media/memento-mori-candle-lighting-umi-kk-vr.

Rashmika Clavain. 2012. "Petition for System Name Change for Vile Rat" (online forum thread). *EVE Online* forums, September 12. https://forums.eveonline.com/default.aspx?g=posts&t=153153.

Red_Oktoberfest. 2013. "Too Soon, Waffles" (online forum thread). reddit.com/r/eve, October 14. http://www.reddit.com/r/Eve/comments/1ogrkf/too_soon_waffles/.

redworm. 2013. "Too Soon, Waffles" (online forum thread). Reddit EVE forums, October 14. http://www.reddit.com/r/Eve/comments/1ogrkf/too_soon_waffles/.

Santino, Jack. 2006. *Spontaneous Shrines and the Public Memorialization of Death.* New York: Palgrave Macmillan.

Thier, David. 2012. "A Look at the Diplomatic Skills of Sean Smith, AKA 'Vile Rat.'" *Forbes,* September 13. http://www.forbes.com/sites/davidthier/2012/09/13/a-look-at-the-diplomatic-skills-of-sean-smith-aka-vile-rat/.

Totilo, Stephen. 2013. "The Amazing Life of Sean Smith, the Masterful *Eve* Gamer Slain in Libya." Kotaku, April 25. http://kotaku.com/the-extraordinary-mischievous-too-short-life-of-sean-481060252.

varoksa. 2013. "Too Soon, Waffles" (online forum thread). Reddit EVE forums, October 14. http://www.reddit.com/r/Eve/comments/1ogrkf/too_soon_waffles/.

Wachowski, Elizabeth. 2008. "Dealing with Real-Life Tragedy in an Online World." WoW Insider, January 15. http://wow.joystiq.com/2008/01/15/dealing-with-real-life-tragedy-in-an-online-world/.

Walter, Tony, Rachid Hourizi, Wendy Moncur, and Stacey Pitsillides. 2011. "Does the Internet Change How We Die and Mourn? Overview and Analysis." *OMEGA: Journal of Death and Dying* 64, no. 4: 275–302.

Wikipedia. 2012. "Sean Smith (Diplomat)." http://en.wikipedia.org/wiki/Sean_Smith_(diplomat).

Wouters, Cas. 2002. "The Quest for New Rituals in Dying and Mourning: Changes in the We–I Balance." *Body and Society* 8, no. 1: 1–27.

Zagdul. 2012. "Petition for System Name Change for Vile Rat" (online forum thread). *EVE Online* forums, September 12. https://forums.eveonline.com/default.aspx?g=posts&t=153153.

# 12

# Imagined Capsuleers

## Reframing Discussions about Gender and *EVE Online*

*Kelly Bergstrom*

*EVE Online* is often described as being an outlier in the massively multiplayer online game (MMOG) landscape for many reasons, including the ratio of male to female players. Unlike games such as *World of Warcraft*, of which an estimated 20 to 40 percent of players are women, the women who play *EVE* are generally understood to make up only an estimated 4 percent of the player population. This gender disparity within *EVE* is widely acknowledged, and yet the reasons for it are not clearly understood. However, in the following pages, you will not find a conclusive list of reasons to explain why so few women play *EVE*. This quite simply is an impossible task, as this exercise in list making would be underpinned with the assumption that "women" can stand as a universal category of shared interests—or, in this case, of shared disinterests. Furthermore, by limiting conversations to why women don't play, the gendered interactions of the other 96 percent of *EVE* players remain underexplored.

## Why Do Some People Play *EVE* and Not Others?

As with all games, playing *EVE* is a voluntary leisure activity. The voluntary nature of game play carries with it an assumption that those who wish to play will be found playing the game and those who are disinterested will not. However, the idea that digital games are a leisure activity can lead to blind spots about the barriers to participation that can (and do) exist. Subscription costs, lack of high-speed Internet, or software that won't run outside of specific geographic areas are material barriers that might prevent participation. Less tangible are barriers that take the form of a player community that is unwelcoming or outright hostile to newcomers. And yet, because play is recreational, lack of participation is persistently attributed simply to a lack of interest rather than being considered the result of barriers a potential player might face.

In this chapter, I investigate how gender-based stereotypes can act as one such barrier to participation in digital games. I argue that discussions about gender and *EVE* are an amplification of the types of assumptions that broadly circulate about women's game play across multiple game titles and multiple game genres. Additionally, I argue that existing discussions about women's (lack of) play in this particular community are often conducted in such a way that obscures other barriers to participation in *EVE*. I begin with a brief overview of the sorts of conversations that tend to happen when gender and digital game play are discussed, providing examples about how this discourse circulates through discussions about gender and *EVE* play. In contrast to the assumption that women's apparent lack of interest in this particular game is a problem to be "fixed," this chapter serves as an argument that *EVE* is an ideal case study to highlight how easily stereotypical notions of gendered play and preferences become reified.

In addition to a review of the relevant academic literature, I draw on four years' worth of research about the *EVE* community, including surveys, fieldwork at Fanfest, and interviews and participant observation within the *EVE* community. Here I use my own experiences researching this player community to illustrate how easily conversations about gender become narrowed to becoming a conversation only about women. After describing my own experience with conflating gender and women, I then shift my focus to describing how the interactions of the majority of *EVE* players can be used to talk about masculinities. As a way to contextualize this research, I introduce Raewyn Connell's (2009) updated conceptualizations of hegemonic masculinities to reframe the discussion about gender to center on the underexplored (male) majority of this particular player population. I use the in-game event Hulkageddon as a case study to talk about the policing of play styles and, in turn, of masculinities within New Eden. The goal of this chapter is to shift the conversation away from Sisyphean attempts to find the specific reasons as to why "women don't play *EVE*" and instead ask the harder questions about who is invited to play *EVE* and, ultimately, who is made to feel welcomed enough to stay.

## What Do We Talk about When We Talk about Gender and Games?

Although it is by no means exhaustive, this section is intended to provide a crash course into the sorts of discussions that dominate academic work regarding gender and digital game play. My intention in reviewing this literature is to highlight how the discussion about gender and *EVE* is hardly an oddity. Instead, how we talk about gender in *EVE* mirrors fairly common assumptions about gender and games—typically focused on women's play (or lack thereof) and where questions of men and/or masculinity are often left underexplored.

Discussions about gender and *EVE* usually begin and end with an observation that very few women play this MMOG. Although *EVE* is a game that has surprisingly few female players (approximately 4 percent) compared to other MMOGs, such as *World of Warcraft* (estimates range from 20 to 40 percent), the overarching idea that games are primarily the domain of men is hardly new. In the opening paragraph of

H. G. Wells's (1913) *Little Wars,* an instruction manual for a tabletop war game played with miniaturized figurines, he explains,

> [This game] can be played by boys of every age from twelve to one hundred and fifty—and even later if the limbs remain sufficiently supple—by girls of the better sort, and by a few rare and gifted women.

This imagined audience of players is made explicit in the book's full title, *Little Wars: A Game for Boys from Twelve Years of Age to One Hundred and Fifty and for That More Intelligent Sort of Girl Who Likes Boys' Games and Books.* Though it may be tempting to view Wells's piece as an example of an antiquated view of gender roles, the idea that games (especially digital games) are by default assumed masculine pursuits has often been repeated (Bryce and Rutter 2003; Burrill 2008; Ivory 2006; Lucas and Sherry 2004; Steinkuehler et al. 2011; Terlecki et al. 2010; Williams et al. 2009).

Two competing narratives are frequently used to account for those women who show an interest in playing games: the first assumes that she is an outlier (to which I return throughout this chapter), the second that she needs to be specifically courted with "female-friendly games" that fall outside the "normal" digital game genres, as she would otherwise be disinterested in playing. These "girl games," "games for women," or "pink/purple games" draw their content from stereotypically feminine interests (such as cooking, raising children, or fashion) and are marketed in such a way that makes them unappealing to "mainstream" (read male) audiences. Even if the title or packaging of the game is not overtly designed to signal that it is explicitly intended for girls or women gamers, advertising will still target potential female audiences differently. Examples of gendered advertising are discussed by Shira Chess (2010), who investigated how Nintendo Wii and the Nintendo DS were marketed in print publications. She found that advertisements appearing in women's special interest magazines focused on productivity and self-help, a significant departure from the way game systems are advertised in other venues that highlight the entertaining or challenging aspects of game play. Chess's research is just one of many examples illustrating that, whether it is through explicitly pink games or gendered advertising, girls and women are continually reinforced as a niche audience that must be persuaded to play rather than assuming that they will come to gaming of their own accord.

There is a depressing lack of diversity among the titles that fall into the category of "games for girls," which can likely be attributed to a lack of understanding of the diversity of girls' and women's play. Mary Flanagan (2005, 1–2) gets right to the heart of the matter: this universalization of the term *girls* within industry is underpinned with the assumption that there is some sort of unanimous experience, ability, and taste shared by all female-identified players, and this can be neatly packaged in a pink or purple box. With many game developers[1] continuing to assume that potential female players are only interested in a limited range of gaming experiences and academic researchers reinforcing the ideas that these specific tropes are what girls and women want, only a limited range of uncontested subject positions are open for women to occupy if they wish to participate in digital games. Indeed, the idea that girls and women prefer collaborative play circulates freely on both sides of the nature versus nurture debate. Whether one believes that it is biology, socialization, or a mixture of the two that leads to marked differences in gender performances, the trope remains that femaleness equates to being less interested in competition and instead that women gravitate toward collaboration, especially in respect to the types of digital games that girls and women are assumed to be more interested in playing.

Although some academic research has seemingly found support for gendered play styles (cf. Hartmann and Klimmt 2006; Williams et al. 2009), feminist researchers continually draw attention to how gender-based stereotypes can cloud research findings by beginning with an assumption that boys and girls want different things from their game-play experiences and then reporting findings to support these hypotheses (de Castell and Bryson 1998). This pattern has been thoroughly critiqued in literature reviews by Jennifer Jenson and Suzanne de Castell (2008; 2010), who identify how research can be used to reinforce gender stereotypes and perpetuate stereotypical claims about the preferences of girls' digital game play. This vein of research begins from the assumption that there is a discernable difference between "male play" and "female play" and produces findings that further cement the gendering of play. And yet, when gender is *not* used as a variable, a different explanation for play styles may be observed, providing alternate explanations for what is frequently presented as "female" and "male" game-play preferences. For example, when observing play within an after-school gaming club and comparing the behavior of girls to that of other girls (instead of girls' behavior being compared or contrasted to male participants' behavior), Jenson, Fisher, and de Castell (2011) argue that what is typically described as archetypical female play actually reveals itself to be *novice* play. The young girls in their study did not have unfettered access to gaming consoles in their own homes and, when first observed playing as part of a girls-only gaming club, demonstrated a preference for cooperative play (a stereotypically feminine approach to game play). However, after being given the opportunity to practice playing in a supportive, girls-only environment, they began to feel more confident in their play. Soon enough, the girls were trash talking, hogging controllers, and being ultracompetitive with each other, demonstrating behavior typically associated with masculine play. Perhaps even more surprising is that this behavior held when boys were introduced into the gaming club. Rather than assuming that collaborative play is linked to femininity, Jenson et al.'s open-ended study design allowed for the possibility to observe that what is frequently described as feminine play (cooperative, noncompetitive) is actually more likely to be attributed to a person's level of experience playing digital games rather than the person's gender.

Returning to the first narrative to explain a woman's participation in digital games—that she is an outlier—this is the narrative that repeatedly plays out in respect to *EVE*. Because of the 4 percent figure so frequently cited, any woman interested in playing this game is immediately positioned as an outlier. This idea that most other women need "something else" other than spaceships to be seduced into the world of gaming is seen quite clearly in the interview with CCP's Andie Nordgren, reported in Joseph Leray's (2013) article for *Destructoid*. Here Nordgren clearly lays out the belief that women are inherently uninterested in science fiction (and, by extension, *EVE*) and would be better targeted by *World of Darkness*, a game with affordances more in line with other MMOGs that do not suffer from as extreme a gender disparity as *EVE*.[2] This narrative of women disliking science fiction conveniently overlooks the long history of women's participation in sci-fi fandoms, such as that surrounding the X-Files franchise (Bury 2001). Francesca Coppa's (2008) investigation of Star Trek fandom is especially relevant, as it describes the female fans who began editing videos of their favorite show set to music ("vidders") and who helped lay the foundation for machinima, the practice of using game-play or specifically rendered footage to tell a story. This statement is sometimes revised to "women don't like *hard* sci-fi," for example, literature, movies, or other cultural productions that are concerned with the scientific accuracy of what is being described. This division between sci-fi and hard sci-fi is an exercise in moving goalposts and, much like the casual–hardcore division discussed earlier, is unhelpful for moving discussions about gender and game play forward.

If women (considered broadly as an exhaustive category) are assumed not to enjoy science fiction, or are assumed to be disinterested in the cutthroat, ultracompetitive environment for which *EVE* is known, this becomes an easy answer to why women don't make up a more equal percentage of the player population and therefore their lack of representation in this community is something that does not need to be addressed. Unacknowledged is *EVE*'s tutorial system, so clearly described by Christopher Paul (2011) (see also chapter 2) as a filtering mechanism for new players. By leaving out key information, new players are forced to seek out external resources and make social connections to guide them through their rocky ascent up the learning cliff. When women's lack of interest in science fiction and/or competition is assumed to be the reason why she (again, considered broadly enough to encompass all women) does not play, information about the assumed ideal *EVE* player, packaged within player-created resources or newbie guides, will continue to remain unaddressed. In my own preliminary explorations of player-created newbie guides, I argue that some of the most readily available new player guides accessible by a quick Google search or linked by communities such as Reddit's popular *EVE* subreddit are buttressed by racist, sexist, and/or homophobic language. Even used in jest, if this is a new player's first encounter with a player-created paratext, it will likely be off-putting to *anyone* (not just women) who finds this sort of language uncomfortable (Bergstrom 2013). Furthermore, the labeling of newbies in the *EVE* community is hardly gender neutral. Elsewhere my coauthors and I have described that the gendered "newbro" is a far more common term used to describe those new to EVE, signaling that the assumed new *EVE* player is already always male (Bergstrom et al. 2013).

## Making Room for Surprise: Researching Women's Experiences Playing *EVE Online*

The research described herein was originally formulated as an investigation of why such a small number of women participate in *EVE*. Given that gaming is often framed as a "boys' club," and that this boys' club is continually reinforced by an industry that perpetuates a "hegemony of play" (Fron et al. 2007), I was primed to expect that female *EVE* players would share narratives of harassment or being made to feel like they didn't quite belong as members of the community (assuming they even disclosed their gender to their fellow players). Indeed, the precedent for this assumption is not entirely reactionary or unfounded. Jessica Beyer's (2012) investigation of the *World of Warcraft* forums found that those who publicly identified as women were consistently blamed for their own harassment because it was assumed they must be using the public display of their gender to garner attention and/or obtain free in-game items from their fellow (male) players. It is therefore unsurprising that Kara Behnke's (2012) ongoing ethnography of a female-inclusive *World of Warcraft* guild finds that most of the participants were specifically attracted to this particular guild as they viewed it as an opportunity to play without being exposed to the "hardcore masculinist rhetoric" pervading the larger community. Through their participation in this particular guild and its supportive environment, Behnke's participants spoke of their newfound willingness to experiment with parts of the game they had previously felt were off limits to them, such as participation in the game's extensive modding and user interface customization community (289). That a supportive environment of one's peers is necessary is made most evident by Kishonna Gray (2011, 2012b, 2012a), whose documentation of the harassment women of color face is a chilling reminder of the sexist and racist discourse that often gets brushed aside by players belonging to dominant groups as "merely trash talking" and/or an "expected part of the game." In Gray's work, similar to earlier research on female *Quake* players by Helen Kennedy (2011), female-only "clans" act as a haven from harassment but also as a support system to draw upon when harassment occurs. These supportive spaces, however, can in turn be used as anecdotal evidence to indicate that the lack of diversity among gaming cultures is now a thing of the past. Genesis Downey (2012, 172) reminds us that "girl gamers should not be seen as some kind of panacea that will right the wrongs present in gaming subcultures," as these opt-in safe spaces merely act as a shield, leaving the toxic dominant culture unchanged.

With so much of the research on women playing in hypermasculine game spaces finding that women tend to come together in affinity groups as a way to shield themselves from harassment, it is not surprising that I expected to find similar supportive enclaves within the larger *EVE* community. Leading up to my fieldwork at Fanfest 2012, I assumed the best way to learn about the lack of women who play this game would be to talk to the women who *do* play and see if they also cluster together in supportive corporations or alliances, as described in Behnke's, Gray's, and Kennedy's work. The first hurdle was to identify a group of women currently playing *EVE* who were interested in talking about their experiences. To facilitate a study of this extremely small player population, I worked in conjunction with researchers at CCP Games to organize a series of focus groups, some open to all, but one specifically advertised toward female *EVE* players. I intended to use these focus groups to recruit participants and subsequently collect narratives about how these female players first became interested in the game and what encouraged them to stay. I theorized that perhaps these few women shared a similar background (previous games played, prior social experiences, areas of study or employment, etc.) that provided particular tools to get over the initial hurdle of becoming proficient at *EVE* and/or that provided a particular tool set to thrive in a predominantly male environment. I was interested in the perspectives of male players, too, especially to see if male players were aware of the extremity of the game's gender disparity and if the game's lack of female players was a concern to them.

During Fanfest, I talked to more than forty individual players either one-on-one or in small groups while they completed a survey about their online gaming habits. In addition to these personal interviews, I ran two focus groups to learn more about why attendees at Fanfest felt that *EVE* is a compelling game. The first was advertised as open to all; the second was geared toward female players. Both were extremely well attended—all available seats around the table were filled. I asked both groups the same set of questions: What attracted you to *EVE*? Why do you play *EVE* instead of other popular MMOGs? What would CCP have to change to attract larger subscription numbers? and, of course, the question that at the time I thought would be the meat of my investigation, Why do you think so few women play *EVE*?

The first session drew primarily male participants and resulted in a lively discussion about the types of players who are attracted to *EVE*, especially when compared to other popular MMOGs such as *World of Warcraft*. A comment made multiple times was the importance of finding an in-game social group to ease a new player's introduction to the game (something that has been corroborated in Paul's 2011 investigations of the new player tutorials). Participants of this focus group described their attraction to *EVE* as stemming from it being a difficult sandbox, but despite the game's challenges, it provides enough rewards to those who are persistent enough to stick with it. When I brought up questions of gender, some conveyed disappointment that their female partners were uninterested in playing *EVE*, a game they themselves loved so much. Overall, there was an interest in having more female players join the *EVE* community, as an increased number of players would ensure the continued success of *EVE* and CCP Games.

When the time came to run the second focus group, this one advertised as specifically focused on women's play experiences, I was pleasantly surprised to see a room full of women (and a few men) sitting around the table, all eager to talk about their experiences playing *EVE*. All had taken time out of a busy Fanfest schedule to spend an hour talking about women's experiences in *EVE*. I asked the same questions as to the preceding group, which again resulted in a lively discussion about what makes *EVE* different from other MMOGs the women have played. Many shared that in their offline lives, they worked or studied in predominantly male environments, so they felt comfortable navigating the predominantly male *EVE* community. The majority of the women were open with their fellow players that they were women, and for a few of the participants, they described distinct advantages to being the only woman in their fleet.

Much like the previous session, the participants in this focus group expressed a preference for the player versus player (PVP) elements of *EVE* game play. Mining and manufacturing were seen as being dull; large-scale fleet warfare, being a pirate, or corporate espionage were more indicative of how *EVE* is "really" played. Where this focus group departed from the previous one was in their response to the question of how to get more female players to participate in the *EVE* community. Here the opinion was that adding more women to the game would somehow break it, as an influx of women would likely only be attracted by adding new elements to the game to allow for more cooperative (or, at least, less competitive) play. If I had been relying only on this particular focus group to understand the small number of women who play this particular MMOG, it would be easy to assume that women who currently play *EVE* are understood by both the larger community and themselves to be outliers. Furthermore, women who do not currently play *EVE* are assumed to require specific modifications to the game world to make this MMOG friendlier to those who would otherwise be disinterested in playing.

Up until this point, my findings seemed to support that the few women who currently play *EVE* came into the game already comfortable navigating a predominantly male environment. However, this is not where the story ends. The room used for focus groups was in high demand, booked for back-to-back sessions by a variety of groups throughout the entire day. As soon as our allotted time was over, the next group slated to use the room began to file in. We ended the focus group, and as I was collecting my belongings, one of the participants who had not spoken during the session asked to speak with me privately. Out in the hall and away from the other participants, she told me that the other women in the room made her feel like she could not speak and share her experiences and what she enjoyed about playing *EVE*. She was, according to the other women in the room, the type of player who "played the game wrong," because rather than engaging in PVP combat, she preferred to spend her time manufacturing in-game items or participating in joint mining endeavors with her boyfriend and their friends. In other words, she was a carebear, a derogatory term used to describe players who do not participate in the game's PVP activities (Carter and Gibbs 2013, 3), a slight also described in Chribba's chapter in this collection (chapter 7). Despite the insults made toward her preferred play style, this was the role she chose to play and how she enjoyed spending her time in *EVE*. The more vocal women in the room did not speak for her and made her feel like her way of playing *EVE* was "wrong,"

but it was important that I knew that this was how *she* played *EVE*. I share this story because this interaction is illustrative of just how easily alternative narratives of play can
be overlooked, even in a program of research explicitly informed by feminist theory.

## Shifting Focus: *Gender* Is Not a Synonym for *Women*

Earlier in this chapter, I provided an overview of the types of discussions that
tend to happen around gender and game play. This literature review being focused on
women is not by accident. In the introduction to *The Postcolonial Science and Technology Studies Reader*, Sandra Harding (2011) writes of the persistent assumption that
*gender*, when used in an academic context, somehow becomes redefined to be synon-
ymous with *women*. Although she is specifically describing science and technology
studies, her statement quoted in the following could easily be applied to the study of
digital games:

> some scholars seem to think there is little reason to raise gender issues in addressing
> topics in this field. Many assume that gender issues are relevant only if women are in
> sight, or perhaps even only if one is actually studying women. (11)

The overwhelming pattern in game studies is that a player's gender, sexuality, or race
does not factor into a researcher's analysis unless the player being described is not
male, not straight, and, frequently, not white. This assumed identity is most clearly
revealed when thinking through the commonly used prefixes attached to the label
"gamer": girl gamer, gay gamer, gaymer, black gamer, and so on. Take a moment to
reflect—when was the last time you heard a straight, white, male player specifically
described as a "straight/white/male gamer"? This framing of the imagined gamer as
being a straight white male colors the assumptions made about who plays games (as
evidenced by the previous section) and immediately positions all other groups as being outliers. As the story of my own developing research trajectory illustrated, viewing
communities in terms of outliers can artificially limit what questions are asked about
the intersections between gender and digital game play.

My interaction following the "Women in *EVE*" focus group at Fanfest was a
turning point in my research about *EVE Online*. By designing a program of research
that emphasized investigation of the women presumed missing from this player community, I overlooked the other gendered interactions between *current* players. I had
become so focused on the outliers' narratives and perspective that I had become
blinded to the norms that pervade *EVE*. Playing out in both focus groups was clearly a
hierarchy of in-game activities, but on further reflection, this also reflected a hierarchy
of gender. Originally, I had considered titling this section "But What about the Mens?"
as a tongue-in-cheek reference to a complaint commonly lobbed at any sort of analysis
that seeks to center the experiences of women. Frequently this question is used as a
derailment tactic, forcing the speaker or writer to justify his or her choice to focus on a

particular population (usually women) at the exclusion of others (usually men). In this instance, it was a question I was left asking myself about the missing majority. What about the 96 percent of *EVE* players who were *not* women? Furthermore, how was masculinity shaping the experiences of all players—not just those who identified as men?

Hegemonic masculinities provide a useful frame for unpacking my experiences at Fanfest 2012. Undergirded by cultural hegemony—the means by which the ruling class maintains the status quo and convinces the oppressed that their subjugation is just (Gramsci 2011)—hegemonic masculinity was a concept originally used to describe men's continued domination over women. Since its original proposal, the concept has been updated and reframed from masculinity to hegemonic *masculinities,* and it serves as a useful lens to explain the continued privileging of certain types of masculinity over all others, including subordinate masculinities and that which is deemed feminine in a particular society (Connell and Messerschmidt 2005). Although only a small number of men may actually embody its qualities, this formulation of masculinity is still maintained as the normative or idealized way to be a man. When used as a lens to understand observations within this MMOG and its associated community, this theoretical framework allows for a possible explanation as to the means by which certain norms have developed, especially with regard to how PVP was described in the focus groups as being the "correct" way to play *EVE.* Just as a plurality and hierarchy of masculinities exist (Connell and Messerschmidt 2005, 846), my research to date strongly suggests that there is both a plurality and a hierarchy of player activities within the *EVE* game world. This narrow interpretation of what counts as "real" *EVE* play (i.e., PVP) obscures other ways of playing (i.e., mining, manufacturing, role-play).

Throughout my interviews with current *EVE* players who prefer PVP, mining and manufacturing are the activities most frequently derided as "boring." These ingame activities are the arena of carebears and, in some players' opinions, should not be considered a "proper" way to play *EVE.* PVP and its related activities, without a doubt, dominate the narratives that are publicly circulated about *EVE* (Taylor et al. 2015). My own first introductions to this game were couched in war stories about the long-standing grudge between Band of Brothers and Goonswarm. Many *EVE* players can tell you about the major players of the First Great War, even if they started playing long after the last ship was destroyed. When gaming blogs and other media discuss *EVE,* coverage frequently focuses on the epic battles and/or scams and other so-called deviant behaviors (Bergstrom et al. 2013; Carter and Gibbs 2013). However, this is not the only way to play *EVE,* and it is not the only story to be told. Most of my interviews were with players who gravitated toward PVP and large-scale combat, largely because these are the players who are most visible (and easily accessible). Since Fanfest 2012, I have continued to interact with *EVE* players as part of my ongoing doctoral research. I have made particular effort to expand my informant base beyond players who participate in PVP combat and to actively seek out the experiences of those whose preferred *EVE* play consists of mining, industry, role-play, and/or any other player versus environment (PVE) content that is ignored and/or derided by the segment of the *EVE* player population that vocally disparages these activities as being those of carebears. But by spending the time to find other players—especially those who do participate in so-called alternative ways of playing *EVE*—it becomes easier to see the homogenizing effect that PVP-oriented play continues to have on this community.

I argue that it is not by accident that most public discussions about *EVE* remain overly focused on combat. Combat and PVP are most readily discussed because these are the activities of the most visible (and valorized) players. Other ways to play can and do exist, but why are they obscured from view? Recall the preceding description of the stereotype that girls and women are somehow more naturally inclined toward collaborative, noncompetitive play. I argue that mining and manufacturing, typically the activities of players who tend to gravitate toward high-sec space, are collaborative and therefore subconsciously gendered as more feminine than PVP-oriented activities. Certainly fleet warfare requires cooperation and collaboration, but any accusation of feminization of this cooperation can be quickly overshadowed by reminding that fleet warfare consists of hunting down and destroying one's enemies. In the following section, I interrogate this gendering of activities further, using Hulkageddon as my frame of reference.

## Hulkageddon and the Policing of Play: Real Players Don't QQ

Other chapters in this collection have made reference to the policing of play styles in *EVE* (see, e.g., Chribba's account in chapter 7). The idea that certain types of play should not be considered the play of "real" players is by no means a unique artifact of the *EVE* community. However, by paying closer attention to what sorts of play within this MMOG become valorized as compared to what sorts of play are derided, the gendered stereotypes underpinning each style of play become particularly apparent. Hegemonic masculinities do not presuppose participation from the majority of a society; in fact, only a small number of people may actually enact this privileged form of masculinity in their day-to-day lives. Similarly, the number of *EVE* players who actively participate in PVP is irrelevant. What matters here is that PVP is valued and exerts a normalizing influence over how communities feel they (and others) should or ought to be playing the game. Broadly reinforced by the elevation of hardcore games as stand-ins for real games and, by extension, hardcore players as the only true or real gamers (see, e.g., Kubrik's 2012 and Vanderhoef's 2013 explorations of this gendered divide), in the closing pages of this chapter, I interrogate how this plays out in *EVE* through those who participate in PVP being perceived as the "real" *EVE* players. I argue that just as casual games are frequently derided as being not real games, mining, manufacturing, and other non-PVP-related activities (if they are even mentioned) are discussed as if they are a less legitimate form of play within *EVE Online* (Taylor et al. 2015).

To illustrate the pervasiveness of the idea that PVP equates with legitimate play, I turn to a player-created in-game event, Hulkageddon, and the subsequent creation of the rival Griefergeddon event. Hulkageddon was a coordinated suicide-ganking contest to see who could kill the most miners in high-sec within a set time period. In other words, Hulkageddon began as a competition to see who could destroy the most ships being used for mining, likely destroying one's own ship in the process. Hulks, mining vessels that stand as a symbol to players who AFK mine in high-sec,[3] were targeted by a group of players who felt that this was an incorrect way to play *EVE*. Although destroying a mining vessel in high-sec would inevitably bring the wrath of CONCORD, the in-game nonplayer character police, the aggressors would allow their ships to be destroyed by this police force. This is key: by not attempting to evade CONCORD, their actions were not against any of the CCP-defined rules of the game. The first Hulkageddon in 2009 saw approximately three hundred miners' ships destroyed, and at the time of writing, the kill-board remains online and accessible.[4]

This was not a one-off event. Hulkageddon II was announced, and the popularity of this in-game event exploded, inflicting 278 billion ISK (roughly equivalent to US$8,340) worth of damage on the victims. This time, more than seventeen hundred ships were destroyed, and prizes of in-game currency were awarded to the most successful gankers. Also included was a competition for who received the best "hate mail" from a victim. Hulkageddon III came and went, and the event continued to attract additional participants intent on hunting miners. At this point, all mining vessels were targets; there was no safety in high-sec. Of the miners I have since interviewed, some described that when the dates of Hulkageddon III were announced, their corporation sent out a notice that all mining vessels should remain docked for the duration of the event. Players were encouraged to remain logged out of the game and to do something else for the week, as the best way to ensure their safety was not to play.

Throughout many interviews with current players (of all genders), as well as in player-authored blogs and forum posts, there has been frequent reference to the "tears" of other players. It seems that much can be gleaned about a player's personality and his or her place within the *EVE* community based on how the player reacts to hostile actions taken against the player's ship. A player who whines, cries, or complains about being attacked—even about being suicide-ganked in high-sec—is held in lower regard than a player who takes his or her demise in stride (as a man is expected to do). Without a doubt, *EVE Online* is a game of hierarchies, and Hulkageddon is an extreme example of a gendered hierarchy at play within the game.

In February 2011, Hulkageddon IV was held. While some PVE-focused players advocated a strike of sorts, refusing to sell their wares during the event, others felt that the week should be spent running missions or playing other games entirely, running down the clock until the hunting season ended. However, this time, the week unfolded in a slightly different manner, as a second coordinated event was set to run concurrently to Hulkageddon. Griefergeddon saw a rival group come together to create a prize pool for killing the players who attempted to hunt and kill the miners. This event was heralded as a way for miners to fight back:

> So it's Hulkageddon again, and you're angry. You can't believe how easy griefers have it, and now they dictate your gameplay style, and if you pay for the game in plex, even your real life income. Maybe you even think CCP should ban Hulkageddon, but we all know CCP won't, no mater now many times you politely ask or insult them. So lets do something about it. (Kodachi 2011)

Though the preceding quote and other player-generated messages in favor of Griefergeddon framed the event as a way to retaliate against their harassers, I wish to draw attention to the original provocation embedded within Hulkageddon: real *EVE* players PVP. And now, Griefergeddon is an event where players who previously were not inclined to participate in PVP are doing so to chase off their tormentors. Their motivations for participating in PVP likely differ from the motivations of players who enjoy this particular play style, but motivations do not change the ultimate result: PVP continues to reign supreme in this particular game world.

## Concluding Thoughts: Using *EVE* to Push Game Studies Forward

Through this example of the Hulkageddon and surrounding events, my goal has been to demonstrate that any meaningful attempt to study gender in *EVE* must move beyond the 4 percent of female players and examine the entire community. Similarly, a wider examination of the play styles that exist within *EVE* must occur beyond the overemphasis on PVP that remains the focus of *EVE*-related reporting (and indeed *EVE*-related academic research). In closing, I wish to stress that the categories of PVP and PVE, much like the categories of "hardcore" and "casual," are not nearly as rigid as the discussions of these categories (including this very chapter) make them out to be. Studying MMOG players is studying moving targets, as play styles are porous and (dis)interests, preferred in-game activities, or even a player's primary game of choice can radically shift over time. It remains unclear to what degree *EVE*-specific scholarship has helped to replicate the gendered stereotypes that pervade conversations about who is likely to be interested in this particular online community. However, by paying insufficient attention to the multitude of ways of playing *EVE* and remaining overwhelmingly focused on the insidious elements of game play, we have certainly helped reaffirm the narrative that *EVE* is a game that only a select few should play.

### NOTES

1  Game developers in this context should be taken to refer to mainstream/AAA developers. Though outside the scope of this chapter, an increasing diversity in the tools that can be used to make games has in turn led to an increased diversity in the sorts of stories that

are told through digital games. See, for an example of this opening up of game design to a wider demographic, Alison Harvey's (2014) discussion of Twine, a tool used by independent game designers for creating text-based games.

2 Development of *World of Darkness* was cancelled in April 2014 (Kuchera 2014).

3 "AFK" stands for "away from keyboard." AFK mining therefore refers to players who, instead of sitting at their computers, set up their ships to automatically mine a large asteroid and do something else outside of the game client until the task is completed.

4 http://hulkageddon.griefwatch.net.

## BIBLIOGRAPHY

Behnke, Kara A. 2012. "Ladies of Warcraft: Changing Perceptions of Women and Technology through Productive Play." In *Proceedings of the International Conference on the Foundations of Digital Games*, 288–89. New York: ACM Press. doi:10.1145/2282338.2282403.

Bergstrom, Kelly. 2013. "EVE Online Newbie Guides: Helpful Information or Gatekeeping Mechanisms at Work?" In *Selected Papers of Internet Research*. http://spir.aoir.org/index.php/spir/article/view/692.

Bergstrom, Kelly, Marcus Carter, Darryl Woodford, and Christopher A. Paul. 2013. "Constructing the Ideal EVE Online Player." Paper presented at the DiGRA 2013 Conference: DeFragging Game Studies, Atlanta, Ga., August. http://www.digra.org/digital-library/publications/constructing-the-ideal-eve-online-player/.

Beyer, Jessica L. 2012. "Women's (Dis)embodied Engagement with Male-Dominated Online Communities." In *Cyberfeminism 2.0,* edited by Radhika Gajjala and Yeon Ju Oh, 153–70. Digital Formations 74. New York: Peter Lang.

Bryce, Jo, and Jason Rutter. 2003. "Gender Dynamics and the Social and Spatial Organization of Computer Gaming." *Leisure Studies* 22, no. 1: 1–15. doi:10.1080/02614360306571.

Burrill, Derek A. 2008. *Die Tryin': Videogames, Masculinity, Culture.* New York: Peter Lang.

Bury, Rhiannon. 2001. "From a Room to a Cyberspace of One's Own: Technology and the Women-Only Heterotopia." In *Feminist (Re)visionings of the Subject: Landscapes, Ethnoscapes, and Theory Scapes,* 55–86. Lanham, Md.: Lexington Books.

Carter, Marcus, and Martin Gibbs. 2013. "eSports in EVE Online: Skullduggery, Fairplay and Acceptability in an Unbounded Competition." Paper presented at the Foundations of Digital Games Conference 2013, Chania, Greece, May. http://www.fdg2013.org/program/papers/paper07_carter_gibbs.pdf.

Chess, Shira. 2010. "A 36–24–36 Cerebrum: Productivity, Gender, and Video Game Advertising." *Critical Studies in Media Communication* 28, no. 3: 230–52. doi:10.1080/15295036.2010.515234.

Connell, Raewyn. 2009. *Gender: In World Perspective.* 2nd ed. Cambridge: Polity.

Connell, Raewyn, and James W. Messerschmidt. 2005. "Hegemonic Masculinity: Rethinking the Concept." *Gender and Society* 19, no. 6: 829–59. doi:10.1177/0891243205278639.

Coppa, Francesca. 2008. "Women, Star Trek, and the Early Development of Fannish Vidding." *Transformative Works and Cultures* 1. http://journal.transformativeworks.org/index.php/twc/article/view/44.

de Castell, Suzanne, and Mary Bryson. 1998. "Retooling Play: Dystopia, Dysphoria, and

Difference." In *From Barbie to Mortal Kombat Gender and Computer Games,* edited by Justine Cassell and Henry Jenkins, 232–61. Cambridge, Mass.: MIT Press.

Downey, Genesis. 2012. "Guilding, Gaming, and Girls." In *Cyberfeminism 2.0,* edited by Radhika Gajjala and Yeon Ju Oh, 171–85. Digital Formations 74. New York: Peter Lang.

Flanagan, Mary. 2005. "Troubling 'Games for Girls': Notes from the Edge of Game Design." Paper presented at the DiGRA 2005 Conference: Changing Views—Worlds in Play, Vancouver, Canada, June. http://www.digra.org/wp-content/uploads/digital-library/06278.14520.pdf.

Fron, Janine, Tracy Fullerton, Jacquelyn Ford Morie, and Celia Pearce. 2007. "The Hegemony of Play." Paper presented at Situated Play, DiGRA 2007 Conference, Tokyo, Japan, September. http://www.digra.org/wp-content/uploads/digital-library/07312.31224.pdf.

Gramsci, Antonio. 2011. *Prison Notebooks.* Translated by Joseph A. Buttigieg and Antonio Callari. Chichester, N.Y.: Columbia University Press.

Gray, Kishonna L. 2011. "Deviant Bodies Resisting Online: Examining the Intersecting Realities of Women of Color in Xbox Live." PhD diss., Justice Studies, Arizona State University.

———. 2012a. "Deviant Bodies, Stigmatized Identities, and Racist Acts: Examining the Experiences of African-American Gamers in Xbox Live." *New Review of Hypermedia and Multimedia* 18, no. 4: 261–76. doi:10.1080/13614568.2012.746740.

———. 2012b. "Intersecting Oppressions and Online Communities: Examining the Experiences of Women of Color in Xbox Live." *Information, Communication, and Society* 15, no. 3: 411–28. doi:10.1080/1369118X.2011.642401.

Harding, Sandra. 2011. "Introduction: Beyond Postcolonial Theory—Two Undertheorized Perspectives on Science and Technology." In *The Postcolonial Science and Technology Studies Reader,* edited by Sandra Harding, 1–31. Durham, N.C.: Duke University Press.

Hartmann, Tilo, and Christoph Klimmt. 2006. "Gender and Computer Games: Exploring Females' Dislikes." *Journal of Computer-Mediated Communication* 11, no. 4: 910–31.

Harvey, Alison. 2014. "Twine's Revolution: Democratization, Depoliticization, and the Queering of Game Design." *GAME: The Italian Journal of Game Studies* 3, no. 1: 95–107.

Ivory, James D. 2006. "Still a Man's Game: Gender Representation in Online Reviews of Video Games." *Mass Communication and Society* 9, no. 1: 103–14.

Jenson, Jennifer, and Suzanne de Castell. 2008. "Theorizing Gender and Digital Gameplay: Oversights, Accidents and Surprises." *Eludamos: Journal for Computer Game Culture* 2, no. 1: 15–25.

———. 2010. "Gender, Simulation, and Gaming: Research Review and Redirections." *Simulation and Gaming* 41, no. 1: 51–71. doi:10.1177/1046878109353473.

Jenson, Jennifer, Stephanie Fisher, and Suzanne de Castell. 2011. "Disrupting the Gender Order: Leveling Up and Claiming Space in an After-School Video Game Club." *International Journal of Gender, Science, and Technology* 3, no. 1: 149–69.

Kennedy, Helen W. 2011. "Female Quake Players and the Politics of Identity." In *The New Media and Technocultures Reader,* edited by Seth Giddings and Martin Lister, 201–14. New York: Routledge.

Kodachi, Kirith. 2011. "Hulkageddon IV and Griefer Geddon Results." *EVE Tribune,* March 14. http://www.eve-tribune.com/index.php?no=6_11&page=1.

Kubrik, Erica. 2012. "Masters of Technology: Defining and Theorizing the Hardcore/Casual

Dichotomy in Video Game Culture." In *Cyberfeminism 2.0,* edited by Radhika Gajjala and Yeon Ju Oh, 135–52. Digital Formations 74. New York: Peter Lang.

Kuchera, Ben. 2014. "CCP CEO on World of Darkness Cancellation: 'We Are Now the Eve Universe Company.'" *Polygon,* May 2. http://www.polygon.com/2014/5/2/5674352/World-of-darkness-cancellation-CCP-Fanfest.

Leray, Joseph. 2013. "Better Design Will Attract More Diverse Players, Says CCP." *Destructoid,* June 3. http://www.destructoid.com/boy-s-club-why-don-t-more-women-play-eve-online--254710.phtml.

Lucas, Kristen, and John L. Sherry. 2004. "Sex Differences in Video Game Play: A Communication Based Explanation." *Communication Research* 31, no. 5: 499–523. doi:10.1177/0093650204267930.

Paul, Christopher A. 2011. "Don't Play Me." In *Proceedings of the Sixth International Conference on Foundations of Digital Games,* 262–64. New York: ACM Press. doi:10.1145/2159365.2159406.

Steinkuehler, Constance, Elizabeth King, Esra Alagoz, Gabriella Anton, Sarah Chu, Jonathan Elmergreen, Danielle Fasher-Herro, et al. 2011. "Let Me Know When She Stops Talking: Using Games for Learning without Colonizing Play." In *Proceedings of the Seventh International Conference on Games + Learning + Society Conference,* 210–20. Pittsburgh, Pa.: ETC Press.

Taylor, Nicholas, Kelly Bergstrom, Jennifer Jenson, and Suzanne de Castell. 2015. "Alienated Playbour: Relations of Production in EVE Online." *Games and Culture* 10, no. 4: 365–88. doi:10.1177/1555412014565507.

Terlecki, Melissa, Jennifer Brown, Lindsey Harner-Steciw, John Irvin-Hannum, Nora Marchetto-Ryan, Linda Ruhl, and Jennifer Wiggins. 2010. "Sex Differences and Similarities in Video Game Experience, Preferences, and Self-Efficacy: Implications for the Gaming Industry." *Current Psychology* 30, no. 1: 22–33. doi:10.1007/s12144-010-9095-5.

Vanderhoef, John. 2013. "Casual Threats: The Feminization of Casual Video Games." *Ada: A Journal of Gender, New Media, and Technology,* no. 2. http://adanewmedia.org/2013/06/issue2-vanderhoef/.

Wells, Herbert George. 1913. *Little Wars: A Game for Boys from Twelve Years of Age to One Hundred and Fifty and for That More Intelligent Sort of Girl Who Likes Boys' Games and Books.* http://www.gutenberg.org/ebooks/3691.

Williams, Dmitri, Mia Consalvo, Scott Caplan, and Nick Yee. 2009. "Looking for Gender: Gender Roles and Behaviors among Online Gamers." *Journal of Communication* 59, no. 4: 700–725. doi:10.1111/j.1460-2466.2009.01453.x.

## The Social System in *EVE Online*

*Mantou (Zhang Yuzhou)*

*EVE* has a high level of freedom. It is a game of very real and complex player interaction. Overall, it is a strong simulation of society. The mode of interaction among the players, style of organization, and causes and effects of behavior are linked to real society in countless ways. Therefore the virtual competition within the game inevitably touches on real problems in the organization of society. In fact, this question is one that many corporation and alliance leaders, including me, have considered. In the real competition of *EVE,* institutional superiority is undoubtedly an important method each alliance will use to outpace its rivals.

In the current world of *EVE,* what kind of alliance structure and basic system is ultimately the most viable and executable? I believe that *EVE,* as a sandbox simulating reality, is in this respect similar to actual society. A theory we all encounter in school is that the economic foundation determines the superstructure, but how do we really understand it? Quite simply, one can't hope for medieval people to bring about a present-day democratic–republican system, because they don't possess the underlying circumstances.

Turning to *EVE,* in an *EVE* alliance, what are the constitutive components of the state? The corporations. One or several CEOs will establish a corporation, recruit new players, and develop logistics, and once the corporation has taken shape, it will join an alliance. What are the corporations in *EVE*? In fact, they are the feudal lords. As far as ordinary members are concerned, they first belong to a corporation, then to an alliance. If the corporation leaves the alliance or changes alliances, the great majority of corporation members will follow. In the same way, people of the feudal era belonged to the lord first, then to the country. For instance, in Japan, the common people are Japanese, but this is just the nationality to which they belong and nothing more. They do not directly belong to a nation or a government; they are first members of the Tokugawa, Oda, or Uesugi clan. Before China brought about the reunification of the nation, the circumstances were the same: people were first Qin or Jin, then members of the Zhou Dynasty. This is what we mean by feudalism. What is called feudalism is simply a means for the country to be divided, distributed into fiefdoms for lords to rule. The monarch rules the feudal lords, and in turn, the feudal lords rule the people. The case is similar in *EVE*: the alliance distributes territory to the corporations, the alliance manages the corps, and the corps manage each player.

Many players in *EVE* mention that the social system is full of backward dictatorships and autocracies. It is hard to find a meaningful success story of democratic–republicanism in the modern sense. The problem is not that we players do not have these concepts; rather, the problem lies in the fundamental form of society, as mentioned earlier.

In this way, corporations constitute the alliance like single feudal lords together constitute the state, so the alliance cannot achieve democratic–republicanism in the modern sense. The system of the division of territory is the core of the problem; rather, the problem lies not just in the division of territory but in how the people in the territory divide it. The ancients said, "Confer ten thousand households and never speak"—to confer a great land is its own justification. The people are conferred territory and simultaneously are subordinated by the lords and nobles. How can they exercise democratic power? Even the founding document of modern democracy, the British Magna Carta, was just a contract between a king and feudal lords and was in no way a contract between the nation's ruler and his people.

Thus serious problems arise for players who do not wish to alter these most fundamental forms of society but simply hope by means of sharing territory to bring about a system of democratic–republicanism. Clearly it is the feudal lords who make up the state. Clearly corporations together form the alliance. The leaders divide and confer the territory, and yet they want to share? Imagine if, during the Warring States period in China, or the Japanese Warring States period, or the European Middle Ages, people practiced sharing territory? They would have easily been subjugated by armed and organized people who would have "shared" their swords.

Second, the state—or, I should say, the alliance—management system also makes it fundamentally impossible to achieve a modern democracy. Running one corporation is OK; running five is OK; running the daily operation of ten corporations, twenty, is fine, but you cannot change the fundamental nature of the constitution of the alliance. The more people who participate in strategic decisions of the alliance, the easier it is to cause an internal power struggle and simply generate more trouble and danger.

Finally, where do we start if we want to probe the theoretical implementation of true democratic–republicanism in *EVE*? The first thing to do is to transform the societal structure, which is to say, smash the system of enfeoffment and of conferment of territory. How do we smash it? The Japan Restoration Party method is "withdrawal." The French method is both to invent a tool quickly to remove the heads of the feudal lords and to propose a great idea: the "citizen." What is a citizen? It means to be directly classified as part of a country, not some feudal lord's property—a national citizen. Only people directly subordinate to the state are able to have the ability, the right, and the power to directly participate in national politics, to push for the transformation of the entire nation. In the case of *EVE*, the first matter is to set up the game system to weaken the management authority of the corporation and to increase the level of authority of alliance management, for example, a system of taxation divided between the corporation and the alliance or a system by which alliance members can vote for or even impeach the alliance leader. We must liberate the people from the system of enfeoffment and from the system of the conferment of territory; only then can we speak of equality for citizens; only then can we speak of power for the masses; only then can we speak of a democratic republic! The people should no longer belong to the feudal lords, to the state, to the government. Let the corps member no longer belong only to the corp but really belong to the alliance. On this foundation, we can begin to speak of a truly democratically elected leader or collective leadership, and only then can we speak of an advanced societal system.

If *EVE* exists long enough to release a version that can finally consider the composition of society on this level, I am convinced that there will eventually be a democratic republic in *EVE* in the modern sense.

# 14

# Do *EVE Online* Players Dream of Icelandic Spaceships?

## The Role and Mechanisms of Co-creation in CCP's Success

*Jedrzej Czarnota*

We are not the gods of EVE. . . . We are her janitors.
—CCP Games employee

This statement accurately reflects the empowered position of players within *EVE Online* and the role of CCP Games as the chaperone of players' creativity. CCP creates boundaries of a system that is essentially designed to enable emergent game play. From this contingency-focused (Malaby 2009) architecture of *EVE Online,* a plethora of innovative patterns of interaction between the game and its users, and among the users themselves, occur. To allow this emergence to play out to its full potential, CCP developers interfere with *EVE* to a low extent. They focus their efforts on reinforcing players' preferences for game play, celebrating and legitimizing in-game events that players have initiated (such as great battles between player alliances), and maintaining the game software's smooth functioning. They do not set any objectives for their players' game play, whose actions are limited only by the terms of service (ToS), the end user license agreement (EULA), and the general "no cheating and no hacking" rules. Thus players take control by playing *EVE* the way they like, constantly testing and pushing the boundaries of the game. Such an emergence-promoting mode of engagement with *EVE,* coupled with specific types of customers who play it (Bergstrom et al. 2013) as well as technoliberal (Malaby 2009) culture dominating among the developers at CCP, paves the way for co-creation of the game itself to take place. What is more, this emergence and, stemming from it, co-creation have been integrated over the years by CCP as one of the core tenets of *EVE*'s business model. This has enabled CCP to sustainably capitalize on *EVE Online*'s competitive position, creating a market niche for a sandbox game of high difficulty, allowing its continued commercial and critical success. As a result, *EVE Online* is characterized by a unique relationship between its players and the studio. Players are highly vocal and interested in the development of the game, while the studio is willing to maintain an open dialogue with the community, closely listening to players' opinions and wishes. This has produced partner-like dynamics between players and CCP, further reinforcing the opportunities for co-creation of *EVE Online*.

The aim of this chapter is to explore this success of *EVE Online* in the context of players' involvement in game development at CCP. It is maintained that the mechanism ensuring this success is indeed the co-creation of the game by both CCP and its customers alike. Key aspects of this mutually beneficial process are explored, together with some managerial insights. The phenomenon of co-creation is investigated, with particular attention to the studio's perspective, thus situating this chapter in innovation studies discourse. In the global games industry, *EVE Online* is at the forefront of embracing players as a resource in game development, and thus close inspection of its model can yield valuable insights for other studios seeking to follow this style of game production. Moreover, this chapter also seeks to contribute to game studies by exploring the relationship between players and game developers, thus advancing our understanding of play experience and the meanings players bring to (or develop from) games and game play.

## Co-creation in *EVE Online*'s Context

Co-creation is a phenomenon constructed by both market and sociocultural forces (Banks and Potts 2010), and its effects play out in both of these dimensions simultaneously. Ample research has explored the motivations and characteristics of co-creating customers (Kohler et al. 2011a, 2011b; Füller 2010), investigating the roles of both intrinsic (such as joy of creating or learning) and extrinsic (such as financial gains or employment opportunities) motivators. The most general definition of co-creation can be summarized as customers seeking to play a greater role in the process of value creation (Hoyer et al. 2010), in which co-creation is considered an important manifestation of customer engagement behavior (van Doorn et al. 2010). Co-creation involves "consumers contributing a non-trivial component of the design, development, production, marketing and distribution of a new or existing product" (Hartley et al. 2013, 21). In the digital games setting, it is a process where players create artwork, provide the studio with extensive feedback, look for bugs, write backstories and lore for a game, produce add-ons, and make game mods, just to name a few manifestations.

To enable co-creation, CCP prides itself on the strong process of communicating with its players: "We provide them [the players] with numerous channels to reach the development team and thus influence the game itself" (CCP employee, personal interview, 2014). Furthermore, CCP also generously reveals information to players about upcoming features, current projects being worked on, and some details of the studio's operations and its esprit de corps. This is also reflected by the technoliberal culture (Malaby 2009) dominant at CCP—one that allows in-game events to play themselves out, with as few interventions from the developers as possible. It also involves the studio's close listening to the players' voices throughout all stages of *EVE*'s development and market delivery. Especially after the "Incarna" expansion, when CCP encountered severe backlash from its player community following the introduction of radical changes to the game (involving a new mode of monetization as well as not delivering on the promises made to customers), the development team working on *EVE* has strongly embraced the paradigm of listening to and working with their users. Such technoliberal culture allows for delegation of tasks as well as designation of time for processing and analyzing customer input at various stages of game development, and in different functions of the firm (development, marketing, PR, community, customer support, and business leadership).

Organizations shaped by technoliberalism are characterized by "their work on new institutional techniques to cultivate the indeterminacy previously anathema to organizations" (Malaby 2009, 16). With the distinction between the game makers and game players blurring in the case of *EVE,* it becomes paramount to allow players the access to the tools, or at least the attention, of the curators of the system where their creativity and agency play out (and bring significant value in the meantime). This also remains closely connected to the distribution of power between the game studio and its players—in a technoliberal approach, the studio relinquishes some of the control over its game, thus empowering players to shape the game's core experience (Taylor 2006). Such readiness to incorporate players' feedback must also be linked to the slack in the game production schedules within CCP, a thing that managers in companies normally avoid, as it is seen as diminishing productivity.

This culture is underscored by CCP's avoidance of heavy-handed regulation of the forms that player creativity assumes in *EVE*. Instead, CCP focuses on creating favorable conditions for this creativity to appear within the game-play limits it has designed—which is matched by studio employees' perceptions of themselves as facilitators, not controllers. *EVE Online,* designed as a complex sandbox system, further reinforces the ample opportunities for players to take the lead in shaping what the game is and how it is played (Boellstorff 2008). Sandbox game design in *EVE Online* relies on formal support and integration of players as productive designers of many aspects of the game experience (Taylor 2006)—especially those that touch on player sociality and competitive game play (see Figure 14.1). This is mostly exemplified by the lack of predetermined game-play structure; instead, players are left alone to come up with their own modes of interacting with the game. In such circumstances of game play, coupled with *EVE*'s unusually committed audience (Paul 2011), allowing players to become more like partners and co-designers than just passive consumers (although in a manner still controlled by CCP) seems like a sound business decision.

One of the biggest challenges that CCP encounters in such an approach to players' creativity is the control over the design vision of the game, especially when it comes to adhering to the business rationale of CCP as a commercial enterprise (Aoyama and

Figure 14.1. A huge battle between numerous player alliances in *EVE Online*, more than seventy-five hundred players were involved. The battle resulted solely from player in-game politics and game play within the sandbox design. From http://community.eveonline.com/news/dev-blogs/the-bloodbath-of-b-r5rb/.

Izushi 2008). This is an opportunity for tensions between players and the studio to arise—players, who are not necessarily expert game designers, may want changes to the game that developers deem infeasible (Banks 2009). Similarly, changes to the ToS or EULA that players may deem desirable may be unsound from a business point of view (e.g., changes promoting aggressive game play can be deterring to new customers buying the game). Incessant balancing of those tensions together with sustainable management of player expectations are among the key components of CCP's co-creative business strategy. Conversely, extensive relinquishing of control over the game could have catastrophic effects on its market performance, as it would lose its design cohesiveness, which could lead to erosion of its unique selling points and thus loss of appeal to a core demographic of players.

High-quality or high-exposure player contributions (e.g., the ones that garner a lot of attention on the forums or that have strong support from many players) are evaluated and reflected on by the CCP developers. Therefore developing new features for *EVE*, or modifying existing ones, can be seen as entailing two essential activities. According to O'Hern and Rindfleisch (2010), those activities are (1) enabling or disabling players to contribute their ideas to game development and (2) selecting which specific concepts and ideas should be pursued. In the first activity, CCP engages in customer co-creation mostly by making available various avenues for player contributions to *EVE Online* (player council, forums, fan gatherings, etc.). Note that some of the game features are developed entirely internally by CCP; that is, the studio does not seek any input from the players during production, and the details of development are kept confidential. In the second activity, CCP allows its players to control the selection of those contributions—albeit to a limited extent. The activity for selecting those resides predominantly within CCP's domain, and the developers have the final say on what player input is incorporated into the game.

## Data Sources and Methods

The data in this chapter come from interviews with CCP employees in all organizational functions—from business leadership through community managers and game developers. The processes, organizational structures, and enabling mechanisms for integrating players' input with the intraorganizational game production practices were of paramount interest to my data collection. Moreover, some of the veteran *EVE Online* players have also been interviewed in the course of this research, with the aim of gathering insights from the "other side" of the firm–customer divide (which, in the case of *EVE Online*, becomes blurred at times by the virtue of co-creative processes), thus allowing for a more complete picture of co-creative dynamics at play in *EVE*.

The interviews were conducted between October 2013 and May 2014 via Skype, with each lasting approximately one hour, and were semistructured (Robson 2011). All data in this chapter, unless otherwise stated, come from those interviews. Some of the respondents' descriptions of processes within CCP have been included in this chapter in the form of vignettes, illustrating CCP employees' perceptions of and feelings about the role of players in game development processes (Braun and Clarke 2013). Those interview data appear anonymized and rephrased to facilitate their reading and to ensure their succinct relevance to the discussion presented in this chapter.

## Community of *EVE*: Those Who Play within the Sandbox

The definition of community is adopted from Cohendet and Llerena (2009, 108) and is described as a "gathering of individuals who accept to exchange voluntarily and on a regular basis about a common interest or objective in a given field of knowledge"—where this common interest is *EVE Online*. Burger-Helmchen and Cohendet (2011) also add that the members of such a community share this knowledge on an informal basis and respect the social norms of the community (which in turn structure their behavior and beliefs in relation to *EVE Online*).

The exceptionally homogeneous composition of *EVE Online*'s player community (Bergstrom 2013), consisting almost entirely of older males working in technical disciplines (such as IT, engineering, and medicine, but also in law and the armed forces), contributes to the relatively stronger relationship between players and the game developer than is found in other games: "The average age of an *EVE* player is thirty-two. Other [massively multiplayer online games, MMOGs] have audiences which are much younger. *EVE* has players from very unlikely demographics; many very highly qualified people are attracted to playing *EVE*. Entrepreneurs hone their skills in *EVE* in the game's economy" (CCP employee, personal interview, 2014). The strength of this community is further reinforced by *EVE*'s unique single-server configuration, the persistent transmedia identity of the *EVE* player, and the player-driven governance of the game (Gibbs, Carter, and Mori 2013). Design decisions made by CCP pertaining to the game's difficulty or that are necessary for in-game survival or interaction with other players (see Figure 14.2) decrease the size of the likely audience for *EVE*, while making its player base more homogeneous and stickier for those who fit the narrowed target demographic (Paul 2011). Other game design elements, such as departures from

| Sandbox type of game play (weak, predetermined game-play structure) | Single-server configuration | Lack of traditional (humanoid avatar) player representation (Carter et al. 2012) | Punishing learning curve (Paul 2011) and difficult game overall |
|---|---|---|---|
| Imperative to form in-game social networks to survive (Paul 2011) | High efficiency of devious and ruthless game-play strategies | Limited amount of graphical detail allowed by game engine | Focus on the economy and military in game-play design |

Figure 14.2. Examples of CCP's design decisions contributing to the formation of cognitive communities of *EVE* players as well as those communities' high uniformity.

conventions of how a player is represented in *EVE,* further contribute to this (Berg-strom et al. 2013).

In such idiosyncratic game-play circumstances, in a system that encourages emergent, sandbox interactions and player self-governance, the community of players as a source of knowledge about *EVE* is an asset of enormous value to CCP. This view is also corroborated by Burger-Helmchen and Cohendet (2011, 321) in their observation that "game players can be considered genuine experts in this field, and as such they are an important source of knowledge, which circulates through . . . channels that lead to the firm." This may sound paradoxical—that developers of a game rely on the knowledge of their players and their ability to fully understand the product—but in a game that welcomes so many divergent approaches to interaction, it should not, on second thought, be surprising.

This is a sentiment many CCP employees express: "Players are experts at playing *EVE* Online, with their knowledge about the game surpassing that of ours on many occasions. . . . Our players are best informed about the ways they like to en-gage with *EVE*" (CCP employee, personal interview, 2013). This can be compared to von Hippel's (2005) work on customers possessing the best knowledge about their needs. Moreover, players of *EVE* have proven their usefulness as developers of soft-ware complementing and enhancing the experience of playing the game. By devel-opment of such toolkits as EVEMon (Battleclinic), the EVE Fitting Tool, and DOTLAN EveMaps, the players have not only contributed to the quality of *EVE's* game play but have also established new ways of playing the game and delivered value to the cus-tomers and CCP as a company.

Therefore, CCP considers players a valuable source of information about their needs and game-play habits as well as a resource for creativity equipped with the skills necessary for game development (many *EVE* players are skilled programmers, talented artists, or competent IT project managers). The community of *EVE* players comprises members with various sets of those skills and interests. Players' reasons for engaging in the community's activities vary, and so do their motivations for get-ting involved in co-creative activities (Füller 2010). Those various motivations can exist both in the sociocultural and market domains of co-creation, contributing here to the observations of Banks and Potts (2010) on the co-evolution of those domains. From this blend of players' skills, as well as their various motivations for engaging in co-creation, Burger-Helmchen and Cohendet (2011) identify four types of game us-ers: average players (forming a community with brand loyalty but not contributing to a cognitive community bringing competencies to the studio), tester type, player type, and developer type (all of the latter three building cognitive communities, contribut-ing to the competence of the studio).

Managing those diverse player types and thus various subsegments of the *EVE* community requires a specific type of competence from CCP, one that is a component of the studio's commercial success with *EVE Online.* It is the ability to build sandbox, emergence-focused game designs for player creativity as well as the capacity to maintain communication and relationships with the player base in the context of those malleable game worlds. It grants CCP a competitive advantage over other studios in the MMOG sector and allows it to succeed in a market niche populated by players of specific tastes for game play with the tendency to form cognitive communities. Thanks to various devices CCP employed in its game design (see Figure 14.2), the community of *EVE* players is predominantly cognitive, according to Burger-Helmchen and Cohendet's (2011) definition. This leads to an increased likelihood for *EVE* players to engage in co-creation, and thus despite being relatively small in size (approximately five hundred thousand users; Roman 2014), it has a community that is a valuable asset to CCP, worth the resources and special attention devoted to it.

## Tools for Co-creation of *EVE Online*

Listening to players' input, as well as integrating that input with the studio's game development practices, is critical to CCP's success with *EVE* (Figure 14.3). CCP undertakes an ongoing review process, reflecting on player input in the context of CCP's vision for *EVE Online*. Various tools for interacting with the community and

Figure 14.3. Appreciating the scale of the battle presented in Figure 14.1 and the number of players involved (as well as player in-game property losses of approximately US$330,000), CCP commemorated the site of the battle by permanently placing the wreckages and destroyed hulls of ships where the fight took place (destroyed player ships normally disappear after some time). Commemorative text was also added to the site. This is an illustration of CCP's general culture of recognizing and empowering players as co-creators of *EVE Online*. From http://community. eveonline.com/news/dev-blogs/the-bloodbath-of-b-r5rb/.

multiple processes through which to engage players in co-creating *EVE* are part of an open dialogue between the company and its customers.

Co-creation of *EVE* occurs via three main channels: physical gatherings, Internet discussion forums, and players' voluntary advisory bodies to CCP (a player council and a volunteer program). All three channels serve to establish organic and undisrupted flow of information between players and developers. Their other roles are to "filter out the noise"—to create outlets for communication that will be transparent to CCP's analysis and that will yield information relevant to *EVE* development efforts. A third application is to produce information that is possible to assimilate into CCP's internal game production processes. Finally, with players continually interacting with *EVE* in new ways, this communication enables CCP developers to gauge whether customers interact with the game's features as planned or generate new modes of game play.

At CCP, internal processing of player input can happen in a variety of ways. An example of such a process for a design issue is given in vignette 1 (CCP uses scrum project management practice; Keith 2010).

> **Vignette 1:** *Description of CCP's Processes for Assimilating Player Input*[1]
>
> Feedback is systematically consolidated and brought on a regular basis to the developers by customer support and community management teams. Those teams use both quantitative (software searching for key words in players' forum posts) and qualitative methods (judging of the players' sentiment by community managers and game masters) to synthesize feedback from the players. One gauge CCP uses for determining the pertinence of an issue is how frequently it appears in the reports on the state of community. If an issue becomes recurrent, it is taken on as a development or marketing project (the issues do not pertain strictly to in-game problems). Alternatively, during a design department daily ten- to fifteen-minute stand-up meeting, one of the developers can bring up an issue he or she encountered on a forum. Then the group checks whether it is a pertinent issue or something not to worry about (the design department on an aggregate level has a very holistic overview of the game and excels at determining the urgency of problems and issues). If the issue can be resolved by the design team, it is taken to the production level, where a senior producer takes it to the product owners and lead game designer, who will then appoint a team to take on the problem, and the problem or issue becomes part of the team's backlog. The business leadership team has many meetings concerning each project, which include representatives from the development, marketing, finance, and community management departments. This team copes with responding to those player issues that require significant or composite changes to *EVE* (if the team is conflicted, the executive producer casts the tie-breaking vote). This team ensures that player-induced changes do not negatively affect *EVE*'s quality as a game or the commercial interests of CCP.

If the issue is technical in nature (e.g., related to a bug in the game code), then the channels will be different. In this case, it is possible to distinguish formal and informal channels, as shown in vignette 2.

**Vignette 2:** *Description of the Differences between CCP's Formal and Informal Channels of Assimilating Player Input Concerning Bug Fixing (Quality Assurance)*

Via the formal channel, a bug petition will be reported, normally by a player or one of the bug hunters (who are volunteer players themselves). Subsequently, it will be formally tracked via a defect tracking system and will go into the bucket of the relevant department, and a person responsible for fixing it will be assigned together with the bug's priority. Via the informal channel, staff members who are involved as players in *EVE* will encounter or hear about a bug and will personally push for the bug to be fixed (despite the fact that bug flagging is not part of their job description)—becoming, in a way, champions of fixing that bug. After such a champion successfully advocates that a bug needs addressing with the relevant members of the development team, the bug is brought onto the official track (for bookkeeping reasons) and processed formally from that point onward.

These processes reveal the attention paid to player input by individual game developers and the deeply ingrained responsiveness to player input within CCP's organizational culture. After all, the main objective is to contrive such a contingency within a game system that will allow for emergent patterns to arise (Malaby 2009).

Over the lifetime of *EVE Online,* the degree of players' influence on the game has also been changing: "In the early days [of *EVE*], player input was quite innovative. Today, long-term vision has become important. So it has become less about players' influence on high-level development and more about giving tools to the players, ensuring that players get the best out of the infrastructure available in the game" (CCP employee, personal interview, 2014). In other words, in the early days of *EVE,* suggestions and input from players had the tendency to be radically innovative (Utterback 1994) and to open up new trajectories for *EVE* game play. Today, mostly because of the existence of a roadmap for *EVE*'s development, as well as other titles designed to be integrated with *EVE Online (EVE Valkyrie* and *Dust 514),* players' input cannot influence the high-level vision for the game, which is controlled more strictly and must be in line with the studio's strategy. Instead, CCP focuses on giving players tools that allow for the maximum level of emergent game play to occur within *EVE*'s existing systems.

## FANFEST AND OTHER PHYSICAL GATHERINGS

The largest and most important of *EVE* player gatherings throughout the year is Fanfest, held annually in the spring in Reykjavik, Iceland. "Up to two thousand *EVE Online* players and fans come to celebrate their involvement in the game, as well as to meet the developers. An additional fifteen to twenty thousand watch the live broadcast from Fanfest on the Internet" (CCP employee, personal interview, 2013). For CCP, this presents an opportunity to connect with players and, more importantly, to gather their feedback about the game in an informal, personal way. For players, it is also an occasion to give suggestions to the developers. Such direct communication allows CCP better insight into players' ideas and concerns: "There have been many instances where *EVE* was changed as a result of those informal chats" (CCP employee, personal interview, 2014). In the accounts given by CCP employees, the motif of superior communication at Fanfest—as being free of the Internet's "information noise"—is recurring (because it is more succinct and less emotional in face-to-face circumstances).

During Fanfest, activities are geared toward enhancing communication between players and developers and ensuring that both formal and informal channels for information flow are open. Fanfest and physical gatherings are not only about player-to-CCP communication—CCP takes this opportunity to announce new expansions and new features and to present upcoming products and the long-term vision for the game. It also uses these events to familiarize the players with business aspects of CCP. Important community announcements, such as Council of Stellar Management (CSM) election results, are also made during Fanfest.

Fanfest consists of various activities, such as roundtables, presentations, keynote talks, and social events. During roundtables, developers sit down together with players and discuss the game. Such events are recorded; their time and location are advertised in the Fanfest program to ensure attendance of interested parties. The discussions pertain to upcoming and existing features of *EVE*. There are dedicated roundtables for player versus environment (PVE) game play, player versus player (PVP) game play, null-sec game play, localization (one roundtable for each of four *EVE* languages), in-game industry, community, CSM, and game lore. Presentations are about developers familiarizing the players with CCP's work and where the studio is going with new or existing features, as well as what will happen in the future of the game. There is always a Q&A session at the end of a presentation, and those discussions yield useful and actionable feedback and ideas for CCP. Throughout the Fanfest, high-profile keynotes are delivered on the topic of all major CCP titles as well as on the company itself. Those talks normally include high-level visions of CCP's products and how the games that CCP makes fit within the company's overall mission. Finally, Fanfest is famous for the rich informal interaction between players and CCP employees. Events such as pub crawls, trips around Iceland, concerts, and spontaneous activities, such as hotel and house parties, become venues for informal and in-depth information exchange between the players and developers about the game and its evolution.

Such rich interaction between the users of *EVE Online* and its developers is possible because of their shared involvement in the game (many of the developers are avid fans of *EVE* themselves). "The game is the topic of many conversations during Fanfest and other fan gatherings as well. We try to be like 'dry sponges' soaking up all the feedback and information throughout the event. Developers record their conversations with fans (to capture all of their feedback and ideas) or write themselves e-mails with notes" (CCP employee, personal interview, 2013). CCP engages with the community to ensure that players' interest in contributing input to *EVE* remains high (Burger-Helmchen and Cohendet 2011) and that their contributions are appreciated. "The community's sentiment is usually at its highest around Fanfest, or right after it, and we try to keep this feeling going throughout the year, for example, by releasing videos from CCP's offices, providing the community with updates, or writing developer blogs" (CCP employee, personal interview, 2014).

Nevertheless, Fanfest is not the only gathering of this type. Other events include EVEVegas (held in Las Vegas, Nevada), EVE Down Under (held in Sydney, Australia), and many other smaller player gatherings throughout the world. Many of those events are organized and run entirely by players. Often CCP sends some developers to participate in the gathering, bringing news and promotional materials. CCP delegates developers even to events attended by as few as forty to fifty people (examples here include Veto Summer Camp and gatherings in pubs in major cities). For other events, CCP developers will often connect with players via Skype (CCP employees, personal interviews, 2013–14).

### FORUMS, SOCIAL MEDIA, AND BLOGS

Online discussion forums serve the function of communicating players' feedback, ideas, concerns and wishes to the game developers. Forums themselves are also indispensable in allowing game-related exchanges between players to occur, and thus vibrant forums are a sine qua non of the emergence of player community. For the purposes of co-creation, the section of the forums most of interest is "Features and Ideas," where players are invited to share their ideas and participate in discussion about existing and upcoming features. Another section instrumental to *EVE*'s co-creation is "Test Server Feedback," from which CCP can gather players' opinions and observe how players utilize game features. Game developers and community managers frequent these forums, keeping their eyes peeled for players' concerns, suggestions, and input. Three interesting cases of such co-creative activities between the player community and the game development studio have emerged (vignette 3).

> **Vignette 3:** *Specific Cases from EVE Online's History Illustrating CCP's Processes for Assimilating Player Input*
>
> The idea of a capital ship arose from a discussion in the "Features and Ideas" section. As players were discussing their ideas for ship design, the developers were listening in (and getting involved in the discussion as well). Eventually the discussion fizzled out, but sometime later, the players' design got incorporated into *EVE* (with some alterations from the original discussion, which resulted from CCP making sure that the design fit within the artistic vision and aesthetics of the game). In this case, CCP sourced some ideas from the community of players for subsequent internal development and introduction into the game.
>
> Ship rebalancing is an important activity for maintaining *EVE*'s playability, especially in terms of PVP game play. In this case, the developers provided the player community with statistics and raw mathematical data about ships requiring balancing. Players started working with the numbers and discussing possible changes, resulting in very long forum threads. The development team was involved in those discussions as well and

went through multiple iterations with the players, listening to their feedback after each iteration. Finally, the CCP balancing team and the community came to a compromise between innovating and staying true to the classic *EVE* feel and game play. This is an example of how CCP delegates some of the tasks that players are adept at solving (because of their deeper individual familiarity with *EVE* and their ever-emergent game-play habits) or of which they have better knowledge to its customer community.

Last, during the "Design a Ship" contest, players were invited to design the graphics for ship hulls. The four best hulls were selected and were introduced into *EVE* a year later: an example of player designs being directly incorporated into the game, without many changes by CCP. The designs submitted during that contest are remembered among CCP's employees as excellent, which is a testament to the general technical and artistic skill of players and their ability to contribute to game development.

Moreover, including player designs in the game serves as a memento to the players, an element of deepening their relationship with the game (which becomes more of their creation with each such successful submission). Therefore co-creation not only serves to improve the game by incorporating the best possible ideas but also works as a PR and marketing tool, drawing customers closer to the product and increasing the likelihood of positive network effects (e.g., manifesting as favorable word of mouth; Banks and Potts 2010).

Finally, one more means of communication between CCP and its players is via the comments feature on the *EVE* Developer's Blog. *EVE* developers will describe their work on new or existing features (which are normally published before the features become live in the main game, e.g., when a feature is tested on the test server), and the player community is invited to leave comments and suggestions. From there, CCP can get a good idea of players' preferences and issues ahead of time, before any tension with the community caused by changes to existing game play can occur. Other valuable outlets for listening to player feedback and ideas include third-party forums (such as Reddit or TheMittani.com) and social media.

## COUNCIL OF STELLAR MANAGEMENT AND VOLUNTEER PROGRAM

The CSM is a democratically elected group of players who are assigned an advisory function to *EVE*'s development (the rules and rationale for this democratic process have been outlined in Óskarsson 2014). The members of the CSM are flown to CCP's headquarters twice during their one-year term, where after signing a nondisclosure agreement, they are invited to participate in *EVE* development meetings with the studio's staff. CSM members also have access to dedicated sections of the forums, where they can discuss *EVE Online* and its community with developers. Communication between CSM members and CCP is further facilitated by CSM members' access to the personal Skype addresses of developers and community managers. The CSM is designed to fulfill the following functions (CCP employees, personal interviews, 2013–14; Óskarsson 2014):

1. represent players' interests and be their voice, influencing the development of *EVE* so that players do not feel that their interests are being threatened as well as ensuring that their feedback is given fair consideration (e.g., when CCP wants to introduce changes to the ToS or EULA)
2. function as a review board for CCP when it is planning to make changes to the game, such as introducing new features, and to highlight any potential problems (e.g., the balancing of the Marauder ship, when the CSM was providing direction to and insight into the many iterations of the developers' work)
3. mediate between CCP and the community in crisis or in other acute situations (e.g., during the "Incarna" expansion's aftermath, when the CSM was a conduit for speaking with the very unsettled community in a controlled manner; the CSM was instrumental in calming things down and acting as a buffer for emotion-laden communications)
4. convey the community's sentiment and mood about the game to CCP (e.g., speaking to the CSM after the release of a new expansion, explaining how the community has received the new features and content)

One of the biggest advantages of the CSM is that "it provides CCP with distilled, coherent feedback aggregated from the players" (CCP employee, personal interview, 2014). Within CCP, a community management team member is entirely responsible for managing the activities of the CSM and for monitoring its interactions with CCP. This is because the incorporation and full use of the CSM's feedback and communications demand a lot of resources. Overheads required to run and manage the CSM include a communication infrastructure, internal mailing lists, and involvement of the CSM in sprint reviews; CSM members also are stakeholders on various development teams. Nevertheless, those overheads also provide an intrastudio framework for processing the CSM's input, which facilitates its integration with game development. This interaction between CCP and the CSM occurs normally via forums, e-mail, and Skype, with the high points of interaction being the summits (for a detailed description of a CSM Summit, see vignette 4). The modes and format of CCP's collaboration with the CSM evolved over the years before reaching their current shape; in May 2014, the CSM was in its ninth term.

**Vignette 4:** *Description of a CSM Summit*

A CSM Summit usually lasts three days. The members are first introduced, and then they sit in meetings with the developers from each development team (separate sessions are held for marketing, PR, community, and business). During those meetings, CSM members are brought up to speed in terms of what CCP is currently working on and are requested to record notes and minutes. After the summit, CCP goes through these compiled minutes and ensures their compliance with the nondisclosure agreement (the minutes are later released to the public). Once the summit ends, those minutes are distributed to respective development teams, and the issues that have been identified as valid during the meetings are put to development. Feedback from the CSM in such forms is tailored to fit into the CCP game development pipelines, and the process of acting upon CSM feedback is established within the studio's production practices.

Apart from the CSM, CCP has established another tool to involve some players in active participation in *EVE*'s development. The Interstellar Services Department (ISD) is a volunteer program that invites players to become "official" collaborators with CCP on some aspects of game development. Similarly to the CSM, after a successful application process, those volunteer players are asked to sign a nondisclosure agreement. The ISD has five divisions, which correspond to various interests of players volunteering in the program: bug hunters, in-game news reporters, game backstory (so-called lore) creators, game wiki curators, and users wishing to help new players find their way around *EVE*. Players involved in the ISD do not become employees of CCP in any way and are under no obligation to fulfill any duties for the studio; nevertheless, they become involved in *EVE*'s development (the ISD displays some basic organizational hierarchy; volunteer players are given tasks by the development team and remain in closer communication with CCP than do regular players). ISD players are not explicitly rewarded by the studio (they are granted no special privileges and are not paid), except for recognition and higher chances of getting employed by CCP—which is one of the first things stated on the ISD's official website (Figure 14.4). ISD members therefore

Figure 14.4. Screenshot of the official ISD website (part of the official *EVE Online* website) showing two of the activities with which volunteer players can get involved. From http://community.eveonline.com/community/volunteer-program/.

have some impact on the way that *EVE Online* is developed, although their creativity and freedom in this process remain severely limited, as they act more like submitters of work commissioned by the studio rather than having an active role in shaping the direction in which *EVE Online* evolves.

## Discussion and Managerial Insights

Co-creation as a strategy is not always suitable for and beneficial to all companies. A number of conditions and circumstances, some of them established by the studio, some emerging from its interaction with customers, must be in place for this mode of game development to generate value. It is the manager's role in an organization to decide whether her company can benefit from co-creation, and in what ways. This chapter has demonstrated how very specific and carefully orchestrated characteristics of *EVE Online,* its player base, and CCP Games as a company (and its culture) come together to enable co-creation. Other firms or studios in the games industry can have different visions for their products, different modes of corporate functioning, or other types of audiences (e.g., games made for children) that render co-creation an undesirable choice for them.

Apart from firms' propensity to co-create, companies may also make mistakes when attempting to take advantage of co-creation. For instance, research has shown that a firm cannot seek to replace its internal competence only with that sourced from customers in a co-creative setup—this quickly leads to the erosion of the community's creativity and their loss of interest in the process (Burger-Helmchen and Cohendet 2011). There are well-known cases of co-creation backfiring and becoming a liability for a firm, with a disgruntled community of players generating highly negative word of mouth, refusing to purchase the final product, and causing the studio to experience severe financial difficulties (e.g., the Auran case discussed by Banks 2013 or the Spar bag contest case discussed by Gebauer, Füller, and Pezzei 2013). What follows here is a handful of observations from CCP's model that might inform managerial practice elsewhere in the games industry.

### TYPES OF PLAYER INPUT

Players' input into *EVE*'s development, whether in the form of feedback on new features, suggestions for EULA changes, new ship designs, or game-balancing changes, can be classified into two broad categories: idea-centric and solution-centric input (O'Hern et al. 2011). These types of user input can be either beneficial or detrimental to CCP, depending on the service development stage at which the input appears (Piller, Ihl, and Vossen 2011). Despite being at first glance superior, solution-centric player input is particularly dangerous to the company's productivity. The input needs to be "translated" from the form in which it is contributed by the players into a form useable by the firm (e.g., in terms of programming language used or type of software required to process such input); its quality needs to be assessed and controlled. Therefore this kind of input can easily distract the development team from its normal tasks and work routines. Consequently, time expenditures and disruptions caused to game development can negatively outweigh any potential benefit from such player-proposed solutions. CCP managers need to understand how to separate various strands of player feedback and when to allow this feedback to be processed by development teams. The type of player input can also be linked to the motivations that drive users to engage in co-creation: intrinsic, extrinsic, or externalized intrinsic, according to one categorization (Füller 2010), or financial, social, technical, and psychological, according to another (Hoyer et al. 2010). This would allow for understanding which player group, characterized by which particular motivation type, is most likely to contribute a given kind of input to *EVE* development.

Furthermore, regardless of the form player input into *EVE Online* takes, assimilation of the input with existing studio practices will remain a problem. One solution is learning how to incorporate slack times into the studio's game development routines, which can serve as dedicated periods during production when developers can process player input (including activities such as evaluation of the contributions, coding, and debugging). Ensuring the ability to sustainably attract and process player input without causing loss of productivity to the studio is one of the key competencies to master (Burger-Helmchen and Cohendet 2011).

## GOVERNANCE AND CONTROL OVER *EVE*

In Malaby's (2006) understanding, under the circumstances of vertical authority, allowing players a high degree of freedom in their mode of engagement with *EVE* (embodied here by the sandbox game design of *EVE Online,* as opposed to the "theme park" game design seen, for example, in *World of Warcraft*), two types of decentralized control exist (Hardt and Negri 2001). These types allow for predicting the patterns of both game play and player input into *EVE Online*. They are implicit governance of cultural convention (the social practices and expectations of *EVE* players) and the architecture of the system, meaning the constraints introduced by the allowances of the game software (which is ultimately controlled by CCP; Taylor 2006). Those two types of governance in *EVE*'s open world direct and shape the interaction of players with the game itself as well as their input into its development under co-creative dynamics. Understanding the allowances and limitations of those forms of control is of paramount importance to CCP in maintaining control over its product. After all, when engaging in co-creation, CCP suffers from diminished control over strategic planning and increased complexity of managing the studio's objectives (Hoyer et al. 2010), and thus all other available forms of control must be recognized by CCP and applied to their maximum potential. Conversely, CCP developers view themselves and their users as particular kinds of gamers and therefore favor a particular kind of game—one that accords with the technoliberal ideology that permeates

*EVE Online.* Also, many of the current CCP employees used to be *EVE Online* players before being hired by the studio (this way, CCP ensures that the developers have good understanding of *EVE*'s mood, audience, and complexities; CCP employees, personal interviews, 2013–14). This unifying identity across the customer–firm divide allows for a degree of trust, which is instrumental to CCP's readiness to allow players' co-creation of *EVE.*

## DECIDING WHEN, OR IF, TO ENGAGE IN CO-CREATION

According to Hoyer et al. (2010), the main firm-level impediments to co-creation include concerns about secrecy, ownership of intellectual property rights, information overload, and production feasibility. There are also challenges to managing potentially negative word of mouth, recognizing valuable ideas from numerous sources of player input, and controlling customer expectations and relationships. These impediments all pertain for CCP, for which the points mentioned earlier must be compensated by the stimulators of co-creation (as the company engages in this form of activity). The stimulators include reduction of development costs, increased effectiveness of CCP's products (through closer fit to players' needs, higher perceived quality, and better differentiation from other games available on the market), strengthening of the relationship with players, savings on marketing expenses (thanks to greater customer enthusiasm and enhanced word-of-mouth effects), and early warning of potential issues with the new product or feature (Hoyer et al. 2010). Understanding the precarious balance of these factors, as well as their application to CCP's business environment, is of critical importance to this studio's market strategy. Moreover, the balance of factors will likely be altered in the near future, as more game development companies begin to embrace the idea of co-creation in their production practices, likely leading to a decrease in number of available customers to provide input (Wexler 2011). From there, the games industry will likely see a new form of competition between studios—competition for customers as co-creative agents and as a resource for generation of value in game development.

## Conclusion

CCP Games's approach embraces the tenets of "customer-centric enterprises" (Piller, Ihl, and Vossen 2011). CCP shares (at the strategic level) interdependencies and values with customers over the long term. At the tactical level, CCP also aligns its processes with the customers' convenience instead of that of operations (seen, e.g., in CCP's internal communication structures enforced by the establishment of the CSM). At CCP, a customer-centric organizational structure (Piller, Ihl, and Vossen 2011) is also adopted, in which traditionally separate functions, such as sales, marketing, and customer service, become integrated (exemplified by the cross-organizational business leadership teams making decisions on changes to game design). Hence, harnessing players as a resource for game development requires not only successful community management but also mechanisms for incorporating the input from those players into internal game development practices. This involves flexible organizational structures (ability to incorporate slack time into production, a move that runs counter to conventional managerial wisdom; Burger-Helmchen and Cohendet 2011) and an appropriate culture embraced by the firm's employees, as well as their unrestricted communications with customers. The enabling mechanism in the case of successful co-creation of *EVE Online* is the committed community of players, who are both willing to and capable of engaging in creatively contributing to the game (because they form cognitive communities). Such a community is rare in the digital games industry, and the establishment, continuing renewal (against the high churn rates of the *EVE* player base; Feng, Brandt, and Saha 2007), and maintenance of this dedicated group of players are among core competencies building CCP's success.

The relationship between CCP and the players of *EVE Online* is somewhat symptomatic of the changes to the games industry at large. Studios are increasingly starting to notice the value that engaged customers bring to their operations. Those engaged customers also enable studios to innovate business models and to experiment with new monetization and distribution techniques (free-to-play, freemium, etc.). At its heart, this relationship attempts to dynamically balance the forces of rationalization that characterize modern game development practices (Tschang 2007), together with the "riot" of unrestricted and difficult-to-manage creativity stemming from players' emotional attachment to the game. Moreover, this relationship plays itself out in the conditions of games as a service (Vargo and Lusch 2004), where the studio is expected to provide ongoing experiences to its customers and where the customers are actively engaged in the creation of value of the game (as it is being experienced by them and as their actions coproduce the game for themselves and for fellow users alike). Those changes do not only pertain to CCP and *EVE Online* alone but have begun to characterize the majority of the global games industry—making CCP's case interesting in terms of its early and prognostic nature for what may soon become a commonplace practice.

Today, tapping into the market niche defined by both *EVE* players' affinity to CCP's uncompromising design decisions (see Figure 14.2) and the close collaboration between CCP and *EVE* players on making the game (so it even further fits the needs of the players populating the niche) has established CCP's sound market position. *EVE Online* is the only MMOG of its age that is not losing players—on the contrary, it has observed a gradual increase in player numbers since its release (Roman 2014). As of today, there are no signs of CCP losing that position—having survived multiple crises (e.g., the "Incarna" expansion or the Mittani scandal), it has emerged stronger and more aware of what it is trying to achieve and to whom it caters. The case of CCP has demonstrated the importance of the lasting relationship between studio and players in achieving commercial success in the games industry, proving conclusively that player communities and studios are symbiotic actors. The other implication of that finding to game studies also comes to the fore—one reaffirming the fact that in academic research of games, not only the players and their communities but also the organizations that make those games and that stage those experiences need to be understood to fully capture the phenomenon of digital gaming.

## NOTE

1 Vignettes are derived from interviews of CCP employees held from October 2013 to May 2014.

## BIBLIOGRAPHY

Aoyama, Yuko, and Hiro Izushi. 2008. "User-Led Innovation and the Video Game Industry." Paper presented at the IRP Conference, London, May 22–23.

Banks, John. 2009. "Co-creative Expertise: Auran Games and *Fury*—A Case Study." *Media International Australia: Incorporating Culture and Policy* 130: 77–89.

———. 2013. *Co-creating Videogames*. London: Bloomsbury Academic.

Banks, John, and Jason Potts. 2010. "Co-creating Games: A Co-evolutionary Analysis." *New Media and Society* 12, no. 2: 252–70.

Bergstrom, Kelly. 2013. "EVE Online Newbie Guides: Helpful Information or Gatekeeping Mechanisms at Work?" In *Selected Papers of Internet Research 14*. Denver, Colo.: Association of Internet Researchers.

Bergstrom, Kelly, Marcus Carter, Darryl Woodford, and Christopher Paul. 2013. "Constructing the Ideal EVE Online Player." Paper presented at DiGRA 2013: DeFragging Game Studies, Atlanta, Ga., August 26–29.

Boellstorff, Tom. 2008. *Coming of Age in Second Life: An Anthropologist Explores the Virtually Human*. Princeton, N.J.: Princeton University Press.

Braun, Virginia, and Victoria Clarke. 2013. *Successful Qualitative Research: A Practical Guide for Beginners*. London: Sage.

Burger-Helmchen, Thierry, and Patrick Cohendet. 2011. "User Communities and Social Software in the Video Game Industry." *Long Range Planning* 44: 317–43.

Carter, Marcus, Martin Gibbs, and Michael Arnold. 2012. "Avatars, Characters, Users, and Players: Multiple Identities at/in Play." In *Proceedings of the Twenty-Fourth Australian Computer–Human Interaction Conference (ozCHI'12)*, 68–71. New York: ACM Press.

Cohendet, Patrick, and Patrick Llerena. 2009. "Organization of Firms, Knowing Communities, and Limits of Networks in a Knowledge-Intensive Context." In *Corporate Governance, Organization, and the Firm*, edited by Mario Morroni. Cheltenham, U.K.: Edward Elgar.

Feng, Wu-chang, David Brandt, and Debanjan Saha. 2007. "A Long-Term Study of a Popular MMORPG." In *Proceedings of the Sixth ACM SIGCOMM Workshop on Network and System Support for Games*, 19–24. New York: ACM Press.

Füller, Johann. 2010. "Refining Virtual Co-creation from a Consumer Perspective." *California Management Review* 52, no. 2: 98–122.

Gebauer, Johannes, Johann Füller, and Roland Pezzei. 2013. "The Dark and the Bright Side of Co-creation: Triggers of Member Behaviour in Online Innovation Communities." *Journal of Business Research* 66: 1516–27.

Gibbs, Martin R., Marcus Carter, and Joji Mori. 2013. "Vile Rat: Spontaneous Shrines in EVE Online." Paper presented at the *EVE Online* Workshop, Chania, Greece, May 14–17.

Hardt, Michael, and Antonio Negri. 2001. *Empire.* New ed. Cambridge, Mass.: Harvard University Press.

Hartley, John, Jason Potts, Stuart Cunningham, Terry Flew, Michael Keane, and John Banks. 2013. *Key Concepts in Creative Industries.* London: Sage.

Hoyer, Wayne D., Rajesh Chandy, Matilda Dorotic, Manfred Krafft, and Siddharth S. Singh. 2010. "Consumer Co-creation in New Product Development." *Journal of Service Research* 13, no. 3: 283–96.

Keith, Clinton. 2010. *Agile Game Development with Scrum.* Upper Saddle River, N.J.: Addison-Wesley.

Kohler, T., J. Füller, D. Stieger, and K. Matzler. 2011a. "Avatar-Based Innovation: Consequences of the Virtual Co-creation Experience." *Computers in Human Behaviour* 27: 160–68.

Kohler, Thomas, Johann Füller, Kurt Matzler, and Daniel Stieger. 2011b. "Co-creation in Virtual Worlds: The Design of the User Experience." *MIS Quarterly* 35, no. 3: 773–88.

Malaby, Thomas M. 2006. "Coding Control: Governance and Contingency in the Production of Online Worlds." *First Monday,* no. 7. http://firstmonday.org/ojs/index.php/fm/article/view/1613/1528.

———. 2009. *Making Virtual Worlds: Linden Lab and Second Life.* Ithaca, N.Y.: Cornell University Press.

O'Hern, Matthew S., and Aric Rindfleisch. 2010. "Customer Co-creation: A Typology and Research Agenda." *Review of Marketing Research* 6: 84–106.

O'Hern, Matthew S., Aric Rindfleisch, Kersi D. Antia, and David A. Schweidel. 2011. "The Impact of User-Generated Content on Product Innovation." http://ssrn.com/abstract=1843250 or http://dx.doi.org/10.2139/ssrn.1843250.

Óskarsson, Pétur Jóhannes. 2014. "The Council of Stellar Management: Implementation of Deliberative, Democratically Elected, Council in EVE." http://web.ccpgamescdn.com/communityassets/pdf/csm/CSMSummary.pdf.

Paul, Christopher. 2011. "Don't Play Me: EVE Online, New Players, and Rhetoric." In *Proceedings of the Sixth International Conference on Foundations of Digital Games,* 262–64. New York: ACM Press.

Piller, Frank T., Christoph Ihl, and Alexander Vossen. 2011. "Customer Co-creation: Open Innovation with Customers." In *New Forms of Collaborative Innovation and Production on the Internet: An Interdisciplinary Perspective,* edited by Heidemarie Hanekop and Wittke Volker, 31–61. Goettingen: University of Goettingen.

Robson, Colin. 2011. *Real World Research.* 3rd ed. Hoboken, N.J.: John Wiley.

Roman, David. 2014. "From Corporate Lawyer to Space Tyrant." *Wall Street Journal,* January 15. http://online.wsj.com/news/articles/SB10001424052702304887104579306663398628476.

Taylor, T. L. 2006. "Beyond Management: Considering Participatory Design and Governance in Player Culture." *First Monday,* no. 7. http://firstmonday.org/issues/issue11_9/taylor/index.html.

Tschang, F. Ted. 2007. "Balancing the Tensions between Rationalization and Creativity in the Video Games Industry." *Organization Science* 18, no. 6: 989–1005.

Utterback, James M. 1994. *Mastering the Dynamics of Innovation.* Cambridge, Mass.: Harvard Business School Press.

van Doorn, Jenny, Katherine N. Lemon, Vikas Mittal, Stephan Nass, Doreén Pick, Peter Pirner, and Peter C. Verhoef. 2010. "Customer Engagement Behavior: Theoretical Foundations and Research Directions." *Journal of Service Research* 13, no. 3: 253–66.

Vargo, Stephen L., and Robert F. Lusch. 2004. "Evolving to a New Dominant Logic for Marketing." *Journal of Marketing* 68: 1–17.

von Hippel, Eric. 2005. *Democratizing Innovation.* Cambridge, Mass.: MIT Press.

Wexler, Mark N. 2011. "Reconfiguring the Sociology of the Crowd: Exploring Crowdsourcing." *International Journal of Sociology and Social Policy* 31: 6–20.

# 15

# *EVE Online* as History

*Nick Webber*

On May 6, 2013, *EVE Online* celebrated its tenth birthday, a landmark anniversary that drove a series of celebratory and media-oriented activities. Significant among these was the launch, a month previously, of a website through which *EVE*'s players could submit what they felt to be "the most important stories of actual events from within New Eden" between May 2003 and May 2013: True Stories from the First Decade. Carrying the tag line "History is made by those who write it," the site offered "a place where people can read the history of our Universe, as told by those that inhabit it" (Ólafsson 2013). True Stories was thus explicitly historical, and the trailer for the site drew parallels between the recording of the stories of *EVE*'s players and those of settlement-era Iceland (CCP Games 2013c). Though conceived, ultimately, as a competition—the stories collected on the site would be open to a player vote, the winners of which would receive prizes—it was also suggested that submitted stories might form the basis of books, comics, TV series, or films set in the *EVE* universe. These stories would help to capture the imagination of the public, potentially driving more players to the game; as *EVE*'s creative director noted, "some of them captured media attention that our PR never gets . . . individuals not only in the *EVE* player base but outside of the periphery want to hear about them" (Ólafsson, as quoted in Corriea 2013). In combination, then, this was a storytelling contest, a PR exercise, and a repository of player and game histories.

Yet irrespective of any corporate motivations underlying the site (perhaps not so out of place in the context of *EVE*), player interest was stimulated, and more than 750 stories were submitted, of widely varying quality (Corriea 2013). The stories themselves, and the debate among players they fostered, demonstrated a discourse incorporating complex concepts and contested ideas about history, including assertions of truthfulness, importance, bias, and propaganda. Notably, the stories were also told in a variety of ways and at a variety of levels: in character and out of character, for example, and from both individual and group perspectives. Some dealt with the political maneuverings of large groups, others with a moment of personal game-play experience (and yet others with stranger things; Xideinis 2013).

In total, then, True Stories provides a rich seam of tales, ideas, thoughts, and responses; even at a glance, it presents a history characterized by complexity, a history distinguished by scale, and, importantly, a history about people. Such a presentation invites us to ask questions, however, about how history functions here, about ownership, about importance and cultural significance, and about whether, as one commentator has remarked, "*EVE* needs historians" (Dinsdale Pirannha, comment on Fiddle 2013). Significantly, an exploration of *EVE*'s history represents a dual opportunity. It can make a contribution to our understanding of the culture of *EVE Online* and its players, while also adding to broader discussions around the ways in which players make meaning from the games they play. At the same time, it offers an important perspective on the nature of history, a subject much debated, and on the relationship of history to video games, a matter of notable contemporary interest (see Webber 2014).

In this chapter, then, I use True Stories, along with other source material from the *EVE* community—blog and forum posts, for example—to explore the role of history in *EVE,* to reflect on *EVE*'s need for historians, and to consider *EVE* as history.

## History

At the outset, however, we must begin with a question: what do we mean by history here? It is typical to use the term *history* in two ways: to describe the sequence of past events and to describe the inquiry into those events conducted by a historian (see, e.g., Carr 1964, 20–21; Oakeshott 1999, 1–3; Jenkins 2003, 6–7)—effectively, an object of study and the discipline of studying it. The accounts collected through the True Stories platform constitute the material of history: a description of the past but also primary source material from which a historian might understand a particular perspective on that past. Yet these stories are not the only elements of the discourse and culture of *EVE Online* that purport to be either of the past or about the past. Indeed, a sense of the past is inscribed within the game in a variety of ways, for example, in a chronology dated in relation to a fictional event, the Yoiul Conference; in-character "employment histories" detailing corporation membership; and in the presence of "ancient" artifacts and locations, notable among which is the EVE Gate, the supposed point of origin for all of New Eden's pilots.

*EVE* is pervaded by a sense of its own past almost as much as, in its space-based setting, it is pervaded by a sense of the future, and these elements of game fabric are overlain with an extended body of material written and produced about and around *EVE* that we might think of as history or, at least, as historical. This material attempts to chronicle, to record, to explore, and to explain aspects of *EVE*'s past, as a game, as a fictional universe, and as a community of players, and also through the interactions between these things. In terms of video games in general, history can be considered to have many different aspects, to be constituted not only by a combination of the political, social, economic, cultural, and technological history *of* games as objects but also by the portrayal of the past (either real or imagined) *in* those games, and by a record of the experiences of those who play them (see Webber 2014). And in the historical activity around *EVE,* we can see an address to all of these elements.

Although it is important to note that these accounts and descriptions do not proceed from any professionalized approach to history, this in no way undermines the historical project taking place here, and there is clearly a sense of authority at play in some areas, as I discuss shortly. The material on the True Stories site consists of accounts written by players, from their own perspectives, both narrating and interpreting *EVE*'s past. This theme remains strong elsewhere, with players recording their narratives and interpretations not only of their own and other players' experiences and activities (a form of documentation I refer to as *player history*) but also of the history of the game as object and of the fictional past of New Eden itself. This material complements historical matter produced by CCP Games, offering an "official" (and perhaps alternative) perspective on the game itself as well as both original and further developed material detailing New Eden's imagined history. This fiction not only introduces and describes the peoples and events that set the context for game play and aesthetics but also offers a justificatory logic for substantial changes in the game's structure, such as the introduction of incursions. Material of this kind is commonly (and hereafter) referred to as *lore.* Lore is a significant component of many online role-playing games, and many players demonstrate a high degree of engagement with it.

In aggregate, these various historical documents constitute a substantial publishing enterprise. Player contributions appear through posts on various forums and blogs, with levels of organization up to and including self-constitution as media organizations and networks, such as EVENews24 (EN24) and TheMittani.com (TMC). These larger networks serve a dual purpose, as "a primary recorder of a shared past" offering the fabled "first draft of history" (Zelizer and Tenenboim-Winblatt 2014, 2) and as a repository of more detailed historical analysis, often produced by those who are established commentators in other *EVE* spaces. CCP's contributions are typically articulated through more corporate mechanisms—the game's main website (http://www.eveonline.com/) and information and dialogue in the game itself—and CCP employees have written and published three novels based on the lore of *EVE* as well as the *Chronicles,* a series of vignettes that tell us a little more about life in New Eden. Yet there are also substantial areas of overlap between players and game provider, in forms such as EVElopedia, a wiki hosted by CCP but contributed to by players, and *EVE: Into the Second Decade,* a book released as part of the tenth anniversary celebrations that "aims to tell the development history of the EVE universe; not just the making of EVE Online and Dust 514, but the influence of the players in shaping New Eden and the community that has served it" (CCP Falcon 2013). Of course, True Stories is also significant here, and player contributions have been combined with CCP's input to produce a series of comic books based on the winning story, with the suggestion that a television series based on a larger body of material is to come (Ólafsson 2014; Williams 2013).

## Credible History

Clearly, then, *EVE* is the locus of a great deal of historical attention, although traditional historians might balk at the notion that *any* of this activity constitutes "real" or "proper history" (see Chapman 2012). The product history of the game itself might perhaps come closest to meeting traditional historical expectations, but certainly the lore of the game world or player histories of in-game activity are likely to be thought of as outside a historical remit. Yet it would be inaccurate to suggest that clear distinctions can always be made here, and there is certainly complexity in disentangling player experiences (both of the game and of playing it) from player activities (within the game and without). Daniel Way (as quoted in Narcisse 2013), the comic writer tasked with the production of the True Stories comics, talked about this very problem in an interview with Kotaku.com:

> I mean, the story's based upon actual events that never "actually" happened, y'know? . . . The trick was to focus upon the initiative and intent of the players behind the campaigns. What they did was real and did actually happen.

For Way, there is clearly an important line between in-game occurrences and human action, and as a writer, he felt the former would prove harder to sell to readers—it would be more difficult to persuade readers to suspend their disbelief (Way, as quoted in Narcisse 2013). The implication is that game occurrences are in some manner less legitimate than those in the real world; even though they may be just as complicated and just as people-centric as occurrences in life, they don't "actually happen." However, although such a line may exist for Way, and perhaps for many others, historians included, the situation may not be as clear-cut as it at first appears.

The notion that there is some fundamental divide between game and world is often summarized through the motif of the "magic circle," drawn from the 1930s work of the Dutch historian Johan Huizinga (translated as Huizinga 1955). In more recent work, particularly that focusing on online games, several scholars have demonstrated that a strict division is misconceived. The circle is permeable; the spatial, temporal, and social frame within which the game occurs is not truly separate; and the ordinary rules of life continue to apply, albeit in competition with other rules (see, e.g., Tyler 2008; Consalvo 2009).

Yet game space apparently retains some kind of privilege as space in which boundaries can be pushed and things can be done differently; players can experiment with behaviors that contradict their personal beliefs and values or that are simply forbidden in real life (Griebel 2006; Consalvo 2007, 186). As Sal Humphreys and Melissa de Zwart (2012, 535) have suggested, the negotiation between in-game and out-of-game versions of structures such as social and cultural norms is one of "dynamic complexity," and they have proposed a move away from a conception of division and toward an understanding of interconnection, drawing on Foucault's notion of heterotopias

(510–14). So although Way's perspective may reflect an instinctive sense of (and comfort with) the unrealness of games, reflected in the common phrase "just a game," any distinction between real and not real is in fact unclear and, as with cultural norms, there to be negotiated.

Clearly, then, the status of this (lack of) distinction has implications for any consideration of history in *EVE*. So, though we have already discussed the breadth of "historical" activity in *EVE*, we must also consider the extent to which such activity and the material generated by it are legitimately historical. We are thus compelled to consider not only what we "mean by history here" but also simply what we mean by history. This has been the subject of extensive debate among historians and philosophers,[1] and we can draw on that debate to inform a perspective on the history of *EVE*.

So, why might we think of *EVE* as history? Writing in the early 1960s, E. H. Carr (1964, 48) indicated that history, although in general about people, is not simply about people: history is "the process of enquiry into the past of man *in society*" (emphasis added). Forgiving him his choice of noun, Carr makes a significant point: history is not about individuals but about the relationship of those individuals to others and about the institutions, practices, and other human creations that tie those individuals together. Thus we might think of *EVE* as history if we can consider *EVE* as a society.

The concept of society is highly contested, however, which in some ways serves only to make the question more complex. There is no consensus view as to its meaning even among historians or game studies scholars, and there is widespread disagreement about the central basis on which our understanding should rest. Some scholars propose, for example, that the emphasis should be economic or political, or both—that society (and thus history) is the result of political and/or economic relations. Furthermore, recent public and governmental initiatives have instead seen participation or citizenship as constitutive of society (or, indeed, the "Big Society"). Yet many contributions to this debate are ideological perspectives on how societies are made or produced, and thus how they should be understood, and they do not necessarily answer questions about how we might define *EVE*.

Dictionary definitions of the term *society* typically highlight three significant points: shared space, order, and community. Sociologist Anthony Giddens (1984, 164) provides a more developed formulation of these ideas, placing significant emphasis on the role of structure and offering the view that societies "are social systems which 'stand out' in bas-relief from a background of a range of other systemic relationships in which they are embedded," because "definite structural principles serve to produce a specifiable overall 'clustering of institutions.'" He also considers the intersection of space and community, highlighting the significance of a sense of "some sort of common identity, however that might be expressed or revealed"—a sense of "belonging" (165).

It seems immediately evident that *EVE* meets all of these criteria and, perhaps, exceeds them. *EVE* is highly ordered: the basic unit of player organization, the corporation, appears in a variety of types and from a variety of origins, much like equivalents in other games—guilds, for example, or clans (see Williams et al. 2006; Ducheneaut et al. 2007). Corporations (and the larger alliances) are often highly structured and hierarchical, enmeshed in political and diplomatic activity, and a number of these structures have declared purposes: education, for example, or banking, or enforcement of a code of conduct.

*EVE* players also, clearly, share space (albeit usually virtual space). Although game providers have made some attempt to define massively multiplayer online games as services rather than spaces, this description breaks down upon analysis, and it has been suggested that it is necessary to legally define such game places to effectively regulate them (see Ruch 2009; Castronova 2004, 201–5). And, of course, this shared space extends beyond the game itself to incorporate online forums, blogs, and other social media; voice chat services; and the physical location of the annual EVE Fanfest, among other places.

Perhaps most evident is the place that *EVE* occupies at the heart of an engaged and active community. Vili Lehdonvirta (2010) has, however, rejected the idea that the player base of a virtual world such as *EVE* should be referred to as a community, suggesting that the term implies too great a familiarity, unity, and intimacy for the mass of players who just happened to have purchased the same game. However, his alternative suggestion of *social world* (following Strauss) is indicative itself of a grouping of people around a specific focus (playing *EVE*) and thus a sense of membership of a broader group of *EVE* players.

Thus, even if this is not (as Lehdonvirta suggests) a community in a classical sociological sense, it would still seem to be a community of interest at the very least. To follow Benedict Anderson (1983), then, we should perhaps refer to the *imagined* community of *EVE* players, constituted by shared consumption of, or participation in, the specific media form. Notably, this is also a community that participates in most cases in intricate social networks, in a thriving economy, and, perhaps most significantly, in a broad range of cultural activities, some of which (as has been highlighted by various scholars) are effectively a form of (free) labor (e.g., Taylor 2006, 88–92). In many ways, the interdependence between *EVE* players is more securely established than that between typical residents of a real-world town.

To claim society status for *EVE*, then, would be to suggest that there is something significant and distinctive about it and that it marks a particular clustering of institutional forms. To claim *EVE* as history is to recognize that this "society-ness" persists across time—that it has a past that is subject to history that is both accessible and discussible. Indeed, *EVE* distinguishes itself as probably more successfully historical than any other online game: it has institutions, it has practices, and it has other human creations that tie its players together. And significantly, vitally, it has versions of all of these things that are *exclusive* to *EVE*, which respond to and exist in the context of *EVE*'s society, and its players write accounts—histories—of these things. So accounts of *EVE* are not only those of individual experience, nor of individual events, but of experiences and events and *institutions* and *practices,* contextualized within an ongoing chronology over a period of ten years. Might we then begin to think of this as some form of credible history? What else might we call it?

## Lore and Player History

Of course, the preceding exploration applies almost exclusively to player histories rather than to the more general fictional "history" (lore) of the *EVE* universe. As with many cultural artifacts, the stories that explain and justify the game are likely to give us rather more insight into the context of their production—the 21st century—than they are into the 234th century. And, to come back to Way's comment, there is seemingly another obvious division: between the historical content in a story about someone who never existed, produced at the whim of its narrator, and the story of things that "'actually' happened." Yet developments during the decade of *EVE*'s activity have made it increasingly difficult to support the perception of a disconnection between player histories and lore. *EVE: Into the Second Decade* notes that, even by late 2004, developer-led histories were increasingly giving way to tales of conquests by player alliances (Shoemaker 2013, 34–35), suggesting that elements of both player histories and lore occupy similar niches and serve similar purposes.

Although separate player-history projects exist (such as the EVEHistory wiki[2]), the creation of EVElopedia, a repository of content generated by both players and developers, further interleaved player-historical and (both CCP and player-authored) lore contributions to *EVE*'s story. EVElopedia features information about the histories of player characters and player organizations alongside those of lore-based races and persons, implying a similar significance and credibility (and "officialness") to each. Most recently, the comics and TV series being produced through the True Stories project promise the completion of this integration, situating player histories within officially sanctioned game lore. Notionally, then, in this fusion of account, experience, and fiction, it will become difficult to determine where any division might lie.

When we consider the relationship between lore and player activity, therefore, and specifically the history expressed in the lore and the history experienced and expressed by players, it seems that an outright distinction is not tenable. This is not least because *EVE*'s players do not relate either to lore or to one another in a consistent manner—not all players play in the same way or feel the same way about game lore. In Blog Banter[3] 48, organized in August 2013 and focused on the importance of lore (Kodachi 2013a), player perspectives varied widely, suggesting that lore was unimportant or uninteresting (Jester 2013b; Kodachi 2013b), that it impeded imaginative play (splatus 2013), that it was important in preventing the game from being soulless (stoicfnord 2013), that it was integral to player processes of sense making (Bryant 2013b), or that it acted as a "fictional cultural heritage" for *EVE* players (Patroller 2013). Certainly, when we consider the case of self-described role-players, whose game-play actions are shaped and guided by their interpretation and understanding of game lore, we can see how lore can be integral to players' game experience and game play (e.g., Ugleb 2013).

Yet though player responses to lore may bridge any immediate divide between conceptions of lore and player history, that there is a divide continues to be widely accepted among the player base. In April 2013, Blog Banter 46 (Westhorpe 2013a) focused on this very issue, inspired by a CCP-run game event, the Battle for Caldari Prime. This event, which advanced the game story line, and thus added to lore, invited the participation of players but in the end proved to be a fait accompli, with some participants complaining that their actions during the event had been meaningless. The discussion of the relationship of players to lore thus hinged on the issue of divide—was it possible to resolve the disparity between player-driven narrative, developed daily through, for example, interalliance warfare, and CCP's "prime fiction"?

Again, diverse perspectives were presented in the resultant blog posts and comments, and although some felt that this division was nonexistent (Jester 2013a) or irrelevant (Woollahra 2013), the general consensus was that such a divide was unwanted and, at one extreme, might be the cause of segregation or fragmentation of the game community (Azariah 2013). Problematically, for players, there was clearly a mismatch between the lore as presented, along with the characters arising from it, and the relationship that players had to that lore and those characters. Thus, though players were responding to lore, lore was not, it was felt, responding to players, particularly in cases where player organizations were building power bases that would notionally threaten the empires detailed in lore (Rhavas 2013a; Zephyran 2013)—and this theme was continued in Blog Banter 48, where the value of lore was in several cases seen to be reduced by its lack of impact relative to player histories (Arcturus 2013; Dredtog 2013). Indeed, some posts sought to address this lack of integration, proposing structures that functioned similarly for both players and nonplayer characters (Grimmash 2013), or through which players might influence nonplayer political organizations (Chiralityeve 2013).

Thus players perceived a stark distinction of agency and of power: lore functioned as a descriptive and explanatory mechanism that contextualized their experience but did not tell a story of human agents nor exercise power over human agents. Conversely, player activity was focused substantially on human agents, and this activity had the potential to exercise a form of power over human agents, both directly and indirectly.

Importantly, both blog banters stimulated discussion about history and the ways in which stories of player activities and achievements were and are recorded and remembered. Here, it appears, lore was considered to be authoritative in a way that player history was not, and contributors wondered how their own experiences might achieve the status of lore and have a "meaningful impact on EVE's history" (Potato 2013). A concern was raised that, although large player-originated events were recorded and noted (such as the winning event on the True Stories site, which hit the mainstream media; Gianturco 2013; Graham 2009), much player history was being lost (Fiddle 2013) and player impact on the game was in most cases evanescent (H 2013; see also Fiddle 2012). "As our own 'story' fades into 'lore,'[4] which is happening more and more right under our feet, the telling, archiving, and meaning of history become even more important," observed one blogger (Javix 2013); yet no formal mechanism existed to obtain this within the game (H 2013). Although this had happened on occasion (Bryant 2013b gives the example of the status of Jita as the main trading hub being a player-driven impact), there was in general an impermeable wall between game lore and player history (Fiddle 2013).

Thus, although CCP recognized that the needs of players and groups "were a better motivation for play than any number of stories about galactic struggle or kidnapped princesses" (Rossignol 2013, 127), and although, in the words of one blogger, "everything that we do is a legitimate piece of game history that can be used" (Kyle 2013), these posts suggested that player histories were valued less highly than *EVE*'s lore and were less likely to be recorded and remembered, and that the players themselves participated in that diminishment. This perspective stands in notable opposition to CCP's own descriptions of *EVE* as a game in which "all player actions, no matter how subtle or bold, always have an impact" (CCP Games 2009), and as the Ólafsson quotations in the introduction to this chapter suggest, player activities and histories have demonstrated significant penetration of mainstream media. True Stories may mark something of an attempt to address this mismatch.

## Ownership and Authority

Although, then, the discourse of sites like True Stories suggests a genuinely democratic form of history for *EVE*, in which history is not only made by those who write it but owned and controlled by them, the reality is seemingly rather less utopian and illustrates a power imbalance at play even in the structuring of players' stories about themselves. This is demonstrated very clearly by EVElopedia, where many lore pages are locked and cannot be edited by the community, but no such restriction exists on the majority of pages about player characters or player organizations. Consequently, these sometimes show contributions from multiple players as well as occasional interventions from CCP staff members.[5] Although players are able to make contributions to many areas of the site that detail non-player-originated material, such as the pages concerning different kinds of ships, the history of the game articulated through lore is apparently not available for modification.

The term *canon* is sometimes used to refer to "official" accounts of this fictional past (e.g., H 2013). Lore material on EVElopedia can be removed where it is considered to be noncanonical and flagged as of dubious reliability when its canonical status is unclear.[6] Players complain that lore is changed without explanation, even retrospectively (Zhaceera Armerarram, response to Priano 2013). Control is exercised not only over player-generated content, however, but also over content created by members of *EVE*'s volunteer program, the Interstellar Services Department and by external authors. Player observations suggested that, for example, story line opportunities opened up in the two novels by author Tony Gonzales were rapidly closed down, although a CCP representative responded that this was just part of an attempt to "shake things up" (CCP Falcon, response to Eko'mo 2013).

In effect, and whatever its intention, CCP's approach to *EVE* lore serves to create two tiers of historical record: an "authorized," canonical history, which informs the design and structure of the game, and creative work deriving therefrom, and an unofficial, unverified, or unauthorized history that is, through a number of processes, reduced in stature, dismissed, or deleted. It is this approach to history with which some players struggle, expressing a sense of oppression that the overemphasis on lore is "smothering" their imagination (splatus 2013) and dominating, rather than responsive to, players and their narratives (Scientist 2013). And certainly, when it comes to the way in which lore plays out in-game, although some players see it as entirely appropriate for CCP to act as a controlling entity, shaping the activities of its players (e.g., Bryant 2013a), one blogger notes that it would be "better for CCP to record player events as history instead of writing history and then giving players a chance to watch it happen" (Potato 2013).

Logically, of course, this is for CCP a natural process. The lore of *EVE* is a substantial component of the valuable intellectual property that *EVE* represents; it is only to be expected that CCP is both keen to maintain control of this material and eager to avoid ceding rights of authorship to potentially unpredictable third parties. Yet, when we return to the ideas underlying True Stories, it becomes clear that this is problematic territory. The media artifacts produced on the basis of the players' stories told on the site will be contextualized within game lore, creating in effect an authorized history that blends protected intellectual property with accounts of human experience. In superficial terms, these are pieces of fiction inspired by the experiences that they relate, and they respond clearly to player requests for "the combination of the player-created stories and history with the CCP-created stories and history" (Wayrest 2013; see also Firstly 2013; ElRandir 2013). Yet they will enshrine a particular perspective and interpretation of what are potentially (and, in the case of the comic, definitely) contentious events. In this, therefore, CCP acts not as a historian but as an empowered commentator on these events, with the consequent potential to represent, not the many voices of those involved, but a singular, corporate, mediatized voice.

In many ways, the position of *EVE* history here is reminiscent of player-created material in games more generally, especially those in which, like *EVE,* the game is dependent on a substantial investment of time in often laborious activities, and it is only through those activities that "the game is made animate" (Taylor 2006, 133), a process sometimes referred to as co-creation. Although this labor is free, and clearly takes place in an uneven power relationship, it is not necessarily exploitative, and it has been suggested that users (players) are not without agency (and thus some measure of power) in such a relationship (Banks and Humphreys 2008, 415). Certainly whether or not players consider their contributions as labor directly, their investment of time and effort prompts them to contest the simplistic model of ownership presented in end user license agreements and terms of service, which typically portray these games and all attendant assets as the developer or publisher's intellectual property, subject to copyright (Taylor 2006, 125–50, de Zwart 2009).

The question of who owns *EVE*'s history is thus an important one, both for those directly involved with the game and for historians more generally. Ludmilla Jordanova (2006, 136, 143) has suggested that accounts of the (real-world) past might typically be thought of as public property; yet "this is quite the opposite of game lore, which is not game lore until it has been recorded and formally identified as such (and, by coincidence, copyrighted) by the owning entity" (Fiddle 2013). True Stories, in the way in which it collects individual accounts and encourages debate, resembles a museum or archival public history project, bringing together material to inform an engaged account of a public past. The active participation and engagement of the game's public, the players, is an indication that these stories matter to them; the material gathered represents a breadth of views and opinions about the stories told.

Much like CCP, then, players have a vested interest here, and indeed a level of ownership of their own experiences, material from which *EVE*'s history might be constructed. Player interests and ownership are perhaps greatest when the history is concerned with the players themselves and with the institutions and other game structures that they create; but many players also have a strong interest in the way in which lore is shaped, especially when their own game play, perhaps over several years, has been predicated upon that material. And here we perhaps reach the crux of the matter. In the case of lore, based on the premise of their ownership of the materials of history, CCP accords to itself the authority to write or to validate that history. Players may make claims of ownership of, and authority over, areas of their own history focused, for example, on player communities and their activities. Yet these lines of ownership and authority are contested by players seeking to embed their activities within the setting of the game and by CCP seeking to retain ultimate control over the history of "its" game. The outcomes of the True Stories project, then, threaten to be distorted by this problem of ownership.

## Discourses of Player History

Such struggles over the ownership and value of history, and of specific histories, are problems that stretch far beyond *EVE*. In recent decades, an increasing access to and engagement with history have led to both a richer and more contested understanding of our past—history has become far more "public" (Jordanova 2006, 126–49).

As we can see from our exploration of the relationship between player histories and lore, discussions within *EVE*'s player community engage with a conception of history substantially beyond the level of authorship and a sense of contribution to a larger endeavor; although the problems we have discussed may, on the face of it, seem of a broadly philosophical nature, they are clearly important to at least some part of the *EVE* player base: "Whether or not it is important to you depends on whether you care about history, and a good story . . . now doesn't it?" (ElRandir 2013). Such engagement, and the discourse of players about history, is also reflected in specific discussions about player histories themselves, offering us further insight into the ways in which publics—in this case *EVE*'s game public—respond to, value, and, importantly, *make use of* history. The idea of the usable past—that through history the past can be put to a variety of (potentially conflicting) uses (Jordanova 2006, 131–34)—is relevant here.

In providing a forum in which perspectives on the history of *EVE*'s players can be co-located and voted on, True Stories stands as a showcase of the discourses and uses of player history in and around *EVE*. The site contains a number of different kinds of stories, including accounts of individual experiences (as a new player, in a battle, etc.; both in and out of character; e.g., Ling Mei-Shin 2013), exploration (e.g., Rhavas 2013b), corporation and alliance histories (e.g., Vodkov 2013), and what are thought of (by their authors) as significant events (e.g., Gianturco 2013). Here, then, are products of the different uses to which history might be put. In some regard, all of these accounts are responses to the competition on the site (setting the direction for these as experiential accounts, however couched), but in presenting particular perspectives on events, other social, cultural, and even political purposes are served, the success of which might be measured by each story's ability to attract attention in terms of both comments and votes (either upward or downward).

This exploitation of the presentation of the past is reflected in the discourses on the site, most strongly through the debates and discussions that take place and that engage directly with what we might think of as core "historical" concepts, such as truthfulness, importance, bias, and propaganda. In its very title, the site itself declares the possibility of truth; it is a place for "true accounts of events that occurred in the *EVE* Universe" (CCP Games 2013a). For commentators, also, trueness is important: the points made in both the debate and discussion section around Xenuria's "We Didn't Listen," for example, indicate substantial disagreement about whether the events recounted occurred or were an elaborate fabrication (Xenuria 2013); another story is simply dismissed as "fake" (Lacuna 2013).

Alongside this desire for veracity is a sense of genuine significance, attached, as might be expected, only to a small number of contributions, of varying kinds. Comments indicate that, for example, Goonswarm's efforts to produce a Nyx supercarrier on the borders of enemy territory were "vital to EVE's history" (Samej Arkanus, debate point 1636, in support of xttz 2013); that "Hulkageddon is important in EVE history" (Burseg Sardaukar, debate point 851, in support of Sardaukar 2013); and that the disbanding of Band of Brothers (BoB) was "probably the single most important thing to happen to EVE" (Jiggle Physics, debate point 1695, in support of Gianturco 2013). That these perceptions are in some cases more generally held is perhaps demonstrated by the use of one event to grant status to another—the Northern Campaign, for example, is described "as important as the later fall of BoB" (Kossaw, debate point 1553, in support of Seleene 2013)—and in any case, through voting in accordance with the ethos of the site, players are seeking to identify the "most important stories" from the game (CCP Games 2013b). Furthermore, some suggestions of importance stretch beyond the boundary of the game and its community: the account of the Guiding Hand Social Club's well-known contract against the CEO of Ubiqua Seraph is considered by its author to be "a significant event in gaming history" (Tyrrax Thorrk, debate point 1464, in support of Thorrk 2013). Thus we can see evidence that many *EVE* players demonstrate not only a clear sense of their game past but a sense of that past as impactful on their present, both within the game and beyond.

## Identity

This notion of importance leads us, however, to some explicitly political uses of history within *EVE*. While responses on the True Stories site express a desire for truthfulness, there is also a sensitivity toward perspective—that some stories are told with a particular position or "take" in mind—and this sensitivity is reflected not only in terms of perceptions of bias but also in comments that suggest an equally purposeful but differently directed use of this material. There is a clear sense, for example, that some commentators feel aggrieved by the presentation of the account of the fall of BoB, which is accused of offering a "one sided view with a stretch on what really happened" (Peter Powers, debate point 1570, in opposition to Gianturco 2013) and of "over exaggerated chest beating" (Kazellis, debate point 1661, in opposition to Gianturco 2013). Elsewhere, bias against particular player groupings is suggested as the reason for certain perspectives or responses (e.g. Assistant Stone, debate point 1716, opposing Archanus 2013; Shank Ronuken, debate point 1614, in support of xttz 2013).

Yet such politicization of these histories also has a more valedictory outcome. In response to the BoB story, under the title "History of the Creation of Goonswarm," one player observed that "it's important for us to know where we came from" (Spike Spiegel-XI, debate point 1741, in support of Gianturco 2013); elsewhere, another noted that the events surrounding it "contributed to the identity of Goonswarm of today" (LakeEnd, May 7 discussion point on Gianturco 2013). Much like real-world histories, then, *EVE* histories can support group identities through self-aggrandisement and the othering of their enemies.

The widespread production of corporation and alliance histories in the *EVE* community demonstrates many developed examples of this use of historical material. As might be expected, these histories often appear on websites associated with specific corporations or alliances.[7] However, and more importantly, they can also be found in a number of public spaces. The section of EVElopedia dealing with player organizations includes almost nine hundred pages devoted to a variety of corporations, alliances, and coalitions, many of which not only provide a current summary of activity but also a history section (although the content of such pages can be contested by the community).[8] Furthermore, histories of such organizations can also be discovered on other public forums, both those about *EVE* (e.g., Dealer 2009) and elsewhere (e.g., Porkbutte 2013).

Although other elements of *EVE*'s history may also be debated in these spaces (e.g., Rein 2007), the achievement-driven nature of corporation or alliance history ("this is what we have accomplished") makes the rationale for public display even more interesting. Again, we are drawn back to the construction of public history, in its radical form, where participants create "politically self-conscious, community-based histories, open to all and usable in political struggles" (Jordanova 2006, 126). In this regard, such accounts offer themselves not only as important in terms of *EVE*, or important in terms of gaming history more broadly, but as culturally significant accounts that can shape player experience and play, both within the game itself and in the metagame beyond.

## Conclusion

With this volume of historical activity, it perhaps seems strange to restate the question of whether "*EVE* needs historians." In the same comment in which that statement was made, its author also remarked, "I just wonder how many would step up to write" (Pirannha, on Fiddle 2013). It seems clear that both of these issues are to some degree addressed by the *EVE* community as things stand: *EVE has* historians, who are apparently writing in droves. Yet their very existence brings to light other, dependent issues that are worthy of consideration. We have seen that history is an important discourse for *EVE* players that can operate at the level of politics and identity—that *EVE* players have an interest in the histories that are told, and that are told about them. The power to make official presentations of *EVE*'s history, however, is not vested in players, and although CCP is superficially supportive of accounts of player experiences, in the ways in which they are recorded and in their direct impact on the game, player histories are evidently secondary to game lore. And though we might see players as agents in the co-creation of the *EVE* universe, it is unclear that this agency extends to the structuring of *EVE*'s history; history is, after all, an act of *curation*, not of *creation*, and *EVE*'s player histories occupy a similar niche to public histories elsewhere: reduced in stature, ultimately, by the mediation of the mechanism of telling.

This connection of player histories with lore leads to other questions about the extent to which histories of *EVE Online* can be considered to be histories at all. How tolerant are we of the fictionalization or embellishment of human interaction? And if *EVE* constitutes a functional society, incorporating institutions, creations, and practices that persist over time, are accounts of this society history? When we write such accounts, are we historians? Or when we encapsulate this blend of lore and experience, are we instead producing fictional history or, indeed, historical fiction?

So perhaps we should ask not whether *EVE needs* historians but whether *EVE can have* historians. To return to an earlier point, if we accept that *EVE* is a form of society, then we must, I think, accept that it is subject to history—that it is both susceptible to study by historians and that it has a credible and complete history (or past) of its own that merits such a study. That part of that history is fictional may present a problem in conceptualizing the relationship between that history and the world around us, but following Jenkins (2003, 31–32), we should not forget that histories are not the presentation of an objective truth but rather a discourse in themselves. As Hayden White has indicated, history is at heart simply one form of story, and even though we tend to distinguish it from fiction, invention plays an important part in the historian's craft (White 1973, 6–7).

Looking back over the traditions of history writing, we have been highly tolerant of the incorporation of fiction, of myth, and of supposition into our histories; even today, there is a fondness among the general population for stories of figures such as King Arthur, preferring the romance of Monmouth and Mallory over the silence of Gildas and Bede. Stories of the origins of modern peoples and nations often hark back to mythological forebears in times before historical record; these were commonplace in medieval Europe, and it is ironic that the trailer for True Stories, in its promotion of Iceland's settlement history as a time of heroes, refers to a period known almost entirely from material from a century or more later, when the sagas and other records were written.

Without doubt, then, *EVE* can have historians, although what sort of history it constitutes is constrained by those who participate in that history and by the extent to which CCP acts as a control upon it. There are two significant problems here: first, that our understanding of *EVE*'s history operates through the practice of a small proportion of *EVE*'s population—there is a huge silent majority (Scientist 2013; Stabs 2013), and even True Stories, apparently successful and popular, only attracted approximately one story for every 650 active accounts, with the winning story up-voted by less than 0.5 percent of the potential electorate. Although engagement is clearly sophisticated, and historical thinking from bloggers like Mord Fiddle (2012, 2013) is developed and insightful, the history of *EVE* may well represent the perspective of only very few voices. It is thus difficult, if not impossible, to speak with authority about the views of the *EVE* community on these matters, and any observations in this chapter (and likely elsewhere) are at best provisional.

The second problem compounds the first: both CCP and players operate as interested parties in the telling of *EVE*'s history, and this inevitably produces partial history. Historical authority, here, is placed with the most powerful and the most interested, and the history produced is dominated by these interests. Yet it is often the case that those who feel most strongly attached to particular histories, who feel the most direct ownership of those stories and experiences, are not the correct people to write those histories; the best historians are, as Jordanova (2006, 143–45) indicates, those who can understand conditions beyond their own immediate experience.

It would appear, then, that *EVE* does in fact need historians able to confidently negotiate these difficulties, with the resources to curate and present a history that reflects the experiences, and perhaps the imaginings, of a broader body of players. Yet, given the increasing volume of human activity that takes place online, it seems that, just as much as, if not more than, *EVE* needs historians, historians need *EVE*. Through projects like True Stories and the efforts of those in its community interested in its history and its lore, *EVE* presents an unparalleled opportunity to reflect on our experience of and engagement with the past. For historians, this means thinking again about what history is and what history means; this is not only a public history created by its participants but a complex interrelationship of fiction and highly subjective experience that presents challenges to more traditional notions of historical truth.

Importantly, also, we can see that this history is impactful and that it is meaningful to players. Although we might have expected that play experiences would affect player attitudes and approaches to play, the activity here demonstrates that these histories are meaningful beyond game play itself. For *EVE* players, history—not only their own history but the history of the organizations to which they belong, the game world that they inhabit, and the game that they play—affects their sense of who they are; how they behave; whom they trust; and how they make sense of the intricate political, social, and economic environment of New Eden. When considering other games, then, we must be mindful not only that history has value to players but also that memories and stories of play experiences are enduring and are a significant way in which players make meaning from the games they play.

## NOTES

1 Well known in this debate is the work of E. H. Carr (1964), G. R. Elton (1967), and Arthur Marwick (1970). For cultural historians, contributions from French philosophers such as Michel Foucault have had a significant impact on our attempts to discern an answer, as have the literary models of writers like Hayden White (1973).

2 http://eve-history.net/wiki/.

3 Blog banters are defined by one of their orchestrators as "single topics discussed across the *EVE* blogging community" (Westhorpe 2013b).

4 Note that the use of lore here seems to refer to the longer-term history of New Eden, fictional or otherwise.

5 See, e.g., the EVElopedia entries for m0o Corp and Chribba, the latter locked to prevent vandalism (https://wiki.eveonline.com/).

6 See, e.g., the EVElopedia entries for the Moon of Ndoria (Chronicle) and Amarr Conservatives and Reclaimers (https://wiki.eveonline.com/).

7   E.g., http://wiki.eveuniversity.org/History_of_the_University.

8   See https://wiki.eveonline.com/en/wiki/Category:Player_Organisations.

## BIBLIOGRAPHY

Anderson, Benedict. 1983. *Imagined Communities: Reflections on the Origin and Spread of Nationalism.* London: Verso.

Archanus, Severus. 2013. "Sukanan Liberation." *True Stories from the First Decade,* April 15. https://truestories.eveonline.com/truestories/ideas/341-sukanan-liberation.html.

Arcturus, Wilhelm. 2013. "You Want the Lore? You Can't Handle the Lore!" *The Ancient Gaming Noob* (blog), August 8. http://tagn.wordpress.com/2013/08/08/blog-banter-48-you-want-the-lore-you-cant-handle-the-lore/.

Azariah, Mike. 2013. "BB 46: The Four Stories." *A Missioneer in Eve* (blog), April 19. http://mikeazariah.wordpress.com/2013/04/19/bb-46-the-four-stories/.

Banks, John A., and Sal M. Humphreys. 2008. "The Labour of User Co-creation: Emerging Social Network Markets?" *Convergence: The International Journal of Research into New Media Technologies* 14, no. 4: 401–18.

Bryant, Mark. 2013a. "BB46: CCP Is King and We Are Its Warrior Subjects." *Mabrick's Mumblings* (blog), April. http://mabricksmumblings.blogspot.co.uk/2013/04/bb46-ccp-is-king-and-we-are-its-warrior.html.

———. 2013b. "BB48: Pile of Bricks." *Mabrick's Mumblings* (blog), August. http://mabricksmumblings.blogspot.co.uk/2013/08/bb48-pile-of-bricks.html.

Carr, E. H. 1964. *What Is History?* Harmondsworth, U.K.: Penguin Books.

Castronova, Edward. 2004. "The Right to Play." *New York Law School Law Review* 49: 185–210.

CCP Falcon. 2013. "Into the Second Decade—A Guest Blog by Zapatero." *EVE Online,* May 18. http://community.eveonline.com/news/dev-blogs/into-the-second-decade/.

CCP Games. 2009. "EVE Online: The Butterfly Effect." YouTube, July 29. http://www.youtube.com/watch?v=08hmqyejCYU.

———. 2013a. "About: Rules of Conduct for EVE Online True Stories." *True Stories from the First Decade.* https://truestories.eveonline.com/truestories/about/contributors.html.

———. 2013b. "True Stories from the First Decade." https://truestories.eveonline.com/truestories/index.html.

———. 2013c. "True Stories from EVE Online's First Decade." YouTube, April 17. http://www.youtube.com/watch?v=vLFVEG9gB20.

Chapman, Adam. 2012. "Privileging Form over Content: Analysing Historical Videogames." *Journal of Digital Humanities* 1, no. 2. http://journalofdigitalhumanities.org/1-2/privileging-form-over-content-by-adam-chapman/.

Chiralityeve. 2013. "The Rule of Law." *States of Entanglement* (blog), April 22. http://spindensity.wordpress.com/2013/04/22/the-rule-of-law/.

Consalvo, Mia. 2007. *Cheating: Gaining Advantage in Videogames.* Cambridge, Mass.: MIT Press.

———. 2009. "There Is No Magic Circle." *Games and Culture* 4, no. 4: 408–17.

Corriea, Alexa Ray. 2013. "'Eve: True Stories' Is Allowing Players to Write Eve's History Book." Polygon, October 12. http://www.polygon.com/2013/10/12/4829942/eve-true-stories-is-allowing-players-to-write-eves-history-book.

Dealer. 2009. "PL: History of Pandemic Legion" (online forum thread). Kugutsumen, March 9. https://www.kugutsumen.com/showthread.php?33849-PL-History-of-the-Pandemic-Legion.

de Zwart, Melissa. 2009. "Piracy vs. Control: Models of Virtual World Governance and Their Impact on Player and User Experience." *Journal of Virtual Worlds Research* 2, no. 3: 3–16.

Dredtog, Grim. 2013. "Blog Banter 48: Stop! In the Name of the Lore!" *Wherein Ships Explode. A Lot* (blog), August 8. http://thatssogrim.wordpress.com/2013/08/08/stop-in-the-name-of-the-lore/.

Ducheneaut, Nicolas, Nicholas Yee, Eric Nickell, and Robert J. Moore. 2007. "The Life and Death of Online Gaming Communities: A Look at Guilds in World of Warcraft." In *CHI 2007: Proceedings of the SIGCHI Conference on Human Factors in Computing Systems*, 839–48. New York: ACM. doi:10.1145/1240624.1240750.

Eko'mo. 2013. "CCP Now Erasing All Trace of the Novels" (online forum thread). *EVE Online* forums, July 10. https://forums.eveonline.com/default.aspx?g=posts&t=257728.

ElRandir, Tumarth. 2013. "BB46: The New Frontier . . ." *A Carbon Based Life* (blog), April 17. http://turamarths-evelife.blogspot.co.uk/2013/04/bb46-new-frontier.html.

Elton, G. R. 1967. *The Practice of History.* London: Fontana Press.

Fiddle, Mord. 2012. "Wine in the Ruins." *Fiddler's Edge* (blog), August 7. http://fiddlersedge.blogspot.co.uk/2012/08/wine-in-ruins.html.

———. 2013. "EVE Lore: Blog Banter 48." *Fiddler's Edge* (blog), August 8. http://fiddlersedge.blogspot.co.uk/2013/08/eve-lore-blog-banter-48.html.

Firstly. 2013. "A Midsummer's Eve: BB46." *Flying Silent* (blog), April 29. http://flyingsilently.blogspot.co.uk/2013/04/a-midsummers-eve-bb46.html.

Gianturco, Alexander (The Mittani). 2013. "The Mittani Sends His Regards: Disbanding Band of Brothers." *True Stories from the First Decade,* May 6. https://truestories.eveonline.com/truestories/ideas/976-the-mittani-sends-his-regards-disbanding-band-of-brothers.html.

Giddens, Anthony. 1984. *The Constitution of Society: Outline of the Theory of Structuration.* Cambridge: Polity Press.

Graham, Flora. 2009. "The Struggle among the Stars." *BBC News,* February 23. http://news.bbc.co.uk/1/hi/technology/7905924.stm.

Griebel, Thaddeus. 2006. "Self-Portrayal in a Simulated Life: Projecting Personality and Values in The Sims 2." *Game Studies* 6, no. 1. http://gamestudies.org/0601/articles/griebel.

Grimmash. 2013. "Making NPCs Matter—Blog Banter 46." *Warp to Zero* (blog), April 16. http://warpto0.blogspot.co.uk/2013/04/making-npcs-matter-blog-banter-46.html.

H. 2013. "BB46—Evanescence." *Aggressive Logistics* (blog), April 17. http://aggressivelogistics.wordpress.com/2013/04/17/bb46-evanescence/.

Huizinga, Johan. 1955. *Homo Ludens: A Study of the Play Element in Culture.* Boston: Beacon Press.

Humphreys, Sal, and Melissa de Zwart. 2012. "Griefing, Massacres, Discrimination, and Art: The Limits of Overlapping Rule Sets in Online Games." *UC Irvine Law Review* 2: 507–36.

Javix, Rixx. 2013. "BB#48: Lore Is Our Soul." *Eveoganda* (blog), August 5. http://eveoganda.blogspot.co.uk/2013/08/bb48-lore-is-our-soul.html.

Jenkins, Keith. 2003. *Rethinking History.* London: Routledge.

Jester (Ripard Teg). 2013a. "No Dichotomy." *Jester's Trek* (blog), April 29. http://jestertrek.blogspot.co.uk/2013/04/no-dichotomy.html.

———. 2013b. "My Story Is the Same as Yours Just One Chapter Ahead." *Jester's Trek* (blog), August 6. http://jestertrek.blogspot.co.uk/2013/08/my-story-is-same-as-yours-just-one.html.

Jordanova, Ludmilla. 2006. *History in Practice.* 2nd ed. London: Hodder Education.

Kodachi, Kirith. 2013a. "Blog Banter #48—Lore." *Inner Sanctum of the Ninveah* (blog), August 5. http://www.ninveah.com/2013/08/blog-banter-48-lore.html.

———. 2013b. "Lore. What Is It Good For?" *Inner Sanctum of the Ninveah* (blog), August 6. http://www.ninveah.com/2013/08/lore-what-is-it-good-for.html.

Kyle, Sugar. 2013. "Blog Banter 46: The Ties That Bind." *Lowsec Lifestyle* (blog), May 2. http://www.lowseclifestyle.com/2013/05/blong-banter-46-ties-that-bind.html.

Lacuna, Vic. 2013. "The Loss of My Widow-Class Black Ops Battleship." *True Stories from the First Decade,* April 3. https://truestories.eveonline.com/truestories/ideas/134-the-loss-of-my-widowclass-black-ops-battleship.html.

Lehdonvirta, Vili. 2010. "Virtual Worlds Don't Exist: Questioning the Dichotomous Approach in MMO Studies." *Game Studies* 10, no. 1. http://gamestudies.org/1001/articles/lehdonvirta.

Ling Mei-Shin. 2013. "Suddenly Pirates: A Cautionary Tale for New EVE Players." *True Stories from the First Decade,* April 28. https://truestories.eveonline.com/truestories/ideas/717-suddenly-pirates-a-cautionary-tale-for-new-eve-players.html.

Marwick, A. 1970. *The Nature of History.* London: Macmillan.

Narcisse, Evan. 2013. "Your Space Battles Shaped the Stories in the New EVE Online Comic Book." *Kotaku*, October 10. http://kotaku.com/your-space-battles-shaped-the-stories-in-the-new-eve-on-1443540885.

Oakeshott, Michael. 1999. *On History and Other Essays.* Indianapolis, Ind.: Liberty Fund.

Ólafsson, Torfi Frans. 2013. "Can You Help Us Find the True Stories of the First Decade?" *EVE Online*, April 3. http://community.eveonline.com/news/dev-blogs/true-stories-of-the-first-decade/.

———. 2014. "Dark Horse Presents EVE: True Stories—Issue #1 Out Now!" *EVEOnline*, February 19. http://community.eveonline.com/news/dev-blogs/eve-true-stories-the-comic-book-based-on-true-events-20.000-years-into-the-future/.

Patroller, Emergent. 2013. "Blog Banter 48—Our Fictional Cultural Heritage." *Emergent Patroller* (blog), August. http://emergentpatroller.blogspot.co.uk/2013/08/blog-banter-48-our-fictional-cultural.html.

Porkbutte, Markonius. 2013. "The Chronicles of Newb." YouTube, November 21. http://www.youtube.com/watch?v=S21-FS8b6uI.

Potato, Samwise. 2013. "Making a Meaningful Impact." *And Other Bright Ideas* (blog), April 17. http://eve-brightideas.blogspot.co.uk/2013/04/meaningful-impact.html.

Priano, Makoto. 2013. "Monolithic Factions in the News, and Fleshing Out Factions." *EVE Forums—EVE Online*, November 20. https://forums.eveonline.com/default.aspx?g=posts&t=297802.

Rein, Kotetsu. 2007. "The Great Eve War" (online forum thread). *Kugutsumen*, February 19. https://www.kugutsumen.com/showthread.php?31002-The-Great-Eve-War.

Rhavas. 2013a. "Consequence (Blog Banter 46)." *Interstellar Privateer* (blog), April 20. http://interstellarprivateer.wordpress.com/2013/04/20/consequence/.

———. 2013b. "SHATTERED—A Yearlong Journey to the Shattered Worlds, an Investigation into the Creation of Wormholes and the Seyllin Incident." *True Stories from the First Decade,* April 30. https://truestories.eveonline.com/truestories/ideas/763-shattered-a-yearlong-journey-to-the-shattered-worlds-an-investigation-into-the-creation-of-wormholes-the-seyllin-incident.html.

Rossignol, Jim. 2013. "Human and Nature." In *EVE: Into the Second Decade,* edited by Richie Shoemaker, 126–27. Reykjavik: CCP.

Ruch, Adam. 2009. "World of Warcraft: Service or Space?" *Game Studies* 9, no. 2. http://gamestudies.org/0902/articles/ruch.

Sardaukar, Burseg. 2013. "General Tso's Alliance Wins Hulkageddon IV." *True Stories from the First Decade,* April 23. https://truestories.eveonline.com/truestories/ideas/554-general-tsos-alliance-wins-hulkageddon-iv.html.

Scientist, Eve (Lorna Sicling). 2013. "Blog Banter 46: The Main Event." *A Scientist's Life in Eve* (blog), April 16. http://eveblog.allumis.co.uk/?p=1239.

Seleene. 2013. "Mercenary Coalition Campaign Report—The North Reloaded." *True Stories from the First Decade,* May 6. https://truestories.eveonline.com/truestories/ideas/1013-mercenary-coalition-campaign-report-the-north-reloaded.html.

Shoemaker, Richie, ed. 2013. *EVE: Into the Second Decade.* Reykjavik: CCP.

splatus. 2013. "Blogbanter: I Reject Your Reality and Substitute My Own." *A Journey through the Mind* (blog), August 10. http://splatus.wordpress.com/2013/08/10/blogbanter-i-reject/.

Stabs. 2013. "Eve: BB46 Player Driven Story." *Stabbed Up* (blog), April 17. http://stabbedup.blogspot.co.uk/2013/04/eve-bb46-player-driven-story.html.

stoicfnord. 2013. "Blog Banter #48—Lore." *How to Be Terrible at Eve: A Guide* (blog), August 5. http://terribleateve.wordpress.com/2013/08/05/blog-banter-48-lore/.

Taylor, T. L. 2006. *Play between Worlds.* Cambridge, Mass.: MIT Press.

Thorrk, Tyrrax. 2013. "Guiding Hand Social Club's UQS Contract, or the Heist Where Mirial and Ubiqua Seraph Have a Bad Day." *True Stories from the First Decade,* May 6. https://truestories.eveonline.com/truestories/ideas/1025-guiding-hand-social-clubs-uqs-contract-or-the-heist-where-mirial-and-ubiqua-seraph-have-a-bad-day.html.

Tyler, T. 2008. "A Procrustean Probe." *Game Studies* 8, no. 2. http://gamestudies.org/0802/articles/tyler.

Ugleb. 2013. "BB48—Lore: The Conflict Driver." *Uglebsjournal* (blog), August 9. http://uglebsjournal.wordpress.com/2013/08/09/bb48-lore-the-conflict-driver/.

Vodkov, Nikolai. 2013. "Pro Synergy—Inception of Eve's First Franchise." *True Stories from the First Decade,* April 11. https://truestories.eveonline.com/truestories/ideas/261-pro-synergy-inception-of-eves-first-franchise.html.

Wayrest, Kalahari. 2013. "Banter 48: Lore." *Chocolate Heaven (blog), August 31.* http://www.minmatart.com/2013/banter-48-lore/.

Webber, Nick. 2014. "What Is Videogame History?" In *Engaging with Videogames: Play, Theory, and Practice,* edited by Dawn Stobbart and Monica Evans, 155–67. Oxford: Inter-Disciplinary Press.

Westhorpe, Mat. 2013a. "Blog Banter 46: The Main Event." *Freebooted* (blog), April 16. http://freebooted.blogspot.co.uk/2013/04/blog-banter-46-main-event.html.

———. 2013b. "Blog Banter Archive." *Freebooted* (blog). http://freebooted.blogspot.co.uk/p/blog-banters-fiction-and-features.html.

White, Hayden. 1973. *Metahistory.* Baltimore: The Johns Hopkins University Press.

Williams, Dmitri, Nicolas Ducheneaut, Li Xiong, Yuanyuan Zhang, Nick Yee, and Eric Nickell. 2006. "From Tree House to Barracks: The Social Life of Guilds in World of Warcraft." *Games and Culture* 1, no. 4: 338–61.

Williams, Mike. 2013. "CCP Creating EVE TV Series with Director Baltasar Kormakur." *Games Industry International,* April 28. http://www.gamesindustry.biz/articles/2013-04-28-ccp-creating-eve-tv-series-with-director-baltasar-kormakur.

Woollahra, Sered. 2013. "Blog Banter 46: Eve's Many Choices." *Sered's Lives* (blog), April 17. http://sered-sl.blogspot.co.uk/2013/04/blog-banter-46-eves-many-choices.html.

Xenuria. 2013. "We Didn't Listen!—The Story of Xenuria and Hydra Reloaded." *True Stories from the First Decade,* May 2. https://truestories.eveonline.com/truestories/ideas/831-we-didnt-listen-the-story-of-xenuria-and-hydra-reloaded.html.

Xideinis. 2013. "Coming of Age." *True Stories from the First Decade,* April 3. https://truestories.eveonline.com/truestories/ideas/159-coming-of-age.html.

xttz. 2013. "A Ship Which Shaped History." *True Stories from the First Decade,* May 1. https://truestories.eveonline.com/truestories/ideas/821-a-ship-which-shaped-history.html.

Zelizer, Barbie, and Karen Tenenboim-Winblatt. 2014. "Journalism's Memory Work." In *Journalism and Memory,* edited by Barbie Zelizer and Karen Tenenboim-Winblatt, 1–16. Houndmills, U.K.: Palgrave Macmillan.

Zephyran, Anshu. 2013. "BB46: Actions Have Consequences." *Structure Damage (blog),* April 25. http://structuredamage.org/2013/04/25/actions-have-consequences/.

## On the *EVE* of Preservation

Conserving a Complex Universe

*Kristin MacDonough, Rebecca Fraimow, Dan Erdman,*
*Kathryn Gronsbell, and Erica Titkemeyer*

We have been persuaded that all that we create in the digital realm is as safe and secure as if it were stored in a bank vault. Hardware and software bombard us with advertisements suggesting that we can do magical things with our personal documents, all the while guaranteeing their permanence. We are in awe of what is happening. . . . There is no one out there, of course, who is so naïve to believe such claims. Is there?

—Richard Cox, *The Future of Archives*

In fall 2012, the Museum of Modern Art's (MoMA's) Department of Architecture and Design (A&D) announced its intention to officially acquire video games for the permanent collection. One of the first fourteen titles to go on exhibit was *EVE Online,* making it the first massively multiplayer online role-playing game (MMORPG) to be acquired by a museum.

Commercially released video games were never intended to be collectible items. Now, as libraries, archives, and museums begin to acquire video games, they are faced with new challenges. Decisions made at every step—from acquisition to prescriptive measures for long-term preservation—will determine how, or even if, a game remains accessible in the future. These procedures depend on the type of institution and its mission "in what is collected, in how works are organized, and in how the institution relates to its users" (Dietz et al. 2004).

Broadly, this chapter considers the work that occurs in the museum setting; whereas libraries are user oriented and archives are research oriented, a museum focuses on unique objects, which carries implications for its preservation practices. Museums that maintain a permanent collection will often make that collection available for research; however, the museum's primary mission is exhibition. Works are presented from a curatorial perspective, and a work gets meaning from its placement within the context of the works around it. In planning for preservation and conservation, it follows that a museum must maintain works in a way that will make them available to future exhibitions and alternative interpretations by other curators.

*EVE*'s unique virtual architecture, its sandbox design, and its tremendous number of players—more than half a million and growing—make it one of the most challenging games to preserve. This chapter addresses the preservation and conservation of *EVE* within the framework of a museum's mission to conserve and exhibit unique works of art and explicates what this implies for video game researchers. Most *EVE Online* scholars are primarily interested in user experience and interaction, and rightly so. However, by incorporating *EVE Online* into the A&D department of its museum holdings, the curators at MoMA have chosen to focus on the underlying technology and digital architecture that provide the playable environment, while keeping player documentation a secondary, but still important, objective. This chapter analyzes MoMA's strategy, addressing concerns for care, handling, and long-term access of the digital game environment, with special attention paid to the current landscape surrounding video game preservation. This is followed by an in-depth examination of the museum's technical approach to preserving *EVE Online* and how an understanding of these practices will add value to the work of current and future researchers.

## Preservation and Conservation of Time-Based Media Art

Although the terms *preservation* and *conservation* may be used interchangeably, there are fundamental differences in the implementation of these processes. *Preservation* refers to the maintenance of an artwork in its original state, or as close as can be approximated with minimal intervention. According to the International Council of Museums (1984) Committee for Conservation, *conservation* is "examination, documentation, treatment, and preventive care, supported by research and education." In conservation, the conservator is active in maintaining the longevity of a piece by treating the work to minimize the effects of chemical or physical damage and deterioration over time. In other words, preservation is the strategic, long-term plan, whereas conservation comprises the daily, monthly, or yearly activities in which the conservator engages to keep the long-term plan on target. There are well-documented conservation standards and guidelines for physical artworks, such as oil paintings or marble sculptures; conservators know what techniques and tools are available to them to care for organic materials. However, over the past twenty years or longer, museums have been collecting works in the realm of time-based media at an increasing rate, and this category includes video, film, audio, and computer-based works.

The phrase *time-based media* is used to describe these formats because the works occur and are displayed over a period of time for the viewer (Guggenheim n.d.). Additionally, these artworks depend on external components essential to the user or viewer experience. Over time, these components may break down and consequently alter the experience or deny it entirely. Next to damage and deterioration, technological obsolescence is one of the greatest risks to time-based media because of the way that the failure of hardware and software can limit access. Artwork created for a specific piece of equipment may become inaccessible if the equipment is no longer manufactured or if it falls apart at a time when maintenance expertise or replacement parts are no longer available. But this physical aspect of technological obsolescence is not the only concern: software obsolescence poses similar threats. Although the hardware of a computer may be running just fine, if the program necessary to access an important file is not functioning or is no longer supported by the developer, then the artwork is inaccessible. In an era in which users are hounded by computer upgrades and software updates nearly every day, this is of great concern to conservators.

To address this need, the Variable Media Initiative (VMI), a project established at the Guggenheim in 1999, conducted research on the preservation of time-based media and ephemeral artworks. The project team recommended four strategies for preserving time-based media, or any complex work: the use of archivally sound storage, emulation, migration, and reinterpretation (or a combination of the four) (Variable Media Network 2013). Storage consists, in this case, of taking in the physical and digital material but does not necessarily include any measures for maintaining the material, making it the most ineffective of the four on its own. Migration involves moving digital content from one format to another. The Digital Preservation Coalition (DPC; 2013) defines *migration* as "a means of overcoming technological obsolescence by transferring digital resources from one hardware/software generation to the next." This is most appropriate in cases when preserving the content is more important than preserving the original technology. Emulation takes the opposite approach from migration, seeking to re-create the original viewing environment by replicating the behavior of the hardware or software. Between migration and emulation, the latter is the more-researched and more-advocated strategy, because the digital content can be preserved in its original form or structure. Reinterpretation (or reenactment) is highly dependent on documentation and can involve reconstructing the game, the environment, or the experience of game play. This solution runs the risk of altering the work or modifying the meaning each time it is interpreted.

## Video Game Preservation: An Overview

As they have edged their way into cultural institutions during the past decade, video games have increasingly been the focus of scholarship and preservation. Recognizing the growing trend in collecting and preserving video games, independent collectors and collecting institutions—libraries, museums, and archives—have started developing practices and standards for evaluating games, preserving them, and making them accessible.

One of the first initiatives to take on the challenge of developing a preservation plan for video games was the Preserving Virtual Worlds (PVW) project. Over the course of a two-year collaboration between libraries and researchers on the preservation of digital games and interactive fiction, the group quite comprehensively identified the general risks to all video games: hardware and software obsolescence; scarcity of media; third-party dependencies developed by the gaming community; complex code (including compilers and information on compiling processes); threats to authenticity; intellectual property rights; preservation of significant properties, such as interactive and artistic elements; and maintenance of context. All of these are pertinent to game acquisition by libraries and archives, and most of these are recognized as risks in the broader category of time-based media conservation as well.

For preservation, PVW recommends a combination of the approaches VMI identified, highlighting migration and emulation to preserve a playable game. Because museums focus on collecting unique works, preservation of both the significant properties and authenticity is especially important to those institutions. Significant properties here comprise the particular design and interactive elements that make the game unique. Authenticity, as defined by PVW, is "[proof] that a digital object is what it claims to be, free from tampering or corruption" (McDonough et al. 2010); what is implied but not stated here is that authenticity in turn relies on the preservation of the significant properties and behaviors that influence the game-play experience.

Following the increased interest in video games among researchers, many organizations have instigated the first step in video game preservation, which is collection. Institutions such as the Computerspielemuseum in Berlin; the International Center for the History of Electronic Games (ICHEG) in Rochester, New York; and the Museum of Art and Digital Entertainment (the MADE) in San Francisco contribute to video game collection practices via their acquisition policies and their preservation and conservation activities. For example, the MADE makes a point of acquiring and preserving the original source code for games, including subsequent versions. In doing so, it documents and preserves not only the original game but also any revisions and additions, allowing the organization to document and bring to light the design process. Along with games, ICHEG collects ephemera, such as publications, packaging, advertising, and other game-related products. The Counterspielemuseum partnered with other organizations in Europe from 2009 to 2012 for the Keeping Emulation Environments Portable Project, an initiative to investigate the legal and technical issues of emulation as a preservation strategy. Each organization also stages engaging and informative exhibitions advocating for video game preservation.

Museums with diverse collections have taken on the challenge of video game exhibition. Two recent examples, *The Art of Video Games,* organized by the Smithsonian (spring 2012), and *Spacewar! Video Games Blast Off* at the Museum of the Moving Image (spring 2013), highlighted the artistic and innovative visual qualities in video games. However, exhibition alone is not preservation—elements such as source code and ephemera acquired by the MADE and ICHEG are necessary for long-term preservation, but they may not be employed in every instance of exhibition.

## Interaction Design at MoMA

According to its mission statement, MoMA is dedicated to maintaining a permanent collection through preservation and conservation activities and by making materials and information accessible for scholarly research and exhibitions. When the museum started collecting interactive media, it needed to construct an approach that was suited to the object but still ultimately rooted in the museum's bedrock principles of conservation and access. This integration was introduced in MoMA's first foray into interactive media, *Talk to Me: Design and Communication between People and Objects* (2011). In the official weblog of the exhibition, the A&D department put forth the museum's general criteria for acquisition, which measure the impact of an object's relationship with people or its environment through form, function, innovation, cultural impact, process, and necessity.

It's important to note that *Talk to Me* did not present interaction itself but rather objects and designs that facilitate or enhance interaction. This selection ranged from computer interfaces and data visualizations to experimental navigation and communication devices. The exhibit encouraged the museum audience to consider the means of communication between humans and technology and the different ways in which humans interact with objects.

Following *Talk to Me,* the A&D department continued to explore and develop its collection in the field of interaction design, eventually making the decision to include video games in its permanent collection. In keeping with their strategy for *Talk to Me,* the curators tried to avoid kitsch or nostalgia when presenting game interaction; their goal was not to present a historical experience of play but rather to create a collection that would provide insight into the art of video game design for its own sake. For their dive into video game acquisition, A&D worked with game scholars, historians, and critics as well as digital conservators and legal advisors to assist in selecting the titles. In the process, they developed four additional criteria for game acquisition: behavior, aesthetics, space, and time.

*Behavior* addresses how players function in and interact with a game, from visual cues to physical devices. *Aesthetics* operates primarily as the visual style, which informs behaviors and works to "enhance a game's identity." *Space* refers to the architecture of the virtual world; "unlike physical constructs, . . . video games can defy spatial logic and gravity, and provide brand new experiences like teleportation and ubiquity" (Antonelli 2012). Finally, in keeping with A&D senior curator Paola Antonelli's maxim that "interaction design is quintessentially dynamic," the department considers the way in which the passage of *time*—both in the real, physical world of the player and in the virtual, diegetic world of a video game—is purposefully designed by the developer and implemented by the player.

Through its consultation with experts and the expansion of its selection criteria, A&D produced a comprehensive acquisition wish list of forty video games. The department determined that it was essential to ingest a game's original software, hardware, and source code along with relevant documentation. For MoMA, these components are the original and authentic game. The procedures and logistics for acquisition vary for all objects; in some cases, it may take years to acquire a single artwork. The process entails more than the mere purchase of a cartridge or console; it also involves contacting developers and negotiating with rights-holders for permission to exhibit and make preservation copies of materials.

Because of this comprehensive process, MoMA's video game collection debuted in 2012 with the following fourteen games from the wish list of forty: *Pac-Man* (1980), *Tetris* (1984), *Another World* (1991), *Myst* (1993), *SimCity 2000* (1994), *vib-ribbon* (1999), *The Sims* (2000), *Katamari Damacy* (2004), *Dwarf Fortress* (2006), *Portal* (2007), *flOw* (2006), *Passage* (2008), *Canabalt* (2009), and, finally, *EVE Online* (2003).

## Preserving *EVE*: Questions and Concerns

The department's interest in exhibiting and acquiring *EVE* sprang from an appreciation of the game's function, design, and virtual architecture that allows players to participate freely. Although its behaviors, aesthetics, and temporal qualities are comparable to those of other MMORPGs, *EVE*'s construction of virtual space (discussed later) sets it apart from other, similar games. The elasticity of the game as an interactive piece and the lack of a linear timeline interested MoMA and its A&D department, but these are also the most problematic aspects in terms of preservation and conservation planning.

As mentioned earlier, all games are dependent on technologies that will (or have already) become obsolete, complex code that needs to run on these technologies, and significant properties that determine authenticity. Additional challenges are introduced to the mix when networking is involved. Both Local Area Network (LAN) games and massively multiplayer online games (MMOGs) are networked games and involve multiple players simultaneously connecting into a central server. However, MMOGs occur in a much more geographically distributed fashion. Players may log in to the game from any sufficiently speedy Internet connection, game play occurs entirely online, and access is granted via a paid subscription service. MMOG players are not usually acquainted with each other (at least initially), and, again in contrast with LAN gaming, the server is controlled and held by some other company or enterprise.

A further evolution of the MMOG is the MMORPG, where an individual player creates an online persona to act as his avatar in a virtual world of the game, a world in which the player interacts with other avatars. The "universe" of the game exists and continues regardless of the individual actions of each player. Probably the most well known MMORPG is *World of Warcraft*. That game, however, segregates its groups of players into parallel, nonoverlapping worlds managed by different servers; *EVE Online* is the first MMORPG to include all players in one consistent world.

Most video games, particularly those meant for individual players or small groups, tend to follow a rigorously linear progression of events. In contrast, *EVE*'s sandbox design, where much of what occurs in the game is the result of the spontaneous, self-directed actions of thousands of players, complicates any efforts at documentation of the events occurring in its virtual world.

For the preservation of *EVE Online*, a number of questions arise. Technologies used for *EVE* are constantly updated, so what hardware and software components must be acquired? How should these technologies be stored? What software should be migrated, and what hardware should be emulated? With more than half a million players guiding the story line of the virtual world, how do we understand the player experience when each experience must be different? How does one measure the impact individual players have on the game? What information should be collected and documented: should the player-developed story line be included as part of the game's preservation? These questions also identify issues related to authenticity—what aspects of these components are recognized as the original game?

## Preserving *EVE*: MoMA's Strategy

As a solution, MoMA's conservators focused on preserving the space, or an offline, virtual architecture of the game, and on creating what they refer to as "*EVE* in a Box." As it turns out, the developers at CCP were already working with a comparable virtual environment. The back end of *EVE* is constructed through online servers hosting the active game, known collectively as Tranquility. However, CCP also owns servers that perform essential game-maintenance functions but do not impact the live and active game. These, known as Singularity, are the test servers that are used to periodically back up the game in progress but also to test out various improvements of the game as they become necessary. While information on these machines is limited, their operation is useful not only for preserving the game as it exists at a certain point but also for maintaining its interactive qualities in an environment where most of the players are not present. Occasional mass-participation tests occur on Singularity that involve live players, but the server must still act as a reasonably accurate replica environment, even without the ability to call on the game's participants to re-create the interactive experience.

MoMA has taken this blueprint and appropriated it for preservation purposes. When a user logs in to MoMA's "*EVE* in a Box" version, she will be directed to an offline server where the game will be emulated in a virtual machine on a server. A virtual machine is a type of emulator: an operating system or software program that exhibits the behavior of a separate computer and can also perform tasks such as running applications and programs. This strategy allows as much as possible of the original game, or original code, to remain the same, preserving the authenticity of the game. Though this strategy will be used for many games in MoMA's collection, it is likely that only a few will be the size of *EVE* and require their own dedicated servers. Like the MADE, MoMA also intends to collect different versions of the software to demonstrate the ways in which the game has evolved over the years and will change in the future.

For the development of further preservation strategies, the curatorial staff in the A&D department and the conservation department will also be conducting interviews with the developers at CCP. MoMA frequently conducts artist interviews for various works to understand the artist's intentions and methods, which in turn influences later strategies for conservation and exhibition. The interview also addresses how exhibition and damage or deterioration should be handled. Again, the museum is very lucky that CCP is interested in helping preserve the game and is willing to provide adequate information, as needed.

For *EVE*'s MoMA debut in the *Applied Design* exhibition (2013), CCP put a call out to players to submit videos to demonstrate "a day in the universe," showing a snapshot of the *EVE Online* universe through the everyday actions of two hundred players from around the world. The developers believed that the complexity of *EVE Online* activity could best be portrayed by submissions of personal game-play recordings from its players. All of those submissions were then combined with 1.2 terabytes of data from *EVE Online* server databases and Big Data storages of player interactions into a larger narrative representing the science fiction game as a whole. Ben Fino-Radin, the MoMA conservator working with the video game collection, plans to continue this practice of collecting player interactions with more documentation, such as videos or still images, submitted by players or re-created in the offline world (Robertson 2014).

*EVE* continues to evolve, and given all the variables in gaming technology, one can only speculate on the form it will take in the future. For researchers to understand the game as it exists now, the ability to access the virtual environment will be an indispensable resource. In an article on *The Verge*, a technology art and culture news website, Torfi Frans Ólafsson, CCP creative director, notes that future historians will be needed to "go back and figure out the story and the human angle." But in the same article, Fino-Radin likens the offline version of *EVE* to a "ghost town." The world that the future researcher, player, or historian will be investigating will be an intact but empty one. Potentially, to generate the crowded feel of *EVE,* many players will be able to log in to the preservation server, but it is unlikely that the anonymity of geographic dispersal and true sandbox culture will be easily re-created. According to Ólafsson, "the entire game exists for you to be aware of people around you and communicate with people around you." Likewise, an article in *Polygon,* a video game news and reviews website, quotes CCP CEO Hilmar Pétursson as saying, "The game *is* the players."

One potential resolution of this dilemma would be to broaden the scope of documentation to include the record of each player's interaction with the game, which would provide a full picture of the user experience by means of simple aggregation. This would include, as per the language of *EVE*'s end user license agreement, "any information relating to your play or use of the Game, including of your game-play statistics, preferred strategies, in-Game transaction history and trends, history of technical issues and support usage, and history of contributed and received User Content." The agreement is also careful to note that "CCP may collect and store User Gameplay Information about you, both as an individual and aggregated with the User Gameplay Information of other users of the Game and the System."

This approach is not without its hazards, however. Although CCP does disclose the fact that it collects such information, it also specifically defines the conditions under which this information will be put to use: "CCP may analyze and use such User Gameplay Information for the purposes of review, research, development, maintenance, operation, administration, and support, and for the marketing of CCP products and services." It is not at all clear that the use of these data as the basis of a preservation project would be covered under those terms. It is true that, in principle, CCP could change the terms to accommodate this, but there is reason to believe that at least some in the company regard that as an ethical gray area. In the *Verge* article, Ólafsson disapprovingly likens such a strategy to "AT&T creating a piece for a museum, and taking everybody's phone records and storing them there."

Conversely, even if MoMA could accumulate all the player information available through the *EVE* servers, it is only documentation of interaction and not interaction itself. Therefore, similar to the works in MoMA's *Talk to Me,* the key elements of player and player interaction, which many scholars and game researchers consider the heart of *EVE Online,* are essentially unpreservable.

## A Lonely Researcher in a Lonely World

For a museum, the video game, no matter its original form, becomes just another object among many and is cared for as though it had a physical presence. Pip Laurenson (2006), head of collection care research at the Tate in London, states that "in conservation the prevalent notion of authenticity is based on physical integrity," that a work must be conserved "as is" as much as possible to preserve its authenticity. For paintings and sculpture, for example, the mildest possible intervention is ideal for preservation. Conversely, hardware and software must be managed and maintained; anyone who has ever experienced hard drive failure can attest to this. The chapter's opening quotation from archivist Richard Cox is most pertinent here: the authenticity of video games must be actively managed. A video game conservator is responsible for frequent reviews of the technology to ensure that it is functioning properly, such as verifying that computers still operate and programs still run. This includes the preservation of significant properties of the games: behavior, space, time, and aesthetics.

MoMA's conservation department has, to an extent, excused itself from imposing significance on the game or from defining the sociological implications through preservation or conservation activities; the work and exhibitions are documented, but the significance is left open to interpretation for researchers. However, as Henry

Lowood (2009), a curator at Stanford University, has written, "future historians of virtual worlds will want to understand what people did in early virtual worlds. . . . Clearly, there is a lot more to the preservation of virtual world history than software and data preservation." Scholars may be keen to address the design of the game through its sociological ramifications, commenting on how the layout of the virtual world shapes how players interact. Those interested in playing an online game in a virtual world with other players are more likely to continue doing so if the world is technologically accessible and visually engaging. So it goes, then, that to understand the virtual and social environments, researchers should familiarize themselves with the underlying hardware and software.

Understanding the technology facilitating a playable environment, both on the front end and the back end, can enhance a scholar's research and analysis of player interaction. What is it about the environment that attracts players? Technological developments within and outside of the game, such as the ability to design new ships or expansion packages courtesy of new servers, influence player activities. Players then respond to these changes and developments within the games as much as they respond to actions of other players, and to ignore these developments is to dismiss the relationship between the player and his virtual environment.

*EVE Online* is an evolving game space. MoMA's preservation strategy generates a primary resource of the software as it exists today, making no assumptions as to why players are attracted to it, the meaning curators will impose on or derive from the game, or the context in which it will be experienced. To understand how the game environment is preserved is to gain more knowledge of it as a primary resource and thus provide additional depth to future scholarship.

## NOTE

This chapter was produced with the original research from the students in the 2013 Handling Complex Media class at New York University's Moving Image Archiving and Preservation program. The class was conducted under the direction of Professor Howard Besser, and the resulting work includes content contributed by Kelly Haydon, Shira Peltzman, Pawarisa Nipawattanapong, Juana Suárez, Chris Banuelos, and Federica Liberi, in addition to the authors listed. Collectively, the class would like to thank Ben Fino-Radin and Peter Oleksik in the Conservation Department at MoMA for sharing their time and expertise.

## BIBLIOGRAPHY

Antonelli, Paola. 2012. "Video Games: 14 in the Collection, for Starters." *Inside/Out* (blog), November 29. http://www.moma.org/explore/inside_out/2012/11/29/video-games-14-in -the-collection-for-starters/.

Dietz, Steve, Howard Besser, Ann Borda, and Kati Geber, with Pierre Lévy. 2004. "Virtual Museum (of Canada): The Next Generation." http://www.chin.gc.ca/English/Members/Next_Generation/pdf.html.

Digital Preservation Coalition. 2013. "Introduction: Definitions and Concepts." http://www.dpconline.org/advice/preservationhandbook/introduction/definitions-and-concepts.

Guggenheim. n.d. "Time Based Media." http://www.guggenheim.org/newyork/collections/conservation/time-based-media.

International Council of Museums Committee for Conservation. 1984. "The Conservator-Restorer: A Definition of the Profession." http://www.icom-cc.org/47/about-icom-cc/definition-of-profession/.

Laurenson, Pip. 2006. "Authenticity, Change, and Loss in the Conservation of Time-Based Media Installations." Tate Papers. http://www.tate.org.uk/download/file/fid/7401.

Lowood, Henry. 2009. "Memento Mundi: Are Virtual Worlds History?" https://escholarship.org/uc/item/2gs3p6jx.

McDonough, J., R. Olendorf, M. Kirschenbaum, K. Kraus, D. Reside, R. Donahue, A. Phelps, C. Egert, H. Lowood, and S. Rojo. 2010. "Preserving Virtual Worlds Final Report." http://hdl.handle.net/2142/17097.

Robertson, Adi. 2014. "EVE, Offline: How Do You Archive a Universe?" *The Verge*. http://www.theverge.com/2014/2/24/5441866/eve-offline-how-do-you-archive-a-universe.

Variable Media Network. 2013. "Strategies." http://www.variablemedia.net/e/index.html.

# Contributors

**William Sims Bainbridge** is a director of a computer science program at the National Science Foundation. He is the author of *The Spaceflight Revolution, Dimensions of Science Fiction, Goals in Space, The Virtual Future, The Meaning and Value of Spaceflight, The Warcraft Civilization: Social Science in a Virtual World,* and *eGods: Faith versus Fantasy in Computer Gaming.* The views expressed in his essay do not necessarily represent the views of the National Science Foundation or the government of the United States.

**Kelly Bergstrom** is a postdoctoral researcher at York University.

**Marcus Carter** is a research fellow in the Microsoft Research Centre for Social Natural User Interfaces at the University of Melbourne.

**Chribba (Christer Enberg)** is a longtime player of *EVE Online* and a community developer. He began playing *EVE* in 2003 and has been developing *EVE*-related websites and services since 2005.

**Jedrzej Czarnota** is a PhD student in business and management at Manchester Business School, University of Manchester. He works at the Manchester Institute of Innovation Research.

**Kjartan Pierre Emilsson** was lead game designer of *EVE Online* at its conception and launch. He is currently cofounder and CEO of a virtual reality entertainment developer called Sólfar Studios.

**Dan Erdman** is an archival consultant, journalist, and writer living in Chicago.

**Rebecca Fraimow** is an audiovisual archivist who has worked with the Dance Heritage Coalition, the New Museum, and WGBH.

**Martin R. Gibbs** is associate professor in Computing and Information Systems at the University of Melbourne and coauthor of the forthcoming book *Death and Digital Media.*

**Catherine Goodfellow** is a PhD student at the University of Manchester.

**Kathryn Gronsbell** is the digital asset manager at Carnegie Hall in New York City. She has worked for archives, museums, libraries, and broadcasters as an asset and metadata preservation consultant.

**Keith Harrison** works for an energy consultancy in Edinburgh, Scotland, and has helped lead his *EVE Online* alliance, Goonswarm, for half a decade. In-game, he goes by the singularly unimpressive nom de guerre "Endie."

**Kristin MacDonough** is a digitization specialist and has worked with Video Data Bank, The Standby Program, and the New Museum.

**Mantou (Zhang Yuzhou)** has been a member of the China-only *EVE Online* Serenity server since 2006. He is the CEO of PIBC Alliance, which is the largest and most powerful alliance on Serenity.

**Oskar Milik** is a PhD sociology student at University College Dublin.

**The Mittani (Alexander Gianturco)** is leader of the Goonswarm Federation in *EVE Online.* His adventures have been chronicled by the BBC, the *Verge,* and the *Wall Street Journal* as well as on his website TheMittani.com.

**Joji Mori** has an academic background in human–computer interaction and is currently working as a user experience designer.

**Richard Page** is a PhD candidate at the University of Hawai'i at Mānoa.

**Christopher Paul** is associate professor and chair of the Department of Communication at Seattle University. He is the author of *Wordplay and the Discourse of Video Games.*

**Erica Titkemeyer** is an audiovisual conservator for the Southern Folklife Collection at the University of North Carolina at Chapel Hill.

**Nick Webber** is associate director of the Birmingham Centre for Media and Cultural Research at Birmingham City University. He is author of a monograph on the medieval Normans, *The Evolution of Norman Identity, 911–1154.*

**Darryl Woodford** is a visiting fellow with the Digital Media Research Centre and the Creative Industries Faculty at Queensland University of Technology. He is cofounder of Hypometer Technologies.

# Index